AF573974

# TELEIOS

*Recovery Through Christ*
*for*
*Adult Children*

# TELEIOS

## *Recovery Through Christ for Adult Children*

*Moira Anderson Allen, M.Ed.*

**Peregrine Press**
**Los Angeles, California**

Cover design by Mona Meisami.



References marked "Strong's Concordance" are taken from *The Exhaustive Concordance of the Bible*, by James Strong, S.T.D., L.L.D., Macdonald Publishing Co., McLean, Virginia. References are designated by concordance number and "G" for Greek or "H" for Hebrew.

Published by:
Peregrine Press
12228 Venice Blvd., Suite 380
Los Angeles, CA 90066

Quantity discounts available for church and recovery groups.

Printed in the United States of America
ISBN 0-9619232-1-0
Library of Congress Cataloging-in-Publication Data: 92-50430

**This book is dedicated to...**

My husband Patrick,
whose love, patience and encouragement
kept me going…
The friends whose prayers provided strength…
And God, whose love and guidance
make all things possible.

Other Peregrine Press books
by Moira Anderson Allen:

**COPING WITH SORROW ON THE LOSS OF YOUR PET**

# Contents

# Introduction

*Jesus answered, "I tell you the truth, you are looking for me, not because you saw miraculous signs but because you ate the loaves and had your fill. Do not work for food that spoils, but for food that endures to eternal life, which the Son of Man will give you. On Him God the Father has placed His seal of approval." Then they asked him, "What must we do to do the works God requires?" Jesus answered, "The work of God is this: to believe in the one He has sent." (John 6:26-29)*

WELCOME TO "TELEIOS."

Perhaps your first thought upon reading the cover was, "What a strange word! What does it mean?"

"Teleios" is a word that, when translated as it is customarily translated, strikes terror into the hearts of most Adult Children. It is the word that is translated as "perfect" in Jesus's command, "Be perfect, therefore, as your heavenly Father is perfect." (Matt. 5:48) This is the one command most of us are convinced that we can never fulfill, no matter how hard we try. We are certain that we can never even come *close*—and so we believe that we are "cut off" from God's "seal of approval."

If God actually expects us to be as "perfect" as Himself—as free of sin, as flawless, as unselfish, as loving, as compassionate, as pure, and as holy—then we have something to despair about. If this is what it "takes" to win God's approval and acceptance, we know that we will never get there.

Most of us never question whether or not this was what God "meant," because this is a "demand" that we have lived with most of our lives. It is what our parents often expected of us. We "failed" them—at least, we never seemed to "be good enough" or "do well enough" to please them or win their approval—and we are sure that we will "fail" God as well. Though we "know" that God loves us, even when we are *imperfect*, we often wish that we could be more than "second-class citizens in Christ."

But is this really what God expects? Was Jesus actually asking something that so few of us would be able to achieve?

I don't believe that God is a "perfectionist." I have met quite a few perfectionists in my life. I have met paranoid schizophrenics who "freaked" at the sight of a single dirty coffee cup in an otherwise spotless sink. I have met alcoholics who had no tolerance for children who did not "measure up" to their standards. I have met parents whose one inflexible "commandment" was "make no mistakes." I have met perfectionists of all types and from all walks of life, and all I can say is that if God is like these people—demanding, critical, condemning, and most of all, *nitpicking*—then something is missing from my Bible. That isn't the God of scripture; that isn't the Jesus of the gospels. If there is one thing we can be sure of—and one thing at I hope you will discover through this book—it is that God is *not* a dysfunctional parent. He does not "think" like an alcoholic, like a child-abuser, like an obsessive-compulsive, like a martyred victim, like an addict. He is *perfect*—but not a *perfectionist*.

If God is not a perfectionist, then, perhaps the problem is that we *learned* about "perfection" from people who *were* perfectionists. Perhaps the problem is that we learned to define "perfect" through the impossible expectations of critical, condemning, demanding, nitpicking people. Perhaps the problem is that some of us learned the definition of "perfect" from alcoholics, child abusers, child molesters, and even paranoid schizophrenics. (Some of us also learned it from parents who were frequently kind, loving, and caring; not all of us came from homes that were blatantly or violently "sick" or "abusive.") Most of us have been struggling to achieve this kind of perfection throughout our lives—or at least to maintain an *illusion* of perfection that will deflect blame and criticism—and most of us are miserable.

I don't believe that Jesus said these words just to make a significant portion of the population miserable. If He said to do it, then it can be done—not just by those who grew up in "good" homes or with the "right advantages," but by all of us.

This book is based upon the belief that we *do* have a hope of achieving, not the perfection that our families (or the world, or even the church) demanded of us, but the perfection that Jesus is actually talking about. We have a hope of achieving "teleios."

"Teleios" does not mean that you never sin or make a mistake. It doesn't mean that you keep your house spotless, dress neatly, raise perfect children, or get all your work done on time. "Teleios" is a word that talks about growth, completion, and wholeness. It means to "become whole," to "reach a goal," and even to "become human."[1] Our lives were designed, by God, to be a *process* of striving toward completion, not a process of *condemning* ourselves for not having "made it yet."

Perfection does not come through works, achievements, or the mask of "Sunday smiles" and charitable sacrifice. These are simply a way of working for "food that spoils," not the food that brings eternal life. Jesus did not tell us that the "work of God" was "good works" or "charity" or "sacrifice" or even "self-improvement." He said, instead: "The work of God is this: to believe in the one He has sent." (John 6:29)

Perfection is not what we have to do to *get* to God. It is what comes *from* God, through Jesus, through His Word and *through His love*. If we are to find "perfection," we won't find it on a volunteer committee or in the office. We *will* find it when we discover how to become "perfected in love," as we are advised in 1 John 4:18. That is what this book is all about.

This book is *not* about learning how to be better, nice, or more "giving" people. It is not about how we can find "recovery" through

[1]Strong's Concordance, #G5046.

"doing more for other people." It is about the love of God, and how we can learn how to apply that love in every area of our lives. We aren't going to find "healing" by nailing our burdens to the cross or laying them at the altar, or by investing a specific number of hours in prayer and Bible study. We can do all those things and never discover love. When we discover love, when we "seek first his kingdom" (Luke 12:31), all those things will be added, not as an obligation, but as a choice.

I don't regard this book as the "last word" on how to become "perfected in love." Rather, I consider it a sort of "first word." It is a beginning, not an end—a beginning that I hope I, and others, will build upon. I believe that love, and becoming "perfected in love," is the foundation of healing for Adult Children, and I hope to see great things built upon this foundation.

Nor is this book intended as a compendium of "everything you needed to know about dysfunctional families and recovery" (though I admit that this was my original vision!). Many excellent books have already been written that describe dysfunctional families and the Adult Child syndrome in compassionate detail. To repeat such descriptions would be a waste of God's trees.

What I am attempting to present is an outline or overview—with some very *detailed* components—about what it means to be "perfected in love." This book explores a love-based approach to understanding our emotions, redefining our self-image, altering our self-destructive self-talk, discovering forgiveness, making choices, and building stronger and more loving relationships with others and with God. The foundation of this approach is the Bible, which not only *addresses* recovery issues, but provides clear and loving assistance to all who need comfort and healing.

I have learned a great deal from writing this book, and I hope that you will make some joyous and healing discoveries as you read it. Most of all, I hope that you discover, as I have, that it *is* possible to "be perfect"—once you know what "teleios" really means.

# - 1 -

# The Quest for Perfection

*There is no fear in love. But perfect love drives out fear, because fear has to do with punishment. The one who fears is not made perfect in love. (1 John 4:18)*

WHAT DOES IT MEAN TO BE A CHRISTIAN?"

It was the standard Sunday school question, and I was receiving the standard answers: It means that we are redeemed, forgiven, loved by God; it means that we shouldn't drink or smoke or sin; it means that we are supposed to be "extra good." The answers from this experimental class for Christian Adult Children were safe and traditional; no one wanted to venture too much yet.

Then one woman raised her hand and said, rather timidly, "It means that we are to be like Jesus."

At last, I thought, we are getting somewhere. People were nodding and smiling around the room. But the woman was *not* smiling. Instead, she was fighting back tears.

"And that means...?" I prompted. (Actually, I doubt I responded with anything so professional—but it was her words that I was to remember, not my own.)

"It means I never *can* be!" she cried. "Jesus was *perfect*, and I can *never* be perfect. I can *never* be like Him. I'll never be good enough."

Perhaps this woman had not quite expressed what it meant to be a "Christian"—but she had certainly expressed what it meant to be a "Christian Adult Child." We are driven to be perfect—and we are certain that we are doomed to fail. And because we regard "perfection" not simply as a *desirable* goal but as one that we have been *commanded* to reach, we suppose that our inability to "get there" will cause us to remain "second-class citizens in Christ."

## "Be Perfect Therefore..."

Adult Children tend to feel like "second-class citizens" under *any* circumstances. We believe that we aren't "good enough," that we don't "do well enough," and that we are a constant disappointment to others (as well as to ourselves). We struggle to be accepted and approved, yet never expect to "make it"—and when we *do* receive acceptance or approval, we don't "believe" it. We absorb every criticism as though it were "gospel," but shrug off praise as inaccurate and undeserved. We tend to think, "If that person *really* knew me, he wouldn't say nice things about me." We tend to think that about *God*, as well.

Many of us grew up in families that had little love to spare for us. Sometimes the love went to other, "favorite" children in the family. Sometimes there was no love at all. Sometimes love was handed out in small doses, or had to be "earned" by good behavior. Sometimes what passed for "love" was accompanied by verbal, physical, or even sexual abuse. No matter where our families fell on the "dysfunctional" continuum, *love* was a precious commodity, one that we hungered for and never seemed to receive enough of.

But we had *hope*. We "knew" that our performance and perhaps even our personality were "disappointing"—but we were convinced that if we could only go that extra mile, give that extra 110%, and find a way to *be* what everyone *wanted* us to be, love would be ours. We hoped that love was waiting for us, somewhere, if we could just "try hard enough" to attain it. Love, to an Adult Child, is rather like the elusive pot of gold at the end of an even more elusive rainbow.[1]

Most of us learned that "love" was something that was "awarded" as the prize for good behavior, and withdrawn to "punish" us for bad. The lesson taught by the vast majority of dysfunctional families is that "love" is something that is measured out on the basis of *approval*—and *approval* is the result of our *performance*. Hence, the obvious conclusion: Improve our performance, get more approval, win love.

We learned to believe that *love* lay just on the other side of *perfection*. If we could become "perfect," if we could stop making so many mistakes, if we could get rid of all our character flaws and personality defects, then nothing would prevent others from "approving" of us. Nothing would "prevent" others from "loving" us. We firmly believe that it is our *own* failures and character defects that "prevent" us from receiving love. The less "loved" we feel, the more we struggle to achieve the "perfection" that we believe will *win* us the affection we crave.

This type of thinking is common to most Adult Children, Christian or not. Christian Adult Children, however, think of perfection as *more* than simply a goal. We think of it as a *command*. We know that Jesus told us, "Be perfect, therefore, as your heavenly father is perfect." (Matt. 5:48) We often suppose that perfection is *required* before we can fully experience the love of God *or* the love of man.

At the same time, we are convinced that it is a command we can never fulfill. We are far too aware of our own shortcomings, our imperfections, our flaws. Every failure reminds us of how "stupid" or "incompetent" or "inadequate" we are—or *think* we are. Every time we fail to meet someone's needs or desires, we suppose that we aren't "caring" or "giving" enough—not enough to measure up to God's standards of giving and sacrifice. No matter how long we pray or read the Bible, we are convinced that a "good Christian" does more. No matter how hard we work, we are convinced that we should be working *harder* and doing *better*.

---

[1]Some of us, on the other hand, struggled not to win love but to avoid hate. Some of us learned to believe that we could *never* be loved because we were completely "unlovable," and our only hope was to become "good enough" to avoid condemnation and punishment.

We are convinced that our "personality" is our own worst enemy. We associate "perfection" with a host of emotions, thoughts, ideas, desires, and preferences that we don't have. We are convinced that we have the wrong emotions, the wrong thoughts, the wrong opinions, the wrong tastes. We believe that it is our moral obligation to "change" ourselves—but we also believe that we must never *reveal* to others that we *need* to change. We struggle for future perfection while striving to conceal our present *imperfection*. And since this struggle is incredibly painful, draining, and hopeless, we regard ourselves as even *more* imperfect for not being able to reach perfection "easily."

You may not know whether or not you are an "Adult Child." You may not know whether you came from a dysfunctional family—or even what "dysfunctional" *means*, precisely. You may be wondering whether or not this book is "for you." The answer is: If you are struggling to "be perfect," if you are desperate for approval because you believe that love "depends on it," this book is for you. If you *hurt*, this book is for you. This book is about *healing*, not about membership in some sort of exclusive "dysfunctional family" club.[2]

Many other books discuss what dysfunctional families are and what it means to be an "Adult Child." This book is about *recovery*—about finding answers and problem-solving techniques to help you heal from your pain. It isn't about *easy* answers or *quick* solutions. It *is* about love, which I believe is the *only* answer. But before we can get to the *answer*, we need to know what the *question* is.

## The Things We Do for Love

Are you a perfectionist? You may not know the answer to that one. You may believe that the quest for perfection simply makes you a "good, dedicated Christian." "Perfectionist" sounds rather like a dirty word—and it is. Nothing tears us apart, destroys our

[2]This book is for you whether or not you are a Christian, as well. The techniques and suggestions described in these chapters are based on love and truth—and those apply to *everyone*. If you are not a Christian, please don't be put off by the number of "chapter and verse" references you find in this book. It is my hope that through this book, you will discover Jesus in a new and perhaps surprising way—even if you *are* a Christian.

hope, or makes us feel more worthless than the belief that we have to "measure up" to an utterly impossible standard of perfection. Yet that is precisely the way many Christian Adult Children live their entire lives. We struggle and pray and work and struggle and pray and read and hope that no one *notices* how stressed and anxious and unhappy we are. We interpret our painful emotions as a sign that there is something wrong with *us* rather than something wrong with the way that we are pursuing our goal—or with the goal itself.

That goal, and our struggle to reach it, leads us into several common behaviors and ways of thinking. *Are* you a perfectionist? If more than two or three of the following sixteen "perfection-seeking behaviors" listed below describe *you*, chances are that the answer is "*yes*."

**1) We are impatient.** Adult Children believe that they are never doing enough, fast enough, soon enough, or well enough. We worry so much about *getting* things done that we are rarely able to appreciate what we have *already* done. We rush from one task to the next, wondering if we have forgotten or missed anything, with our minds always focused upon (and dreading) what lies ahead.

We believe that we are supposed to get things right "the first time." We are often impatient with the learning process; we consider ourselves "failures" when we undertake a new project and can't do it perfectly *right away*. Whenever we face a new challenge or task, we don't think, "I should do that," but rather, "I should have done that already." We do not think in terms of process or progress; instead, we continually condemn ourselves for not having "failed" to achieve a final "product" or "goal."

Most of us believe that we should "improve ourselves"—but we believe that we *should* have done it *yesterday*. We blame ourselves for not *already* being the kind of person we think we should be, or that we assume other people want us to be.

We don't know how to take time "for ourselves." If we aren't doing something "constructive" or "productive," we often feel terribly guilty for "wasting time." We don't know how to relax over a cup of coffee or a book, or how to play, or watch a sunset, or simply do "nothing." We feel lazy and selfish when we aren't doing something for *other* people. We may even believe that "self-care"—such as eating or sleeping properly—takes time that we don't have the right to spend upon ourselves.

When we enter recovery, we are often discouraged because we don't "improve" or "become perfect" as quickly as our impatience tells us we should. Instead of being able to look forward to change and growth, we blame ourselves for not having "already solved" each new issue that we confront. We may also expect others to blame us for not having "resolved" our personal issues by now. When our loved ones ask, "Why can't you just leave this behind and move on?" or "Why haven't you gotten over this yet?" we are sure we are doing something wrong, that we aren't moving "fast enough."

We don't imagine that there is time for us, or our needs, in God's universe. We expect other people to be impatient with us, and we expect God to be impatient as well. In recovery, we often suppose that God is waiting for us to "get our acts together" so that we can become better servants and better Christians. We want to "hurry up and be better" so that we can win the respect and approval of others, of God, and of ourselves.

**2) We are unkind to ourselves.** Adult Children rarely see themselves as due the same degree of respect, consideration, or kindness that they offer to others. We often believe that "kindness" is the result of "worth"—and we struggle to increase our "worth" so that we can become more "deserving" of better treatment.

We often think nothing of being put down, humiliated, insulted in public, called names, "chewed out" for the slightest mistake, ignored, or treated without respect—even by our closest friends or loved ones. Such treatment is often precisely what we give ourselves. We "punish" ourselves with unkindness in an effort to "motivate" ourselves to do better. We don't think that we have the right to be "nice" to ourselves until we manage to *become* the sort of person who *deserves* "niceness."

We have no kind words for ourselves. We grant ourselves no favors, no leeway, no mercy. We drive ourselves with punishments, not with "treats." We overwork and overstress our bodies, starve our emotions, and fill our minds with self-abusive thoughts. We often fail to take proper physical care of ourselves, and may neglect to give ourselves a balanced diet, enough sleep, or even medical treatment when we are ill.

We also tolerate unkindness from others. Many Adult Children believe that they would not *receive* abuse if they did not *deserve* abuse—and thus submit to inappropriate behavior they would never dream of inflicting upon another. Some "submit" because they believe that this is the "scriptural" thing to do—either as part of "turning the other cheek" or of "submitting" to a husband.

We don't expect kindness, gentleness, or caring from God. Instead, many of us dread His criticism, punishment, and rebuke—and expect to receive this treatment from other Christians as well. While we know that we are expected to *be* "good neighbors," we can't imagine that God expects others to be good neighbors to *us*.

**3) We wish we could be more like other people.** Though we would be slow to admit it, many of us feel as though God "favored" others with more advantages or better attributes than He gave to us. We feel lacking, inferior, and unable to "compete" with people we regard as "naturally" gifted or superior. We tend to assume that everyone around us is smarter, more capable, more confident, more attractive, and more *lovable* than we are. While we struggle to achieve the qualities we think we lack, we also often feel a twinge of envy toward those that we believe "attained" those qualities "without effort."

We often burn with anger and self-hate because we believe we lack the personality, looks, achievements, and abilities that we perceive in others. We believe that we are inherently incapable of doing as well or being "as good" as other people—and that we are therefore eternally cut off from the benefits that we believe are available only to the "deserving" or "worthy."

Most of us have learned from childhood on to compare ourselves to others—and to find ourselves lacking. Many of us were asked why we "couldn't be more like" a more favored brother or sister—and some of us hear this sort of message from loved ones today! We have learned to attempt to be what *others* are, instead of to discover what *we* are. We have learned to measure ourselves against impossible and unrealistic standards of perfection and performance, and when we "fall short" of those standards, we blame ourselves. We assume that other people are "meeting" those standards with ease, and that there is something wrong with us that prevents us from doing the same.

We often envy the "ease" with which other people pray aloud, or seem to "hear" God, or seem to "walk in victory." Most of us are convinced that *no one else* has the problems (or the feelings) that we have—and that, therefore, there is something wrong with us for having them. We envy the happiness we suppose others have, certain that they have total peace in their relationships with God and others. We spend our lives trying to "do better" so that we can be "more like" people that we believe "are better."

**4) We "boast."** Most Adult Children think of "boasting" as claiming lots of wonderful qualities and abilities that one does not have. Many of us have encountered boastful people—people who use their claims of "superiority" as an excuse to be abusive. We often believe that if a person is "smarter" or "stronger" or "more capable," that person has the *right* to treat us as an "inferior."

One woman, for example, believed for years that her husband's put-downs, criticisms, "silent treatment," and belittling words and actions were "justified" because he was "smarter" than she was—or so he claimed. By claiming "intellectual superiority," this man was actually claiming the right to emotionally abuse his wife. The real problem, however, lay in the wife's willingness not only to believe the claim *itself*, but to accept it as a valid rationale for abusive treatment.

Most of us would never consider "bragging" in this way, because we honestly believe that we have nothing to brag *about*. We believe ourselves to be hopelessly inferior, and we are certain that if we attempted to proclaim even our *genuine* abilities and achievements, no one would believe us. Nevertheless, we still practice a subtle form of "boasting"—if one accepts that "boasting" is a way of claiming something that isn't really true.

Adult Children have learned to declare that everything is "fine," that we are "feeling fine," that we have no "problems," that we have no needs, that we really don't *mind* knocking ourselves out for others, that we actually *enjoy* being miserable. We often claim that we are perfectly happy, content, and secure in the Lord. We want the world to believe that *nothing is wrong*.

We "boast" for the same reason a braggart boasts: We want people to like us, to think well of us, and to approve of us. We don't believe that people will accept us if they know that we hurt, that we have problems, or that we aren't as "spiritual" as we think we "should" be. We are afraid that if anyone discovers the truth, we will be rejected or condemned. So we have learned to say what we believe people want to hear—even when it isn't true.

Unfortunately, we are often correct: Many people *don't* want to hear the truth. They don't want to know that we hurt—and if we confess our pain, we are often greeted with simplistic platitudes like, "If you would just give it all to Jesus, that pain would go away." Many people don't want to know that our lives are falling apart, that we are terrified, that we don't trust God, and that we have no desire to run the next church luncheon. When we experience negative reactions to the truth, it only confirms our original impression that it is safer to "lie."

We even "boast" to God. We are often as afraid of losing *His* love and approval as we are losing the approval of people. We fear that if we admit to Him how bad things really are, how unhappy we feel, or that we are filled with doubt and distrust, He will be angry with us and perhaps even reject us. Some of us have been taught that we must never say anything "negative" to God, but that our "confession" must always be "positive" if we are to receive God's blessing in our lives. We often do not realize that one reason we do not *get* the help that we need is that we are unable to *admit* that we *need* it—even to God!

**5) We are hindered by pride.** A great many of us have been taught to believe, as though it were gospel, that there are certain problems and feelings and concerns that we *absolutely should not have*. Some of us have learned to believe that the greatest sin of all is to be "weak," and we often define "weak" as having emotions, pain, or needs. Some of us have learned that the greatest sin is to be "sick," because we were taught that "sickness" places a tremendous burden upon others. Some of us learned to believe that we should never ask for help for our problems, but that we were "supposed" to solve all our problems on our own.

Some Christian teachings reinforce these beliefs. Some churches teach that "affliction" is a bad sign, and that if we had "faith," we would never be afflicted. Some teach that negative or painful emotions are "wrong" and need to be "corrected" with the "right attitude." Some teach that if we are sick, it is because we have "failed to receive healing," which convinces us that it must be *our* fault. Some teach that all we need to do to "solve" a problem is to "turn it over to God," and that we are being "unspiritual" if we seek any other kind of assistance.

Pride frequently locks us into "roles." We strive to be the

"perfect spouse," the "perfect parent," the "perfect employee," the "perfect Christian." We try to appear "sin-free," "spiritual" and "committed." We often fall for the teaching that it is more important to "look good" than to "be good"—or that if we *focus* upon "looking good," we will somehow *become* good.[3] Yet we know that we aren't *really* as "good" as we pretend to be, and we live in constant fear of "discovery."

As a result, our pride often prevents us from seeking help where we need it the most. If we are convinced that we are "bad" for having the wrong emotions, we will do everything we can to avoid revealing that we *have* those emotions, and most especially, we will not admit that we need *help* for them. We are often too proud to cry, too proud to admit that we are angry, too proud to admit that we have been hurt or still feel pain from past hurts. If we associate "recovery" with "being sick," we may stubbornly resist the notion that we need to do anything to "heal" or "get better." If we believe that we are supposed to be "able to handle our own problems," we may refuse to seek guidance or assistance from others (or even from God) in our recovery process.

This form of pride can be a tremendous barrier to change, because before we *can* change, we must admit that we *need* and *want* to change. Before we can solve a problem, we must first acknowledge the existence of that problem—and accept that it is no *shame* to have problems.

**6) We are rude to ourselves.** Our self-talk is filled with name-calling, put-downs, sarcasm, ridicule, accusations, condemnations, and other forms of "toxic talk." Most of us don't know any other way to "talk" to ourselves. We believe we "deserve" this kind of language—even from our own minds—and we often believe that we "deserve" it from others as well.

When we make mistakes, we have a host of vile names for ourselves. Our automatic response is usually a nasty variant on "You stupid idiot!" We curse ourselves with profanity and obscenity, "chew ourselves out" for the slightest error or flaw, and use language against ourselves that we would shudder to use against our worst enemy.

---

[3]I am not making this up. I have heard this teaching in more than one church—and you may have heard it as well.

Most of us came from households that were, at the very least, verbally abusive. This is the language that we learned to consider "normal"—at least when applied to ourselves. While many of us learned the importance of "politeness" in our verbal transactions with the rest of the world, we learned that *we* did not rate that same politeness. Many of us still accept this form of communication from friends and loved ones, and even from our own children.

We also learned to take many other forms of "rudeness" for granted. We expect to be interrupted, ignored, criticized, or treated with contempt. We take it for granted that our feelings and our time are far less important than anyone else's. We often believe that "politeness" is something that we simply don't "deserve," and that we are the "kind of people" that others are automatically rude to—as we are rude to ourselves.

Rudeness—whether from others or from ourselves—makes us feel small and worthless, hurt and bitter, defenseless and stupid. At the same time, many of us learned to believe that we weren't supposed to be "hurt" by cruel and abusive language, or that we were silly to "take it seriously." Dysfunctional families often repeat maxims like "Sticks and stones may break my bones, but words can never hurt me," or ask, "Can't you take a joke?" The implication is that "mere words" do no harm and have no lasting effect.

The Bible says otherwise, however. It speaks of the tongue as "a restless evil, full of deadly poison. With the tongue we praise our Lord and Father, and with it we curse men, who have been made in God's likeness." (James 3:8-9) Far from condoning name-calling, Jesus says, "But I tell you that... anyone who says to his brother, 'Raca,'[4] is answerable to the Sanhedrin. But anyone who says, 'You fool!' will be in danger of the fire of hell." (Matt. 5:22)

**7) We are selfish.** This may come as a shock, for most of us have spent our lives desperately trying to be "unselfish," or to live down parental labels of "selfishness" and "lack of consideration." We have learned to believe that to be "unselfish," we must do whatever others ask of us, meet everyone else's needs before our own, "give until it hurts," and never complain. Since most of us have been *doing* precisely that for years, how could we possibly be

[4]An insult meaning "worthless" or "empty" one.

selfish? Indeed, many of us are concerned about beginning "recovery" precisely because we are afraid that it *is* selfish.

Often, however, when we are doing the things that *seem* the most unselfish, we are actually acting out of selfish interests—though we may not be aware of it. We do not strive for achievement and accomplishment because we hope to benefit from success and growth, but because we fear that we will be rejected and condemned if we do not "do more" and "do better." We struggle to become "perfect" not out of a sincere motivation to improve or grow, but out of a desperate desire to "cover up" our perceived character flaws and weaknesses.

We give to others, sacrificing our own desires and needs, because we fear that people will stop loving us or approving of us if we stop "giving." One woman, for example, was deeply concerned that though she did her best to do everything her friends asked of her, she seemed to "lose" those friends the first time she "failed" to meet their needs. A classmate asked her if it was possible to be a "friend" without being a "rescuer." Her startled dismay would have been comical if it was not also tragic: The thought had never occurred to her. We tend to suppose that the only thing people "like" about us is what we can "do" for them.

Because we are so afraid of being rejected or punished, we will often allow the demands of others to drive us to exhaustion. At the same time, we may never discern what is actually in the "best interest" of others; instead, we do whatever we are asked, and we may only vaguely wonder why we are surrounded by adults who act so much like spoiled children.

Our Christian walk may also be based on "self-interest:" We struggle to avoid sin, read and pray for a specific number of hours, volunteer on lots of committees, and prove what dedicated and selfless Christians we are *so that we can win the approval of others and of God.* We have learned, from painful experience, that we may be rejected if we fail to do what others want of us—and we have learned to believe that these are the things that *God* wants of us. We seek to avoid God's anger, and to avoid censure from critical Christians, not realizing that these are actually "selfish" acts.

Becoming "unselfish" means more than "doing less for me and more for others." It means identifying what is in the *best* interest of everyone involved, rather than what is "demanded" or "expected" or supposedly "required." Adult Children don't *want* to be selfish or *intend* to be selfish—but it takes a major change in thinking to suppose that we could actually be *less* selfish by learning to take better care of *ourselves*.

**8) We are angry at ourselves.** Adult Children are constantly angry at themselves. We are angry at ourselves every time we make a mistake—or think we do—and we are angry at ourselves the rest of the time for being the *kind* of person who *makes* mistakes. Whenever we say something wrong, upset someone, or express the wrong feeling, we are angry at ourselves because of how *other* people react to us. We are angry at ourselves for our past, for the things that we may have "gotten into." We are angry at ourselves for not being good enough or doing well enough. We are angry at ourselves for all the things that we haven't done yet. Our anger is a constant companion.

We don't like ourselves, and we are angry at ourselves for not being "someone else," someone "better." We are angry at ourselves when we don't live up to the expectations of others, or our own. We think that everything that has gone wrong in our lives is our fault. When someone else gets angry with us, we become even *more* angry with ourselves for having "provoked" that anger.

Many of us lived with constant anger from our parents. We were often the "safe targets" on which our parents could vent the anger that had accumulated from other, external pressures. Most of us never knew that our parents were actually upset about office problems or difficulties in their relationship; all we knew was that whenever we did anything wrong (and sometimes when we didn't), all that anger descended upon *us*.

Some of us learned to accept the blame for family problems that we had nothing to do with. We may have learned to believe that we were "responsible" for a parent's drinking problem, or a parent's violent rages, or even a parent's sexual abuse. Quite often, we heard, "I wouldn't have had to do this if you hadn't driven me to it," or "You made me do it. It's your fault." We learned to *believe* these messages, and today many of us carry hidden anger toward ourselves not only for our *own* problems, but for having been the cause of our *family's* problems.

We have a hard time being nice to ourselves, or speaking to ourselves gently, because inside we are *furious* with ourselves. We take our anger out on ourselves in any way we can. When it becomes extreme, we may even punish ourselves physically. We may deliberately (or "accidentally") hurt ourselves, or punish our bodies with eating disorders, or drive ourselves to an accident-prone state of exhaustion. Carried to an extreme, anger at self can lead to suicide.

**9) We condemn ourselves.** The "sin" Adult Children dread the most is the sin of "making a mistake." We believe in instant condemnation—from ourselves and from others. We don't perceive mistakes as something to be "forgiven" for, but as something to be "punished" for. Nor does it matter *why* we made the mistake—whether it was because of circumstances beyond our control or expectations beyond our ability. The only thing that matters is that we *made* one. Indeed, we even condemn ourselves for mistakes that we make in the *process* of learning how to do a task *correctly*.

We believe that we are responsible for doing things "right" 100% of the time. Even a single error makes us "total failures." Nor do we blame ourselves simply for our mistakes; we blame ourselves for being the *kind* of person who *makes* mistakes.

In our minds, if there is any sin greater than making a mistake in the first place, it is *repeating the same mistake twice*. We think there is "no excuse" the second time; we should have "known better." When we repeat the same mistake, we think we are stupid, careless, or simply not "trying hard enough."

For this reason, we do not allow ourselves to *forget* past mistakes. One young man was enthusiastically telling his father how wonderful it was to understand forgiveness, rather than to "kick himself" for mistakes that were ancient history. His father responded by recalling a mistake that *he* had made on his honeymoon, forty years before. "Oh, I'm not kicking myself for it," he declared to his son. "But I don't want to forget it, so that I can be sure that I never do it again!"

We rarely remember our successes (if we notice them in the first place). However, we keep a "record of wrongs," a personal rap sheet of every mistake we have ever made, real or imaginary. Whenever we do something wrong, it not only goes on our record but *reminds* us of that record: It adds to the "weight of evidence" against us. We are our own accusers, our own prosecutors, and our own judges—and we offer ourselves only one verdict, "Guilty."

When others condemn us, we assume that they are "right". If someone can find fault with us, we are certain that there must be "fault to be found." We accept criticism as deserved, but reject compliments as inaccurate and unmerited. We make ourselves the scapegoats for every problem in our lives, every trouble in our families, and even the difficulties that our parents experienced. We see ourselves as hopeless disappointments to ourselves, to others, to God. Our motto is "if only I could have been better." We hope that our constant "self-conviction" will somehow inspire us to become better people—but it only succeeds in increasing our fear, self-hate, anger, and drive for impossible standards of perfection.

**10) We succumb to evil.** The quest for perfection is stressful and agonizing. We never relax; we never rest; we never feel "good" about ourselves or anything else; and we hurt continually. We can't stand to live like this *all* the time; it would kill us. But when we don't believe that we can "change" the perfection quest itself, we often find that we have to do something *else* to "ease the pain."

Quite often, the things we turn to for "pain medication" are destructive and evil. This is a part of our lives that we don't like to talk about, think about, or admit—but many of us are keenly aware of that "dark side" to our search for perfection. Indeed, it is the "dark side" that makes us feel even *more* guilty and even *more* determined to "become perfect," even as it drags us farther and farther away from the perfection that we seek.

We may medicate our pain through alcohol or drugs. Adult Children of alcoholics are at a high risk of *becoming* alcoholics, or finding another addictive behavior through which we can "handle" or "control" our feelings. Some Adult Children turn to various forms of sexual activity to "feel good" or to "feel loved." One young man became suicidal over his inability to break free from sex addiction that drove him to seek "love" from prostitutes. Some turn to pornography and masturbation. Some turn to various forms of occult activities, such as fortunetelling or Ouija boards, or worse. These activities make us feel guilty and ashamed, and we promise ourselves over and over again that we will stop, that each time is the *last* time—but we can't stop.

Some of us find release in "socially acceptable" addictions. It is quite possible to get "hooked" on work, on achievement, on power, on money, or even on religious activities. When such behaviors "take over" our lives, no matter how "good" they may appear on the surface, they have become addictions—and addictions destroy.

I have encountered Adult Children who have gotten "hooked" on romance novels, food, exercise, relationships, success, shopping, and on such "noble" pursuits as prayer and fasting. None of these things are "evil" in themselves. But they *become* evil (yes, even prayer and fasting) when we are no longer able to control them, when they control us. Paul writes, " 'Everything is permissible for me'—but not everything is beneficial. 'Everything is permissible for me'—but I will not be mastered by anything." (1 Cor. 6:12) When we become addicted to an activity or a substance, we are "mastered" by it; we become the slaves of evil.

We can't stop because we haven't learned any healthy way to free ourselves from the pain, or from the feelings that we have learned to consider "unacceptable." Because we believe that *we* are evil, and that what we *feel* is evil, we keep trying to "stuff" the part of our nature that we don't know how to accept or deal with. The fact that we can often only "stuff" our feelings and "unacceptable thoughts" through addictions and "medications" is a good indication that "stuffing it" is itself an "evil" way to handle that part of us that we don't understand yet.

**11) We believe lies.** Our quest for "perfection" is often based upon what we have been taught to believe about ourselves. Most of us have been taught to *believe* that we are hopelessly imperfect, that we are failures, that we are disappointments. We believe that we are stupid, incompetent, inconsiderate, selfish, inadequate, worthless, unlovable, and unacceptable. We believe that we have done nothing worthy of "approval" and many things worthy of "disapproval." We have learned to accept a host of negative, destructive labels as our "identity."

When people tell us that we are wrong, we believe them—and we try to come up with the "right" answers or the answers that will "please" others. When people tell us that our opinions are invalid or stupid, we believe them—and we try to reflect the opinions of others. When people tell us that our dreams or ideas are ridiculous, we believe them—and we often give up our hopes and dreams because we have been *told* that we have no chance of success. When people tell us that we aren't "considerate" enough, we believe them—and struggle to prove how "loving" and "giving" we can be.

We believe every criticism of our performance—beginning long before the days when our parents shook their heads in disappointment over an A- on a test. We believe that we never do well enough, and that we will never be good enough. We often believe that we are not "spiritual enough"—especially when others regale us with tales of how many hours they spend "on their knees" or impress us with their knowledge of the scripture.

When people tell us that we don't have the right attitude, or that we aren't trying hard enough, or that our feelings or reactions are "inappropriate," we believe—and we try to change. We are at risk of living our entire lives in an endless effort to become what we "should be"—simply because we have learned to believe a set of lies about what we *are*.

Moreover, we often ignore the truth even when we *do* hear it. Which would you be more likely to believe— "You're doing excellent work" or "I'm really disappointed in your performance"? Most of us believe criticisms, but ignore and dismiss compliments. We feel very uncomfortable when someone tells us that we look nice, or that we are fun to be with, or that we did something well, or that they are impressed with us. But we take to heart the slightest indication that we may have done something "poorly."

Not only do we believe lies, we may also believe that we *have* to lie to protect ourselves. We may have learned that the truth brings pain. Many of us have been rejected or condemned for having the wrong opinion, the wrong idea, the wrong thought, or the wrong feeling. Many of us have learned that a sure way to destroy a relationship is to discuss its problems honestly.

We may even have found that to confess our "sins" to fellow Christians is not the way to find help and forgiveness, but the way to find rejection, condemnation, and humiliation. One woman, a victim of emotional and verbal abuse in her marriage, asked her church for emotional support as she struggled to leave a lesbian relationship. Instead of receiving help, she was condemned and rejected for a sin that she had *already confessed and repented of.* One church member told her, "I could have understood if it had been a *normal* affair..."

Such lessons may teach us to believe that we need to "lie" to God, that we can't come to Him with our troubles or thoughts or feelings. Instead, we suppose that we need to pray the "right" things or express only "positive" thoughts in prayer. This keeps us locked into the ultimate lie: That God won't "love" us if we reveal the "truth" about ourselves to Him.

**12) We do not protect ourselves.** Many of us have become so accustomed to pain—either from childhood or in adulthood—that we honestly think we must be doing something *wrong* if we *don't* hurt. We often believe that we aren't "doing enough" unless we are "giving until it hurts," working ourselves to exhaustion, and finding other ways to "crucify the flesh."

When we believe that self-care is self-*ish*, we may abuse *ourselves* by failing to take proper care of our bodies. We may fall victim to eating disorders in an attempt to control, or even to punish, our bodies or our looks. We may work ourselves until we are physically stressed and exhausted—and then *blame* ourselves for *feeling* tired and "burnt-out." No matter what our physical "breaking point" is, we assume that a "strong person" could and *should* do "more"—and we assume that we are "weak."

We often do not provide ourselves with adequate nutrition, rest, or medical care. Some of us learned that it was "wrong" to be sick—and as adults we have a very hard time admitting that we need treatment. One woman became trapped in a web of conflicting messages: Though she became very upset when people didn't "believe" that she was physically ill, she also did her best to *convince* everyone that "nothing was wrong" when she was sick. She often refused to go to doctors even for serious medical problems because she predicted that "they wouldn't believe her." When she finally recalled that she had been "punished" for being sick, or for injuring herself, as a child—and when she realized that this punishment was actually "unfair" rather than "deserved"—she was able to change her approach to self-care.

Often, we fail to protect ourselves from the abuse of others. We may "allow" others to abuse us verbally, physically, or even sexually, either because we believe we have no alternative or because we believe we "deserve" it. Many Adult Children who were physically or sexually abused in childhood grew up to believe that they *deserve* abuse or that any abuse they receive is "their own fault." Some believe that it is an inevitable part of "loving" relationships, or that they must "put up with it" to *keep* a relationship. We may even abuse ourselves, inflicting physical injury upon ourselves as "punishment" for our mistakes and flaws.

Even when our relationships are not sources of "harm," they may not be sources of "protection" either. Our parents often had too much stress of their own to want to hear about *our* problems. We often learned not to "bother" other people with our troubles—including our spouses or closest friends. One woman's husband, for example, refused to help her deal with a problem of sexual harassment at work: This was "her" problem, not "his." When this is our experience with loved ones, we often assume either that God has no interest in protecting us (or we wonder where He was when we needed Him), or that He, too, may actively "harm" us.

**13) We don't trust.** Adult Children expect promises to be broken, commitments and obligations to be forgotten or put aside for "more important things," and trust to be violated. We don't expect people to be honest about their intentions or their feelings. When someone says "I love you" or "I will never hurt you" or "I won't let you down," we rarely believe them.

When we *do* trust, we are often disappointed, because we have not learned how to determine who is *trustworthy*. Instead, we learned to believe that the keeping of promises and honoring of commitments depends upon *us*, not upon another. Many of us were told, as children, things like "I won't take you to the zoo like I promised because you haven't been good enough this week to *deserve* it." We often believe that promises depend upon the "worth" of the recipient rather than the "character" of the giver.

More than anything else, we are afraid to trust others with the "truth" about ourselves. We fear that if we reveal "who we really are," others will condemn or reject us. We often hide our personality (or, more often, our *perception* of our personality) under the characteristics we believe others *want*. We fear that if we reveal what we think or believe, others will ridicule us, criticize us, or condemn us as "stupid" or "ignorant." We fear that if we express our feelings, we will make people angry, be told that we are "overreacting," or give people a weapon to use against us. We fear that if we "confess" past mistakes, they will be held against us. We fear that if we reveal painful secrets, they may be used as "ammunition" to hurt us or manipulate us in the future. We're afraid of revealing our true desires and needs, for fear that these may be used as a form of "emotional blackmail" against us. Some of us believe that to let anyone know what we care about or want is the best way to have those things taken away from us.

Nor do we trust ourselves. We do not trust our own judgment, our ability to make the correct decisions, or our likeliness to "do the right thing." Instead, we often seek rules and guidelines from others or from institutions to tell us "what is right" or "what to do." We are afraid of taking risks, making choices, or determining our own actions, because we are convinced that we will "do the wrong thing." We aren't sure that others will tell us the *right* thing, but at least if *others* "steer us wrong," we won't be to blame.

Finally, we do not know how to trust God. We have learned that people with power over us will often use that power to take advantage of us, manipulate us, or abuse us. Since God has more power than anyone else, we may find Him more threatening than anyone else. We have little experience with people who would use their power in our best interest. Instead, we are often afraid that if we really "surrender" to God, He will take everything away from us and send us off as impoverished missionaries to some remote, hostile, and bug-infested part of the world. We fear that He, like others, will condemn and reject us for who we are and what we think. Yet because we know that we are *supposed* to trust Him, our inability to do so—or to do so "100%"—makes us feel like hypocrites, and fills us with guilt and fear.

**14) We lose hope.** Adult Children approach life with a strange combination of high hopes and hopelessness. Many of us received promises that "things will get better" or "it will never happen again." Such promises took us on a rollercoaster ride of hope and disappointment: Though things might seem to "turn around" for awhile, they always got worse again.

Many of us came to believe that if we could only escape the chaos of home, we would find a perfect world outside of it, a world in which all our problems would disappear or be solved. Some of us came to believe that finding the "perfect partner" would end our sadness and pain, only to find that our rescuers were often as abusive as what we sought to be rescued *from*. Some of us sought the perfect job, the perfect career, the perfect look, the perfect community, or the perfect church. We came to believe that if our current situation was the source of our current *unhappiness*, changing the situation would bring us *happiness*.

Yet, over and over, we find our hopes shattered. The "perfect job" turns out to be as unfair or difficult as the last one. The perfect church contains imperfect people. The perfect look doesn't bring us the attention or affection we desire. The perfect partner has feet of clay. Most of all, our own efforts to improve seem unsuccessful, and we begin to regard *ourselves* as "hopeless."

Many Adult Children become caught in one of three "hope traps." The first is to continue searching for the "perfect solution" in the outside world, moving from one relationship to the next, one job to the next, one church to the next, always hoping to find the "cure" in something external. The second is to look at "self" as the "problem," and to try to improve ourselves, become more what we think others "want" us to be, work harder, do better, or wear a more perfect "mask" of conformance and acceptability. The third is to give up hope altogether and assume that because we haven't found the solution yet, it does not exist.

Many Christian Adult Children enter into a relationship with God with this same combination of unrealistic expectations and hopelessness. We may start out hoping that God will provide an instant, miraculous "cure" for all of life's problems, and that once we enter into a relationship with Him, we'll never have "trouble" again. When troubles *do* occur, as they invariably do, we begin to doubt. We may then shift into the "performance" trap, believing that if we pray more, read the Word more, and "do" more for God, *then* our troubles will be removed. When the desired "outcome" of our "performance" does not materialize, we may feel as though God has betrayed us and let us down, and that there is no hope left.

**15) We do not persevere.** Adult Children often find it very difficult to finish what they start. We may not put off the *beginning*, but we procrastinate over completion. We often doubt that our "finished" work will be "as good as it should be"—and in consequence, we sometimes never "finish" at all. Many of us have closets filled with unfinished craft projects, unfinished novels, unfinished dreams. Many of us feel as though we are living in perpetually unfinished *lives*.

When we are afraid that our work won't be "perfect," we often find it difficult to complete. As soon as we suspect that it isn't going to "turn out" exactly the way we wanted, or the way we think others expect, we may abandon it altogether. We are often afraid to move forward, take a chance, accept a promotion, or attempt the career of our dreams—because we are afraid that we have to be perfect when we *start*.

We are like people who, upon beginning a class on some unfamiliar subject, assume that we are expected to be able to pass the final exam *before we have begun the course*. If we can't be perfect "immediately," we assume that we are failures. We do not make allowances for progress; we have learned to believe that the only thing that "counts" is completion—and perfect completion at that. We believe in *products*, not in *process*.

We often take this approach to change and recovery in our own lives. We want to be "better"—but we don't believe that we have the right to take time to *get* better. We search for the quick fix, the overnight solution. Once we determine that we *aren't* perfect, we don't perceive this revelation as an opportunity or a challenge. Instead, we see it as another source of condemnation: We think we should have "gotten there" already. We may hop from one "quick fix" recovery fad to the next, looking for the one that will "complete" the process as opposed to the one that will *begin* it. We may feel pressured to "recover *now*" because our own loved ones are impatiently asking, "Why can't you let this go and move on already?"

We can be susceptible to condemning messages about recovery from the church. Many Christians believe that "recovery" should be an "overnight" miracle from God, not a long-term process of healing and growth. When people tell us that "all we need to do" is "give it to the Lord" or "receive our healing" or "let go and let God," we believe it—or feel guilty for having "failed." Many Adult Children spend their lives going through what I call the "revolving door of rededication" in the hope of "getting it right *this* time."

Because we are so often looking for "quick" results, we may not give any approach time to "work." When we read of a new technique or a new way of thinking that might be helpful, we don't say, "I'll *do* it." We say, "I'll *try* it." We *do* try it—for a few weeks. But when we don't experience *immediate* results, we often assume that it "doesn't work," and we give up.

Recovery can only *begin* when we realize that we may have *no idea* where it is going to end. The "end" is not seen; it can only be hoped for. We don't know where we are *going* because we don't know where we *are*. Nor can we "undo" the effects of *years* of false

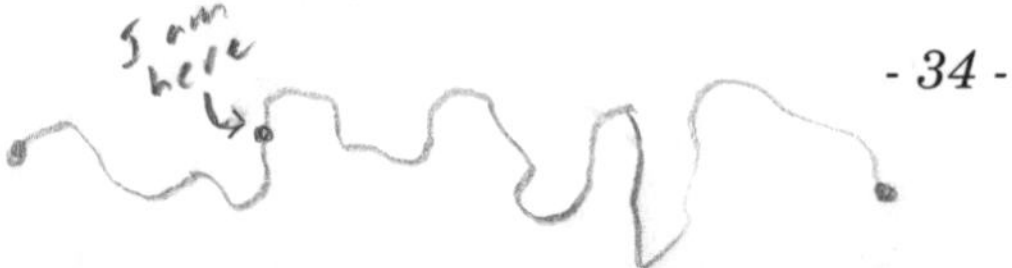

teachings and perceptions with a few *weeks* of positive affirmations or prayers. Recovery is the result of perseverance, and perfectionism is perseverance's worst enemy.

**16) We fail.** As long as we pursue the goal of "perfection," we are bound to fail. We *do* fail—over and over and over again. Every night that we go to bed with the realization that we aren't "perfect" yet, we feel like failures. Every morning when we realize that there is "more to do," we feel like failures.

We have learned to believe that if we can say, "I could have done that better," or "I could have done that more quickly," or "I could have done more," we are automatic failures. Saying that something could be done *better* is the same, to us, as saying that it wasn't done "well enough." If it wasn't done "well enough," then it wasn't perfect. And if it wasn't *perfect*, then it was *imperfect*, and if it was *imperfect*, it was meaningless.

We apply the same standard to ourselves. If we can say, "I could be more considerate" or "I could be less impatient," we regard ourselves as failures. We have not achieved "perfection," so we are imperfect—and in our world, "perfect" and "imperfect" are like darkness and light. We don't see in "shades of gray." We don't notice that we are "better" than we were yesterday; we only notice that we aren't "as good" as we want to be *tomorrow*. And since we can *always* say that we could "do" more or "be" better, we believe that we are *always* failures.

We believe that we have "failed" if we get sick instead of "succeeding" in remaining healthy (even though we may do nothing to *keep* ourselves healthy). We believe that we are "failures" if we need help, if we need advice, if we need ministry. We believe that we are "failures" if, in any way, we suspect that we are a "burden" to someone else. We believe that we are failures if we don't have the "right" emotions, if we are unhappy, if we are what we consider "weak" rather than "strong." We believe that we are failures every time someone has a need that we have not met. We believe that we are failures if *we* have a need at *all*.

When we fail, we get angry with ourselves, we condemn ourselves, we lose patience, and sometimes we even punish ourselves. Because we *believe* that we are failures, we believe that others are justified in condemning us, rejecting us, and "punishing" us as well. Nor do we expect any "better" treatment from God, whose standards, we suppose, are considerably higher than our own or those of others. If people see us as "failures," we suppose that God sees us as *colossal* failures.

## Failure and Fear

If you have been involved in the "perfection quest" for very long, you have discovered one thing: It rarely produces the *love* that you have sought. Instead, it tends to produce something else. It produces *fear*.

The more we struggle for perfection, the more we fear that our *imperfections* will be discovered. The harder we try to succeed, the more we fear failure. Instead of getting smaller, our fear of disapproval, rejection, condemnation, and punishment grows. Often, we try to fight the fear by struggling *harder*, perhaps believing that if we could reach "perfect," we would have nothing more to be afraid of. But as we struggle, we become increasingly aware that we are *never going to get there*. We become convinced that we *are* failures, that we *are* hopeless, and that we *deserve* the abusive treatment we apply to ourselves and accept from others.

Fear hurts. It drives us to do things that we later regret. It is a feeling that we want desperately to get rid of, but because there seem to be so many *things* to fear in our lives, we don't know *how* to get rid of it. We believe that our worst fears could come true any day. We live in a nightmare of dread and apprehension; anxiety and tension are our daily companions. We have lived in this condition for so long that we can't imagine what being "fearless" or "free" would actually be like. All we are really sure of is that *we* could never live that way.

The Bible, however, tells us differently. It tells us that "God did not give us a spirit of fear." (2 Tim. 1:7 KJV) If God did not give us such a spirit, it stands to reason that we are not "doomed" to live with it for the rest of our lives. But what can we do about it?

John tell us that "fear has to do with punishment." (1 John 4:16) But he *also* tells us that "perfect love drives out fear." We are not afraid because we haven't managed to become *perfect* yet; we fear because we have not become perfected in *love*.

That, at last, is an attainable goal. None of us is ever going to be as good, as loving, as giving, as understanding, as self-sacrificing, as pure, or as holy as Jesus. That doesn't mean that we stop *trying* to be "imitators of God"—but it *does* mean that we can stop *condemning* ourselves for not having *made* it yet.

The answer, then, does not lie in more and better "works." It does not lie in trying to "be a better person." It does not lie in trying to "get rid of all the sin in our lives." All of these may be worthwhile goals—*when* they are undertaken in the right way and for the right reason. When we pursue them as the way to get us *closer* to God or more *approved* by men, we are doing the wrong thing for the wrong reason. Works and sacrifice and "personal goodness" will not get us any closer to God. Only love can do that. To find healing, to find an alternative to the quest for perfection, to find release from fear and pain, we have one alternative: We must "Follow the way of love." (1 Cor. 14:1)

# - 2 -

# The Greatest of These Is Love

*Love is patient, love is kind. It does not envy, it does not boast, it is not proud. It is not rude, it is not self-seeking, it is not easily angered, it keeps no record of wrongs. Love does not delight in evil but rejoices with the truth. It always protects, always trusts, always hopes, always perseveres. Love never fails. (1 Cor. 13:4-8)*

Life offers endless opportunities. If you are an Adult Child, however, you may feel as though it offers endless opportunities for *failure*—and little else.

Every step we contemplate confronts us with agonizing possibilities: Will it lead us closer to "perfection"—or will it plunge us into failure and defeat? We may have little hope of ever *achieving* perfection, but the thought of failure fills us with dread. Failure means condemnation, humiliation, shame, rejection, and possibly punishment. Failure "proves" how stupid and worthless and incompetent we are. While "perfection" may not bring us much *closer* to the approval and affection we seek, we believe that every "failure" drives us farther away. While our "successes" are forgotten as soon as they happen (by us and often by others), evaporating like mist behind us, we believe that every *failure* adds to a never-to-be-forgotten backlog of shame, guilt, and unworthiness.

Such beliefs provide us with an endless supply of *fear*. Fear lurks like a shadow behind every anticipated joy, like a nightmare at the edge of every dream. It's the "dark side" of every promise made to you, every opportunity that comes your way, every gift you are offered. It's the heart-pounding feeling of panic that comes late at night, sometimes with no apparent cause, or the stomach-twisting pang of anxiety that accompanies the demands of the day. Fear is a thief, robbing us of joy, confidence, strength, trust, and hope. It keeps us locked in patterns of self-defense designed to minimize pain and risk to our vulnerable, traumatized selves. It is our constant companion. Many of us can't image what life would be like without it.

We often suppose that we fear the "unknown," the "future." But that isn't precisely true. What we *fear* is the *known*—the painful experiences that we have had *before* and that we don't want to have *again*. We fear rejection because we *know* what it feels like to be abandoned and unloved. We fear humiliation because we *know* what ridicule and shame feel like. We fear to take risks because we *know* what it is like to be condemned and penalized for making mistakes. We fear failure because we *know* how it feels to be labeled "not good enough."

Adult Children, however, don't simply fear the "bad things." No one enjoys humiliation, shame, or rejection. What sets us apart is that we *also* fear the *good* things—because many of us believe that whenever something "good" happens, something "bad" will follow.

We have learned, for example, that recognition may be followed by shame, or trust by betrayal. We have learned that "openness" leads to "vulnerability," and that intimacy often leads to pain. We often consider the *start* of a new relationship virtually "the beginning of the end." We crave love but we expect to be abandoned; we crave intimacy but we expect to be rejected as soon as someone gets to "know" us; we crave approval but we are certain that it will never last. Even when our lives are going *well*, we are "on edge," constantly "waiting for the other shoe to drop."

We are caught in a double bind of desire and dread. The closer we come to what we want, the more terrified we may become of actually "getting there." Until we learn how to resolve these conflicting messages and expectations, our lives can become an endless effort to compensate for competing and often contradictory fears. We may find ourselves struggling to attain what we want—only to pull away or "sabotage" our own efforts just as "success" (or love) seems to be within our grasp.

We don't know what to do with our fears. We aren't sure where they came from. It seems as though they have "always been there."

It *seems* as though they have always been there because they *have* always been there. Our fears, our search for perfection to attain love and *conquer* those fears, and our sense of hopelessness and imperfection, are not a reaction to a frightening future, but a legacy from a frightening past. We learned these fears and beliefs in childhood and *brought them with us.*

## A House Built on Sand

Critics of the "recovery movement" are reluctant to acknowledge that an adult could still be the victim of fears and experiences that happened "way back in childhood." Some argue that, since Christians are "new creations" (2 Cor. 5:17), what happened "in the past" should no longer have any effect upon us.

The Bible, however, stresses the importance of foundations—and childhood is the foundation of adulthood. Parenting is the process of *building* a foundation for a child's future life, and scripture neither discounts nor ignores the importance of that process. When the Bible tells us, "Train a child in the way he should go, and when he is old he will not turn from it," (Prov. 22:6), it does *not* go on to say, "But if you *don't* train a child properly, don't worry; good parenting doesn't matter. He'll figure it out eventually."

God designed His children to receive a prolonged period of care and training from their parents—longer than any other creature. God was obviously able to create creatures that could feed and take care of themselves in a few months or a year; why didn't He design *us* the same way, if "childhood" was to have no "meaning" in terms of adulthood? The implication of scripture *and* of God's design is that parenting is *very* important—that it was *intended* to be the foundation of our adult lives.

The Bible also indicates that different types of "foundations" are possible. A strong foundation doesn't happen by accident. It happens through the *application* of the Word of God—and not just "knowing" the Word or having good intentions, but upon *doing* that Word. Jesus declared, "Therefore everyone who hears these words of mine and *puts them into practice* is like a wise man who built his house on the rock. The rain came down, the streams rose, and the winds blew and beat against that house; yet it did not fall, because it had its foundation on the rock. But everyone who hears these words of mine and does not put them into practice is like a foolish man who built his house on sand. The rain came down, the streams rose, and the winds blew and beat against that house, and it fell with a great crash." (Matt. 7:24-27, emphasis mine.)

The Bible contains much advice about how to "do" healthy relationships. We are told, "Do not let any unwholesome talk come out of your mouths, but only what is helpful for building others up according to their needs, that it may benefit those who listen." (Eph. 4:29) "Get rid of all bitterness, rage and anger, brawling and slander, along with every form of malice. Be kind and compassionate to one another, forgiving each other just as in Christ God forgave you." (Eph. 4:31-32) "Have nothing to do with the fruitless deeds of darkness, but rather expose them." (Eph. 5:11) "Do not get drunk with wine, which leads to debauchery. Instead, be filled with the Spirit." (Eph. 5:18) "Husbands, love your wives, just as Christ loved the church and gave Himself up for her... In this same way, husbands ought to love their wives as their own bodies. He who loves his wife loves himself." (Eph. 5:25, 28) "Fathers, do not exasperate your children; instead, bring them up in the training and instruction of the Lord." (Eph. 6:4)

God does not have one set of standards for families and another for the rest of the world. The institution of "family" does not provide some sort of sanctifying umbrella for "deeds of darkness." On the contrary, the family is the *first* and *most important* place for these scriptures to be practiced and honored, for the family is the "learning ground" for all other relationships (including one's relationship with God). Dysfunctional parenting can be measured by how far it departs from these basic relationship commandments.

Building healthy relationships, however, does not mean sweating through the Bible to uncover a host of "do's" and "don'ts."

Nonchristians are as capable of having *healthy* relationships as Christians are of having *unhealthy* relationships. These commands *themselves* have a foundation upon which *they* are built. That "foundation" is summed up in Jesus's command, " 'Love the Lord your God with all your heart and with all your soul and with all your mind.' This is the first and greatest commandment. And the second is like it: 'Love your neighbor as yourself.' All the Law and the Prophets hang on these two commandments." (Matt. 22:37-40)

The foundation of all foundations is *love*. Love is the foundation of functional parenting, parenting that God models for us by personal example. Love is more than warm feelings or good intentions. We are told, "let us not love with word or tongue but with actions and in truth." (1 John 3:18)

If we were raised by a family that did not *practice* love consistently—even if it was loving at heart—our foundation is not firm. It is shaky, unstable, "sandy," and full of cracks that allow fear to creep into our spirit and take root there. Salvation does not automatically change this foundation, for salvation does not miraculously erase or replace our misperceptions, beliefs, thought patterns, feelings, or fears. After salvation, we are *still* called to "be transformed by the renewing of your mind. Then you will be able to test and approve what God's will is—His good, pleasing and perfect will." (Rom. 12:2)

Recovery is the process of replacing these sandy foundations with something solid and firm. It means replacing a foundation of fear with a foundation of love, for "he who abides in love abides in God, and God abides in him." (1 John 4:16 RSV) And therein lies the primary problem, for those of us who were not raised upon a foundation of love *often do not know what love is.*

## I Will Love You If ...

Love is a popular word. We all like the sound of it and we all want it. But L-O-V-E is a word that can be overused, misunderstood, and misinterpreted just like any other word. Before we can become "perfected" in love, we need to know what it means.

Most dysfunctional families—with some traumatic exceptions—consider themselves "loving" families. However, they also tend to apply the word "love" to a number of things that are *not* love. Many

of us learned, for example, that when someone says, "I love you," what they really mean is "I expect something of you." Many of *us* say "I love you" when we really mean, "I need you so much that I am willing to do *anything* for you." When we hear that God loves us, we may believe that we must work extra hard to please Him. We believe many things about love that have nothing to *do* with love.

- We believe that "love" is something that one must earn by working hard to prove one's worth—by getting good grades or doing one's chores or by keeping everyone "happy."
- We believe that "love" is something that is handed out like a reward for achievement or good behavior—but rewards, by definition, are something "special" and not something that one receives every day or all the time.
- We believe that "love" is something that can be taken away from us if we fail to please or to live up to someone's expectations, or if we make someone angry, or if we are "disappointing."
- We believe that "love" may be available only in limited quantities, which is why we need to work "extra hard" to get a share. We may have learned that there was never enough to "go around," and that if someone else had "more," it might mean that we would have "less."
- We believe that "love" isn't something that can be counted on, that it isn't always available when we needed it or wanted it, or that it depends upon the "mood" of the giver.
- We believe that "love" depends upon the quality of our personality, and whether or not we are "good" enough or "worthwhile" enough to receive it.
- We believe that "love" indebts us to the giver, and that if we receive love, we are obligated to "repay" it through our works, gratitude, or sacrifices.
- We believe that "love" is something that we can receive only if we prove our own love *first*.
- We believe that "love" may be associated with pain, broken promises, let-downs, disappointments, demands, condemnation, untrustworthiness, neglect, and even abuse.

There is a word for what we have learned to pursue in the name of "love," and that word is "approval." Approval is conditional; unlike genuine love, it is not given as a gift, but must be earned. It is based upon performance, not upon person; it teaches us that we are valued for what we "do," not for who we are. While love says, "I love you because you are my child," approval says, "I love you because you are such a *good* child."

When "approval" is offered (or withheld) in the *name* of love, we learn to believe that "love" comes only to the deserving, to those who have worked hard enough to be "good enough" to receive it. This belief locks us into a lifetime struggle to become "perfect." At the same time, because approval is fleeting and unsatisfactory, we never *feel* loved—and we suppose that we must be doing something wrong. We believe that we aren't "loved" because we aren't "good enough" to be loved, and that we have no hope of *ever* being loved.

Christian proponents of "self-esteem" have tried to counter the devastating effects of our sense of worthlessness and "unlovableness" by arguing that, because we are children of God and created in His image, we have "infinite value." Others argue that God loves us not because of our inherent "value" but *in spite of* our unworthiness, and conclude that God's grace "proves" that we are completely *without* value. The trouble with this controversy is that both sides are approaching the issue from the wrong direction. God does not love us because we have value; we have value *because God loves us*. Love is not the result of value; value is the result of love, and God demonstrated how much He valued us by the price He was willing to pay to redeem us. John writes, "This is love: Not that we loved God, but that He loved us and sent His Son as an atoning sacrifice for our sins." (1 John 4:10) Jesus did not die for us because we were worth dying for; He died because He loved us.

## Self-Love Without Sin?

Most of us know that God loves us. Most of us know that we are supposed to love God. Most of us know that we are supposed to love others. What most of us do *not* know, however, is that we are supposed to love ourselves.

The very thought of "loving ourselves" raises a loud outcry among many Christians. "Self-love is a sin," many declare. If we love ourselves, surely we will become selfish and prideful, forget the grace of God, and begin to "exalt" ourselves. Some point to the scripture that tells us, "Love your neighbor as yourself" (Matt. 22:39), as "proof" that we "already" love ourselves.

Adult Children would probably join in the outcry against the idea of "loving self," not because we think we *already* love ourselves "too much," but because we are convinced that there is nothing to love in the first place. Most of us don't even *like* ourselves. Many of us hate ourselves. We hate our personalities; we hate our looks; we hate our feelings; we hate our behavior. We wish that God would transform us into someone else, someone "worth" loving. One young woman hated herself so much that she went forward in a healing service to ask God to "replace" her personality.

We may be tempted to mistake this self-hate for spiritual humility, but it is not. It is a matter of scriptural ignorance—as is the attitude that we must avoid "self-love" at all costs. When we don't know what love is, it is easy to be persuaded that self-love is "bad" and "sinful." If we take a closer look at Matt. 22:39, however, another picture emerges.

This scripture commands each of us to "love your neighbor as yourself." That word "as" means "*in the same way that.*" We are to love our neighbors *as much as* or *in the same way as* we love ourselves. Putting aside for a moment the question of whether this implies that we "naturally" love ourselves, how is this verse telling us to love our neighbor?

If love for "self" was truly sinful and selfish, would Jesus *really* instruct us to love our neighbors *in the same way*? Would He command us to apply self-exalting, "undeserved" love to *others*?

He would not. Jesus does not tell us to love our neighbors (or ourselves) with "sinful" love. Instead, He tells us, "A new command I give you: Love one another. As I have loved you, so you must love one another." (John 13:34, emphasis mine.) He tells us to love our neighbors "as I have loved you"—with His love, not with selfish love. And if we are to love our neighbors "as ourselves," then it follows that the kind of love that we are meant to have for ourselves is *also* His love. We are to love our neighbors as ourselves, and ourselves *as He has loved us*.

The love of God is without sin. It is not, by definition, "self-seeking," (as we'll see below). We have God's love not because we deserve it or earned it, but because He has given it to us as a gift. If we do *not* apply His love in our own lives as well as in the lives of our neighbors, we are literally throwing away the gift of God.

Nor can we skip that part about "as ourselves" and try to simply love our neighbors. Love is not something that we are called upon to practice "part time." It is something that we are meant to operate in 100% of the time. It is not a garment that we put on and take off at will; it is to be our way of life. God does not tell us to love our neighbor, whom He loves, yet hate ourselves, whom He *also* loves. We are to love as God loves—and *God loves you just as much as He loves your neighbor.*

When we act in self-hate, we act in sin. We are told, "Get rid of all bitterness, rage and anger, brawling and slander, along with every form of malice. Be kind and compassionate to one another, forgiving each other, just as in Christ God forgave you. Be imitators of God, therefore, as dearly loved children and live a life of love, just as Christ loved us and gave himself up for us as a fragrant offering and sacrifice to God." (Eph. 4:31-5:2) This verse does not tell us to get rid of "some" bitterness and anger and malice. It says "all." We are not told to *retain* the bitterness and anger that we feel toward ourselves. We must get rid of *all* of it. We cannot be "imitators of God," nor can we "live a life of love" as Christ, when we hate ourselves.

## Prescription for Recovery

How can we begin to love ourselves, however, when we don't know what love is or how to apply it in our lives? Fortunately, God provides us with a clear definition of His love: "Love is patient, love is kind. It does not envy, it does not boast, it is not proud. It is not rude, it is not self-seeking, it is not easily angered, it keeps no record of wrongs. Love does not delight in evil but rejoices with the truth. It always protects, always trusts, always hopes, always perseveres. Love never fails." (1 Cor. 13:4-8) When we learn how to understand this definition and promise, we will learn four important skills: How to recognize the love of God (and distinguish what is *not* from God), how to recognize genuine love in others, how to act in love toward others, and how to *live a life of love ourselves.*

God's love has sixteen components—and each of those components "counters" one of the sixteen "perfection-seeking behaviors" described in the previous chapter. As we learn to understand and practice each of these sixteen components, we will learn how to become "perfected in love" instead of struggling to "perfect *ourselves*" so that we can *be* loved. It isn't easy. It won't happen quickly, overnight, next week, or even next year. You may look at some of these steps and say, "I could *never* do that! I could *never* treat myself that way!"

But it is necessary. To replace the sandy foundation of fear and perfectionism that we have built our lives upon with a *firm* foundation of *solid love*, we must learn what God's love means and how to apply it in our lives. To heal, we must have love. God has given us a sixteen-step prescription for recovery, and His promise tells us that this prescription will work, if we will follow it.

**1) Love is patient.** Impatience springs from worry, and worry springs from a combination of lack of information and lack of time. When we wonder if we have "done enough" or done our work "soon enough," it is because we worry about what *might* happen if we "don't get everything done." God, however, has an infinite supply of time *and* information—so He has no reason to be impatient.

God is not frustrated or angry with our "lack of progress." Instead, He watches over us like a gardener tending a beloved garden, well aware that no amount of rushing and pressure will cause a flower to blossom any faster. Each of us is "like a tree planted by streams of water, which yields its fruit in season and whose leaf does not wither." (Psa. 1:3) When we live in impatience, our "fruit" often resembles those supermarket tomatoes that are picked long before their time and artificially "ripened" so that they can be rushed to the store. They may *look* perfect, but one bite tells you the results of this sort of "impatience."

God does not attempt to push us to "ripeness" before our season. He knows where we are, where we are going, and how long it will take us to get there. He also knows that when we *do* "ripen" or "mature," our fruit will be sweet and nourishing, because it grew according to His timing, not according to ours.

When we accept God's patience, we begin to learn how to be patient with ourselves. We can begin to learn how to relax. We can slow down and become involved in "process and progress," rather than in condemnation. We can stop telling ourselves that we aren't "doing enough" or "moving quickly enough." Once we realize that there are no "ultimate destinations" on the recovery journey, we can begin to shed our impatience to "get better" and "get it over with." We can take time to savor success in the tasks that we *have* completed, rather than blaming ourselves for what we *haven't* done yet. We can stop telling ourselves, "I should have done that already" or "I should have known that already."

As we learn to walk in love, we will stop berating ourselves in the harsh, impatient "inner voice" that we are so accustomed to. We will listen, instead, for the nurturing and comforting voice of God. We will learn to appreciate the roses, and the sunsets, and the sound of the waves, not as "luxuries" that we don't have time for, but as part of God's creation that were given expressly to us to care for and enjoy.

As we discover the patience that comes from love, we can stop struggling to earn God's approval and start seeking His peace instead. God does not always promise approval; He *does* promise peace. We will find ourselves bearing healthier, happier "fruit" when we learn how to reach for what God guarantees, rather than the elusive goals of perfection that we have pursued for so long.

**2) Love is kind.** Most of us find it easy to believe that God is kind and gentle to others—but few of us imagine that He applies that same kindness to us. We need to realize that God is not "double-minded": He does not give gentle treatment to some of His children and abusive treatment to others.

God is not a slave-driver. He does not stand over us with a whip, driving us until we are ready to drop with exhaustion or despair, then punishing us when we stumble. God is a tender parent, with a quiet voice, who stands ready to minister to us as He ministered to a tired, despairing Elijah in the desert (see 1 Kings 19:3 on). He is not waiting for us to "be good" so that He can "be kind" to us; God is *already* kind.

We may have lived most of our lives in fear of punishment for doing the "wrong" thing. Healing and peace become possible when we realize that whether our next step is right or wrong, God is still standing by us with His hand held out, not in punishment but in kindness. As we learn to understand God's love, we realize that He is there with tenderness, with comfort, with compassion, with mercy, with words of strength and encouragement. He is there to support us, pick us up if we have stumbled, guide us if we need direction, and hold us when we don't have the courage to go on. He is not waiting to condemn us for every "wrong step"—but waits patiently and kindly to guide us back to the right one.

As we learn to walk in God's loving kindness, we will begin to learn how to treat ourselves the same way. We learn to stop abusing ourselves with our own bitter self-talk, our own accusations and put-downs and name-calling. We learn to stop driving our bodies and minds as though we were slaves under a whip. We stop chasing elusive goals of achievement and perfection, and start discovering what God's goals are for us instead. We can begin to realize that if God does not become "unkind" when we make mistakes or stumble, we do not have the right to be "unkind" to ourselves either, for in doing so, we are counteracting God's work in our lives.

Once we begin to do this, we will see growth. Our "inner man" will respond to this consideration and begin to flourish and blossom. We will begin to see confidence, change, strength, and joy where once we found only pain and fear. We will see healing as our inner wounds are treated with kindness for perhaps the first time.

Treating ourselves with kindness also means avoiding the unkindness of others. God does not condone the abuse of any of His children. "Don't you know that you yourselves are God's temple and that God's Spirit lives in you? If anyone destroys God's temple, God will destroy him; for God's temple is sacred, and you are that temple." (1 Cor. 3:16-17) We have no right to destroy that temple with our own unkindness—nor do we have a right to *allow others* to destroy it. When we permit ourselves to be abused, punished, and enslaved by the unkindness of others, we are counteracting God's loving kindness by participating in a sin.

**3) Love does not envy.** A major obstacle to recovery is the assumption that God is "jealous" of any effort we spend upon ourselves. Christian Adult Children are often convinced that because recovery does not seem to directly serve God or others, it is "selfish."

Many of us were raised by parents who seemed to care only about what they could "get" from us. Loving parenting, however, is not the process of raising slaves or imposing obligations; it is the process of bringing healthy, functional human beings to maturity.

That is God's purpose in our lives as well. Just as a genuinely loving parent wants to see a sick child recovery, not so that he can get back to washing the dishes and scrubbing the floors but so that he can be *well* and stop *hurting*, God wants the same in our lives. He is not angry or jealous if we are "sick" or if we need "help." His desire is for all His children to grow and become strong. He is not "jealous" of whatever is required to bring you joy and strength and wholeness—for you can hardly deprive God of "resources" that come from Him in the first place! Recovery is not time that we have "stolen" from God, but time that He has given us so that we can discover what it means to be His beloved child.

As we stop fearing the jealousy of God, we can begin to give up our own forms of jealousy and envy as well. We begin to realize that God does not "favor" some of His children over others, or provide some with "better" abilities or benefits. Instead, He created us all as unique individuals—different, but not "inferior."

Through His love, God has made each of us an equal heir to His limitless resources, including love, joy, peace, strength, comfort, and encouragement. God's resources are not based on worldly measures of "worth." Paul reminds us: "There are different kinds of gifts, but the same Spirit. There are different kinds of service, but the same Lord. There are different kinds of working, but the same God works all of them in all men." (1 Cor. 12:4-6) No matter who you are or what you do, God works in you in love.

**4) Love does not boast.** A more accurate translation of this verse is "Love vaunteth not itself."[1] "Vaunteth" isn't a word we hear every day—but it is something that we have often experienced. Many of us had parents who "vaunted" their love, whose motto was "Look how much I have done for you!" We were never allowed to "miss" the sacrifices involved in every gift we received and everything that was done for us. We were taught that "love" required an endless debt of "gratitude."

This verse tells us, however, that love does not "boast" about itself. When love is accompanied by "boastfulness," it is not a gift, but something that is offered with the expectation of gratitude or repayment. Love does not indebt.

God's love is a gift. When you receive it, you don't have to worry about "getting the bill" later. God does not say, "Look how much I have done for you! Look how much you owe me in return!"

Nor do we have to "boast" to *receive* God's love. We don't have to "prove" that we are better or more "deserving" than we are. We don't have to be perfect—or appear perfect—to be loved by God. We

[1]Strong's Concordance, #G4068.

can't fool Him anyway—but He honors the truth, and delights in our honesty, even when the truth is painful.

When we begin to experience God's love, we realize that there is no need to "lie" to Him, no need to pretend that we are happier or healthier or more trusting and faithful than we are. Instead, when we express our true feelings and troubles to God, we discover that we really do have "the Father of mercies and God of all comfort, who comforts us in all our affliction, so that we may be able to comfort those who are in any affliction, with the comfort with which we ourselves are comforted by God." (2 Cor. 1:3-4)

If the truth is that we are falling apart, terrified, overwhelmed with feelings that we don't understand or know how to control, and even filled with self-destructive thoughts, we can tell Him. We do not have to wear a Christian "happy face" or a "Sunday smile" to convince God (or other Christians) that our walk is 100% victorious and joyful. When we give up "boasting," we can begin to admit our hurt, angry, and confused feelings. Only then can we actually begin to *do* something about those feelings, and about the situations that are *causing* them.

When we stop attempting to conceal our hurts from the world, we will also discover who actually "walks in love" toward us and who doesn't. When others turn away from us because they don't want to know about our pain or our situation, this is not a sign that there is something wrong with *us*; it is a sign that we are probably better off without that relationship in the first place. If our relationships are built upon approval that is itself built upon our carefully maintained illusion of perfection, those relationships will be destructive to everyone involved. When we become free, in love, to confess the truth, we will find ways to build relationships with genuinely loving and caring people.

**5) Love is not proud.** When Jesus walked among men, He showed us what God means when He says that love is not proud. Jesus did what no "righteous" Jew would do: He ate with sinners, He associated with tax collectors and prostitutes, He spoke with Samaritans. "And when the Pharisees saw this, they said to His disciples, 'Why does your teacher eat with tax collectors and sinners?' But when He heard it, He said, 'Those who are well have no need of a physician, but those who are sick. Go and learn what this means, "I desire mercy, and not sacrifice." For I came not to call the righteous, but sinners.' " (Matt. 9:11-13) Jesus associated with those that the "solid citizens" of that day rejected and scorned.

Through Jesus, God tells us that you can never be so bad, so worthless, or so "unclean" that God is too proud to associate with you. You can never descend so far that God won't be willing to reach down to where you are and not only lift you up, but embrace and comfort you in all your filth. We don't have to "get clean" to come to God. We come to God so that we can "get clean." God says, "Though your sins are like scarlet, they shall be as white as snow; though they are red as crimson, they shall be like wool." (Isa. 1:18)

We may feel that we don't have the "right" to come to God unless we are "perfect." Many Adult Children are enmeshed in sin and shame, in behaviors that they feel guilty about, in thoughts and feelings that disgust them. We often suppose that we need to "get rid of" these things before we can come before God. We know we don't "deserve" His love. But God tells us that He will walk with us, talk with us, eat with us, forgive us, and love us—not *after* we have "cleaned up our acts" but *before*. God is not "too proud" to get His hands dirty. Instead, He stands ready to cleanse us of all the dirt we have ever gotten into, and as we stumble and fall back into the very same behaviors that we have been trying to get out of, He stands ready to help us out and clean us off again and again.

Recovery may be a step backward for every two steps forward (and it may seem like the other way around sometimes), but God is with us every step of the way. We don't have to "get perfect" to come to Him; when we discover His love, we become able, instead, to partake of His perfection.

**6) Love is not rude.** There is no rudeness in love, or in God's interaction with us. God will never rudely dismiss us, or ignore us, or ridicule us, or treat us sarcastically. He will never call us names, put us down, or make fun of us. He will never treat our dreams and ideas and thoughts as though they (and we) were stupid and silly. He will never shame or humiliate us. God does not make us feel small or worthless. He will never "brush us off" or walk out on us. No matter what we have come to expect from the rudeness of others, we will *not* receive this kind of treatment from God.[4]

[4]You will never hear "rudenss" from God in answer to prayer , for example.

It is, in fact, impossible to be rude "in love." When someone attempts to justify rude behavior by claiming, "You know I said that in love," that person is mistaken. He may have *intended* to act in love, but rudeness is not loving. One man found that an officer in his church continually interrupted him and refused to listen to him or let him finish what he was saying. At the same time, this officer continued to declare, "You know I'm telling you this in love." When the man pointed out that interrupting was rude, and that love is not rude, he was finally able to be heard!

When we learn to walk in love, we will begin to learn the importance of putting all rudeness out of our lives—including rudeness to ourselves. Even though "rude self-talk" has become virtually second nature to us, it is a nature that we can do without. Every time we say to ourselves, "You idiot," we contradict the Word of God. Every time we say to ourselves, "You're so hopeless and worthless, you'll never get anywhere," we contradict the love of God in our lives. And when we tell ourselves that what we have done is "unforgivable," we contradict the redemption of God in our lives. When we learn to address ourselves in Godly language, the meaning of what God has done for us and how much He loves us will begin to become real to us.

Instead of resorting to rudeness, we can learn to simply confess our mistakes, without adding bitter words of shame and condemnation to that confession. When we do not meet our own expectations, we can learn to explore those expectations themselves, rather than automatically labeling ourselves as worthless failures. In our personal lives, we can begin to walk in love when we practice the command, "Do not let any unwholesome talk come out of your mouths, but only what is helpful for building others up according to their needs, that it may benefit those who listen." (Eph. 4:29) We are "listeners" to our own talk—and if it is not helpful for building us up, if it does not "benefit" us, then it needs to be changed in love.

**7) Love is not self-seeking.** Have you ever received an unexpected, last-minute Christmas gift that sends you running to the mall in a frantic search to find a way to "reciprocate?" We learned that "gifts" obligate us to the "giver," and that we are selfish and ungrateful if we do not "give back" more than we receive.

We often expect the gift of love to have the same "strings" and requirements. We have never learned how to receive a "free" gift, a gift that is not "self-seeking." Even though we often expect no "return" on our *own* gifts, we believe that we will be *expected* to "pay for" every gift that we receive—including the gift of God's love.

God's love is the "costliest" gift we will ever receive. It cost the life of God's "only begotten Son." Nothing we do can ever "pay God back" for this gift—and that realization often makes us feel very guilty, and obligated to do our best to "try" to pay Him back even though we can't. We feel required to show God, through hard work and sacrifice, how much we *appreciate* His gift.

A true gift, however, is one for which the giver has already chosen to "bear the cost," rather than one in which the giver attempts to pass that cost along to the receiver. Many of us respond to God's love as though we were still under an obligation to "repay" the debt that Jesus died to pay in the first place. Paul tells us: "Now when a man works, his wages are not credited to him as a gift, but as an obligation... But the gift is not like the trespass... For the wages of sin is death, but the gift of God is eternal life in Christ Jesus our Lord." (Rom. 4:4, 5:15, 6:23)

"Self-seeking" love seeks reciprocation: It gives only because of what it hopes to receive. God's love is *given* because He seeks our best interest, not His self-interest.

Many of us have learned to believe that God's love is "self-seeking" (though we would never have used that term) because we have experienced jealousy and condemnation whenever we do something that does not directly serve someone else. Many of us have sacrificed personal interests, needs, desires, relationships, friends, finances, and even our health and well-being on the altar of "selflessness." Yet no matter how much we "give up," as long as we have "more to give," it is never enough. We often believe that God makes the same sort of demands upon us: We believe that anything we do that does not *obviously* contribute to His service or worship is "selfish." One family expressed this attitude perfectly when, after having dinner and games with another Christian family, they bemoaned the fact that they had "wasted" time that they could have spent "praising and worshiping God."

Jealousy is the ultimate form of selfishness. It is a way of saying, "Whatever you have, I want, and if you don't give it to me joyfully, you are bad and you don't love me enough." Some of us have learned to believe that this is *precisely* how God reacts to us—

yet His Word tells us differently. "To do what is right and just is more acceptable to the Lord than sacrifice." (Prov. 21:3)

We often wonder if "recovery" is "just and acceptable." It may *seem* to be "selfish" because we are doing something for *us*. Most of us have learned to believe that "being sick" *and* needing time to "get well" are "selfish," because we aren't able to "help out" when we are in *need* of help. We believe that we are "doing something good for God" if we take care of one of God's *other* children, but not if we take care of *ourselves*. We also suppose that it is "selfish" to *need* care. We are caught in quite a contradiction: Each of us tends to perceive ourselves as the *only* child of God who is not entitled to His mercy, patience, or healing.

God wants us to be well, not sick. "Jesus said to them, 'It is not the healthy who need a doctor, but the sick. I have not come to call the righteous, but sinners.' " (Mark 2:17) A loving parent wants his child to heal because *he loves the child*—because he wants that child to be well *for the child's sake*. God's love is not self-seeking; His desire is for our well-being. God is not "honored" by having a flock of sick, miserable children "glorifying His name." He is *honored* by joyful Christians who have learned to understand "what this means: 'I desire mercy, not sacrifice.' " (Matt. 9:13)

**8) Love is not easily angered.** We often perceive God as a perpetually angry deity, who talks to us only when He is mad at us (which, we think, is most of the time). We imagine that the only thing God wants to "tell us" is what we are doing wrong or what is not "pleasing" to Him. In consequence, we spend a great deal of our lives trying to anticipate and avoid those things that we suppose make God *mad*—because we can't imagine that anything about us makes God *glad*.

While the Bible does not say that God is *never* angry, neither does it say that He is *always* angry—as our parents may have been, for example. "The Lord is compassionate and gracious, slow to anger, abounding in love." (Psa. 103:8) Nor does He "hold" anger against us, "For His anger lasts only a moment, but His favor lasts a lifetime; weeping may remain for a night, but rejoicing comes in the morning." (Psa. 30:5)

Learning how to walk in love means learning how to step *out* of anger and *into* peace and forgiveness. God is not interested in beating us over the head with our mistakes and imperfections.

Instead, He holds out a loving hand to lead us forward, so that we can leave our mistakes behind. He offers forgiveness, telling us to "put away" wrath and bitterness, and to allow His tenderness and acceptance and mercy to enter our hearts.

When we live in anger, we cannot heal; we can only hurt. To move forward, we need to find ways to free ourselves from that anger—and from the constant fear and expectation of anger from others and from God. We need to forgive our mistakes instead of condemning them, heal ourselves instead of punishing ourselves, and accept the "self" that we have rejected for so long. We can stop blaming ourselves for not being who we think we "should" be. When we begin to model our walk on God's "slow to anger" love, we learn that it is safe to make mistakes and to be ourselves. Only in this way can we discover who we really are, take risks, and grow. We can begin to feel safe, not only with others, but with God—and with ourselves. When we learn to walk in love, not anger, we will stop being our own worst enemy, and stop expecting *God* to be our second-worst enemy.

**9) Love keeps no record of wrongs.** God forgives. He keeps no record of wrongs. He is not the "keeper of the eternal rap sheet."

A "record of wrongs" is a powerful mechanism of control, one that we often learned from our parents and experience with our current loved ones. When we know that everything we do "wrong" is going to be held against us, perhaps indefinitely, our lives become a constant struggle to do what others *want* us to do. We struggle to "make up for" our failures, "live down" our mistakes, and "prove" that we can "do better next time." Many of us have been shamed and humiliated not only by the "record" that others hold against us, but that we hold against ourselves. A record of wrongs keeps us looking forever backward, trying to "do better" than we did before. It is the exact opposite of forgiveness, and of love.

God does not "control" His children by continually reminding them of, and making them feel guilty for, the things that they have done wrong in the past. All of us *have* done wrong and we know it. God tells us, however, that we are not to think on these things. Jesus says, "But do not think I will accuse you before the Father." (John 5:45) God does not *need* to "control" us through shame and guilt. Instead, He liberates us with forgiveness.

Rehashing old mistakes is a way of looking backward. God

looks forward, not back. He helps you find solutions for the problems that confront you, instead of placing blame for those problems. He has redeemed your past for all time. He took the burden of your mistakes so that you could be *free* of that burden, not so that you could haul your record of failures around like a concrete backpack, or so that you could feel even *more* guilty and indebted to Him for what He has done.

When we begin to understand forgiveness, we can begin to let go of our "rap sheet." This is what Paul is telling us to do when he writes, "But one thing I do: Forgetting what is behind and straining toward what is ahead, I press on toward the goal to win the prize for which God has called me heavenward in Christ Jesus." (Phil. 3:13-14) We are called to *forget* past mistakes, and *press on* toward future goals. We may start by "forgetting" mistakes that we made years ago, and then progress to mistakes we made months ago—until eventually we are able to do what God does, and "forget," through forgiveness, the mistake we made yesterday or in the last few minutes.

Once we stop worrying about mistakes, and begin to realize that they are forgiven and "over" instead of something that we will never "leave behind," we can begin to take risks. We can take the chance of *learning* something new, without worrying about *how well we do*. We can try new things, decide whether or not we like them, and move on to other things. We don't have to get everything right *the first time*, or even the second or third time, or *ever* in some cases. Instead, we can keep the confidence that God loves us just as much when we make mistakes as when we don't.

**10) Love does not delight in evil.** We often suppose that God thinks "the worst" of us, perhaps because we are sure that He "sees the worst." We know that we have done bad things, wrong things, and self-destructive things. Some of us may be caught in addictive behaviors that fill us with guilt and shame. The more we strive for perfection, the more we realize how imperfect we are, and the more we expect to be condemned and rejected.

A better way to translate this verse would be that "love does not keep an inventory of evil." The word "delight" means to "take an inventory of."[5] When we believe that God "keeps a record of

[5]Strong's Concordance, #G3049.

wrongs," we often suppose that He is keeping an "inventory" of all our "evils." Yet the Bible tells us just the opposite.

God does not keep lists of our faults, flaws, personality defects, character deficits, and failures. This is not His picture of our "self." He does not think of us in terms of the labels that we have become accustomed to—labels like "stupid" and "incompetent" and "inconsiderate" and "boring." When God looks into our hearts, He does not inventory all the negative things that He finds there; instead, as the next verse discusses, He delights in the "good things."

This is the ultimate definition of acceptance. It is not that God is blind to our faults. He knows that they are there, far more clearly than we do. Yet He loves us enough to *overlook* these imperfections, rather than inventory them and, perhaps, present us with "lists" of our unacceptable qualities. While others may have presented us with lists of flaws and told us, "I'm only telling you this out of love," this scripture tells us that love does *not* "inventory evil."

God keeps no "inventory" of our flaws because He does not want us to concentrate upon flaws but upon Himself. God is both flawless and the source of all flawlessness. When we concentrate upon Him, we learn how to emphasize what is good, not what is rotten or disappointing or inadequate. We are not told to keep an "inventory of evil," but to focus upon what *God* focuses upon: "Finally, brethren, whatever is true, whatever is honorable, whatever is just, whatever is pure, whatever is lovely, whatever is gracious, if there is any excellence, if there is anything worthy of praise, think about these things." (Phil. 4:8)

**11) Love rejoices with the truth.** This is the second half of the statement above. Not only does God *not* keep an "inventory of evils" about us, He also "rejoices in the truth" about us. This has an interesting implication: It suggests that the "truth" is worth "rejoicing" about.

It is unlikely that God would "rejoice" in the "truth" that you are a worthless slimeball, less lovable than pond scum, an excrescence upon the face of the planet. It is unlikely that He would be "delighted" by the alleged "fact" that you are stupid, incompetent, inconsiderate, and hopeless. So there are only two possibilities: Either God *does* rejoice (for whatever reason) in these unpleasant "truths," *or*, these things *are not the truth*.

We imagine that the "truth" is bleak and ugly. Our personal

"truth" is built of our record of wrongs, our history of failures, our perception of "self" as weak and imperfect. We see the truth as something to be concealed and changed, not rejoiced in. Yet the truth is that we don't *know* the truth.

It is time to take a closer and more loving look at ourselves, and at what we have believed for so many years. Maybe we *aren't* hopeless; maybe we aren't incorrigible failures; maybe we aren't stupid and worthless and ugly; maybe we aren't selfish and uncaring and disappointing. If these things were "true," God would not be rejoicing. But if God is rejoicing, we had better discover what He is so happy about.

When we learn to walk in love, we discover and accept the truth about ourselves. We begin to realize that we are *not* as bad as we thought. We discover qualities and abilities and characteristics that we never noticed before. We begin to see our flaws and imperfections not as cause for despair and shame, but as opportunities for growth and development. Most of all, we begin to discover *who we are in Christ*, which is a truth worth rejoicing in.

**12) Love always protects.** Most of us experienced, at the very least, "verbal" abuse in our homes—including yelling, shrieking, hysterical accusations and scolding, and name-calling. Many of us experienced physical and sexual abuse at the hands of "loved ones" as well. We learned that "love" rarely protects, and often harms.

Many of us don't trust God to protect us. Some Adult Children wonder where God was when they needed Him—when they were being physically or sexually abused—and then feel guilty for their anger at God for "failing" them. Because we were often punished for having the "wrong" feelings as children, we may expect *God* to punish us for having the "wrong" feelings toward Him.

We may believe that God will only "protect" us if we are obedient and good. Some Christians teach that "sin" removes God's "hand of protection" from us, and that if we stray, we will "get what we deserve." Such an attitude, however, portrays God as a highly dysfunctional parent, one who would stand by and let His child run over the edge of a cliff simply because that child "disobeyed" His command to stay away from that cliff. Sometimes God *does* let us "hit bottom" because it is the only thing that will cause us to *turn* from our own self-destructive behaviors—but He doesn't *require* us to "hit bottom" just to "teach us a lesson."

The truth is that God does not consider it "OK" to abuse His children. We are told, " 'Because he loves me,' says the Lord, 'I will rescue him; I will protect him, for he acknowledges my name. He will call upon me, and I will answer him; I will be with him in trouble, I will deliver him and honor him.' " (Psa. 91:14-15) Paul asks, "What, then, shall we say in response to this? If God is for us, who can be against us?" (Rom. 8:31)

If the answer is "us," something needs to change. As we learn to walk in love, we will also learn to *stop* being our own worst enemies. We will learn, instead, to take proper care of God's temple, God's child. We will learn to stop hating and abusing what God loves. We will learn how to avoid self-destructive behaviors, addictions, and interactions. We will learn, instead, ways to create for ourselves an environment of safety and love, an environment in which we can model our *own* behavior upon the behavior of our gentle, loving Parent. Perhaps most of all, it means that we will choose to protect *ourselves* from the abuse of others, instead of submitting to it because we believe we deserve nothing better.

**13) Love always trusts.** We know that we are "supposed" to trust God, and that part of learning to love Him means learning to trust Him. But how can "trust" be a part of learning how to love ourselves? How can we possibly be called to "trust" ourselves? The word "trust" means to "put faith in."[6] Does that mean that God puts His faith in *us*?

Parents who do not "trust" their children often *remove* a child's right to make decisions and choices. Instead, "untrusting" parents choose what a child is to wear, what he is to study, whom he is to play with, what he is to eat, and even what he is supposed to "like" and what career he is expected to choose. When a parent feels unable to "trust" a child to do what is "best" for himself, that parent robs the child of any chance of living his own life. The parent may *believe* that she is acting in "love," or in the child's "best interests," but what she is actually doing is creating a helpless, frightened adult who has no idea how to make choices or live independently.

We often suppose that the world would be a better place if God did precisely that—but the reality is that He does not. He gave us

---

[6]Strong's Concordance, #G4100.

free will—and free will is the ultimate expression of "trust." God trusts us to make the right decisions even when He *knows* that we will often make the wrong ones. If He did not, He would remove our right to make decisions and choices in the first place! Instead, He gave us this right, knowing that it is only through His trust (and our own mistakes) that we can learn to grow, become strong, and distinguish *good* choices from *bad* ones.

God does not withdraw His love when we "violate" His trust. If we do something wrong, God does not tell us, "Well, I *thought* I could trust you, but I see I was *wrong*." Instead, He uses the power of forgiveness to free us from the *consequences* of our errors, enabling us to learn and move on and try again.

God does not fence us in with rules and guidelines and restrictions—even though it may seem that way to some of us. We are not bound by a host of laws. We cannot learn how to "be good" by learning the "rules." Paul writes, "I would like to learn just one thing from you: Did you receive the Spirit by observing the law, or by believing what you heard? Are you so foolish? After beginning with the Spirit, are you now trying to attain your goal by human effort?"[7] (Gal. 3:2-3)

Instead, God frees us, in love, to make choices and decisions. He permits us to take risks and make mistakes, to come back to Him for forgiveness and guidance, and to step out again to make *more* choices and decisions. He trusts us to *learn* how to choose "correctly" even if we aren't capable of doing so *today*.

Once we realize that God trusts us, we can begin to trust ourselves. He knows more than we do! He trusts us to succeed tomorrow, despite our failures today. He trusts us to do His will tomorrow, even if we can't perceive or understand that will today. Once we realize that we don't have to "get it right" the first time, that we have a God of "second chances," then we can begin to trust ourselves. We can trust ourselves to complete the journey that we have started, knowing that we are not required to complete it alone, for "He who began a good work in you will bring it to completion at the day of Jesus Christ." (Phil. 1:6)

---

[7]The word translated as "attain your goal" comes from the same root as "teleios" (Strong's Concordance, #G2005).

**14) Love always hopes.** If we regard ourselves as "hopeless," as having no chance for the future, as being incapable of change or growth, then we are not walking in love. Love hopes, and when we have love in our hearts, we will have hope not only for others but for ourselves.

Adult Children are accustomed to measuring the future by the past. We accept our perceived "character flaws" as our permanent identity, something that we have little hope of changing. We look at our past mistakes and believe that we are doomed to repeat them. We "predict" the future by what has gone before. In effect, we are like people who walk through life backwards, always looking into the past and believing that it is what lies ahead.

Bringing "hope" into our lives means shifting the direction of our focus. Instead of looking back, we need to learn how to look forward. Who we "were" (or who we think we were, which is not always the same thing) is not who we will be. What we have done is not what we will do. As we learn to walk in hope, we learn to believe that "I can do everything through Him who gives me strength." (Phil. 4:13)

Hope is not based upon what we have *already* seen. It is based upon what we *haven't seen yet*. Paul tells us, "But hope that is seen is no hope at all. Who hopes for what he already has? But if we hope for what we do not yet have, we wait for it patiently." (Rom. 8:24-25) We may not have seen "growth" yet, but we will. We may not have seen "change" yet, but we will. We may not have seen much "progress" yet, but we will—when we wait for these things with patience. When we walk in love, we walk in the hope that our feelings may change: Hurt and fear may disappear. We walk in the hope that our thoughts may change: No longer will our inner voices whisper shame and condemnation to us. We walk in the hope that our lives may change, in ways that we cannot even imagine today.

God never gives up on us. His hope is that of one who plants a seed and stands back, never doubting or anxious, but confident that what He has planted will grow. He knows exactly when that seed will blossom, and what fruit it will bear. He doesn't plant radishes and "hope" for apples; instead, He plants the seed of a sturdy tree, *knowing* that even when the *tree* can hardly be "seen," the apples will come in their season.

God has planted the seed of recovery in you. Each of us will learn our own ways to water and tend that seed—but it is our hope in the "one who brings the growth" (1 Cor. 3:7) that keeps the seed alive. God assures us, "Do I bring to the moment of birth and not give delivery?" (Isa. 66:9) When we realize that God will never throw up His hands in despair and walk away from us, we can allow *ourselves* to hope again. Our hope lies in the certain knowledge that God will never abandon us or fail to "bring to growth."

**15) Love always perseveres.** Many Christian Adult Children fear that if they do not "heal" fast enough or "improve" fast enough, God will "give up" on them. Many of us have been "given up on" in the past. Many of us have given up on ourselves. When God tells us that "love perseveres," however, He is telling us that no matter how hopeless and bleak the future *appears*, He will *never* give up on us.

In recovery, there will be many times when we are tempted to quit. We will be tempted to "give up" when we don't see visible progress, or when we don't think we are moving "fast enough." We will be tempted to quit when we look ahead and see "how far we still have to go." We will be tempted to quit when the going gets tough—when old memories or issues are more difficult to face and resolve than we expected. We will be tempted to quit when *others* threaten to quit on us, when loved ones refuse to support us or actively oppose our recovery. We will be tempted to quit when problems that we thought we had "resolved" return to plague us.

As we learn to walk in love toward ourselves, however, that temptation to "quit on ourselves" will grow less. The temptation to quit is based on the assumption that we aren't "worth it"—that we aren't worth the effort, that we are wasting our time, that we should just try to be what others want so that they will "love" us. But as we learn that God never gives up on us, that He is there with us and holding our hands during the darkest and most frustrating times, then we begin to realize that *He thinks we're worth it*. He will never decide that we aren't worth saving, that we aren't worth healing, that we aren't worth "standing by."

Recovery is not a "delay" in God's lifetime plan for us. It is *part* of that plan. God is not "surprised" by our need to find healing, for He already knows where we are, how we got there, and what we need to recover. Recovery is not a "disease" with a "time limit"; it is a process of growth, and growth is the process of *life*.

Gradually, as we walk in love, we learn that *every* journey has its setbacks, its detours, its holes in the road. We learn to understand that our "delays" are not because there is something wrong with *us*, but signs that we are actually making progress. If we never came to a valley to cross or a mountain to climb, it would mean that we weren't traveling at all. As we learn to persevere, we learn that attacks are not defeats, that a detour is not a "derailing," and that a fear is not a failure. We learn, instead, that "in all these things we are more than conquerors through Him who loved us." (Rom. 8:37) Victory does not come in an instant, but it comes—to those who persevere.

**16) Love never fails.** God will always be with us. He will always be there *for* us. He keeps His promises, and He has made this promise to us. It is His *Word*, and He says, "so shall My word be that goes forth from My mouth; it shall not return to Me empty, but it shall accomplish that which I purpose, and prosper in the thing for which I sent it. For you shall go out in joy, and be led forth in peace; the mountains and the hills before you shall break forth into singing, and all the trees of the field shall clap their hands. Instead of the thorn shall come up the cypress; instead of the briar shall come up the myrtle; and it shall be to the Lord for a memorial, for an everlasting sign which shall not be cut off." (Isa. 55:11-13)

That promise doesn't change, for God does not change. "Jesus Christ is the same yesterday and today and for ever." (Heb. 13:8) His promises are not based on moods or whims, or upon our worthiness, but upon His own unchanging and eternal nature.

As long as "love" never fails, not a single *component* of love described in this chapter will fail us. God will never cease to be patient and kind, forgiving and protecting. Nothing in this chapter will ever "pass away" from our lives. God's love comes with an "eternal lifetime guarantee."

But this statement is not only telling us not only that love will not fail us and that God will not fail us. It is also telling us that if we *do not walk in love, we will fail.* We can have great spiritual wisdom and knowledge; we can read the Bible from cover to cover; we can memorize scriptures and post them throughout our house; we can pray for hours; we can attend miracle crusades and powerful teachings and "fall under the power" and receive anointings and manifest the gifts of the spirit—but without love, we will fail. Paul, who ought to know, writes, "If I have the gift of prophecy and can fathom all mysteries and all knowledge, and if I have a faith that can move mountains, but have not love, I am nothing." (1 Cor. 13:2)

We can learn many skills and coping strategies that will help us recover. Many techniques are available to help us address and resolve the issues of the past—and the issues of the present. But if we pull down strongholds of "dysfunctional thinking" and do *not* change the unloving foundations upon which those strongholds are built, they will rise up again, in different forms. As long as the basic fears remain, our lives will not change at the most fundamental level. We may "conquer" our addictions—but simply by transferring them to less obvious, more socially acceptable outlets. We may get rid of some false beliefs, but we will replace them with others that are equally false.

Only love—genuine, agape love from God—casts out fear. John tells us, "There is no fear in love. But perfect love drives out fear, because fear has to do with punishment. The one who fears is not made perfect in love." (1 John 4:18) *If* we love, God tells us that "love never fails"—that love will not fail to accomplish what is promised throughout the Bible.

In recovery, "love" is not an optional extra. It is the basic requirement. Without love, we will fail.

# - 3 -

# Didn't God Take Care of All That?

*Praise be to the God and Father of our Lord Jesus Christ, the Father of compassion and the God of all comfort, who comforts us in all our troubles, so that we can comfort those in any trouble with the comfort we ourselves have received from God. For just as the sufferings of Christ flow over into our lives, so also through Christ our comfort overflows. If we are distressed, it is for your comfort and salvation; if we are comforted, it is for your comfort, which produces in you patient endurance of the same sufferings we suffer. And our hope for you is firm, because we know that just as you share in our sufferings, so also you share in our comfort. (2 Cor. 1:3-7)*

MANY CHRISTIANS WONDER whether God *really* promises "recovery," or whether that word is simply so much "psychobabble." There is some confusion about what "recovery" means, particularly in the context of the modern "recovery movement." In the spiritual and scriptural sense, however, that word can be regarded as active as well as passive: God will not only guide us in "recovery," He will also "recover" us. He will "bring us back" to wholeness and health.

"Recover" is one of the meanings of the word translated as "restore" in a verse that many Adult Children find of great comfort: "The Lord is my shepherd, I shall not be in want. He makes me lie down in green pastures, He leads me beside quiet waters, He *restores my soul.*" (Psa. 23:1-3, emphasis mine.) That word "restore" could also be translated as "recall, recompense, *recover*, refresh, relieve, requite, rescue, retrieve, return, reverse, reward," and my personal favorite, "to fetch home again." Genuine recovery is a combination of all of these things—and of growth, forgiveness, freedom, truth, revelation, wisdom, and understanding. All of these are promised to us by God, and we do not have to be ashamed of our desire or need for them. God will truly "fetch us home again" and bring genuine, life-changing recovery and healing to our lives.

The next question we often ask (or are asked by others), is, "But didn't God take care of that already?" Many people interpret God's promises not as something that He *will* fulfill but as something that He *has* fulfilled—and that, therefore, we no longer have any right to ask Him to do more for us than He has done already. A great many people teach that God has literally "done all that He's going to do, and the rest is up to you—you have to 'receive' it."

That perspective makes about as much sense as claiming that a parent's job "ends" at giving birth—as though this is all the parenting that a parent is going to do or should be asked to do. While some of us may have had parents who seemed to think along very similar lines, most agree that the job of parenting *starts* with birth, instead of ending there. God is the perfect functional parent, and His parenting begins with our birth; He hasn't *already* given us all the parenting that He's "going to give."

This issue raises mixed feelings in Christian Adult Children. Some greet this idea with a surge of hope: "If God took care of all that, maybe I won't have to!" We know that if we begin to poke around in the "past," we are going to hurt. We don't *want* to dig up the fears, pains, and lies that are buried within us. One way to avoid it is to claim that "God already resolved all the issues from my past, so I don't have to."

Others, however, react to this issue with worry and guilt. When we *do* poke at past memories, or explore our present issues and concerns, we are very aware that the pain is still there. "Healed" wounds are rarely painful, though they may leave scars; thus we realize that our pain must be coming from something that *hasn't* healed yet. But if God "took care of it" already, we wonder why we are still hurting. Have we done something wrong? Have we failed to "receive" God's healing and deliverance?

Before we examine the question of whether or not God *did* "take care of all that," we need to examine why we ask that question in the first place. Though the question is valid, it often has its roots in one of five "foundational beliefs" that spring directly from those very fears that we are trying to overcome.

**1) We believe that we have no right to be "sick."** The very word "recovery" implies that we are somehow "sick," that there is something "wrong" with us that we need to "get over." Many of us have learned to believe, for a variety of reasons, that to be "sick" is virtually a sin and something to be avoided at all costs.

Many of us learned to believe that when we were sick, we created an unfair "hardship" for the rest of the family. We learned to believe that we placed a "burden" on others by being in need of extra care and attention. We learned to feel guilty and ashamed for the "trouble" we caused our parents.

Besides the burden we placed on our family by requiring care, we may have also learned to believe that we were a burden because we were temporarily unable to carry "our share of the load." While we lay in bed, others had to handle our chores and responsibilities. We learned to believe that the pain and suffering we were experiencing was "nothing" compared to the pain and suffering we were "inflicting" on others. We learned to believe that it is "bad" to hurt because our pain is an inconvenience to everyone else.

We were often isolated or ostracized in some back bedroom while sick, cut off from the family and family life. Family members rarely came to see us, and then only begrudgingly, when we needed something. We were often denied any source of entertainment to relieve our boredom: A common refrain of a dysfunctional family is, "If you're too sick to go to school, you're too sick to watch television." From these practices, we may have learned to believe that "no one wants to be around a sick person," and that it is somehow "wrong" to "have fun" while one is sick—that one should not only suffer *from* sickness but *because* of sickness.

Our sicknesses may have been *denied* by our parents until we were so ill that our symptoms couldn't be ignored. "You're not sick," many dysfunctional parents declare with God-like omniscience. "You just want to get out of doing your work." Thus we often learned to ignore our own symptoms, or to believe that they didn't really "mean anything"—which is why many Adult Children neglect their physical health and allow minor problems to flare into major illnesses. We may also believe that "sickness," no matter how genuine, is a form of "laziness." In addition, some of us learned that it was better to suffer in silence than risk the *consequences* of being sick.

Finally, we learned to believe that "sickness" was equivalent to "weakness," which is often the ultimate sin in dysfunctional families. We may associate "being strong" with having no weaknesses, needs, feelings, desires, or hindrances to our primary task of "taking care of everyone else." When we enter recovery, those same messages rise up to haunt us.

We often believe that God reacts to "sickness" the same what that our families did (and, unfortunately, some Christians *do* perpetuate these same critical attitudes toward "illness"). We may believe that it is "selfish" for a Christian to enter into personal recovery, because we are doing something for "self" rather than "doing for others." We may believe that we become a "burden" to God if we need recovery, not only because we may need ministry, but because we may be temporarily unable to minister. We may believe that other Christians (and even God) won't want to be around us while we're sick. Some Adult Children in recovery put aside all forms of personal "fun" or entertainment because they feel that this is "wasting time" that could be spent on recovery—not realizing that part of recovery means learning how to live a life of joy rather than one of self-induced hardship.

We could bypass these unhealthy attitudes toward recovery simply by realizing that Adult Children are not "sick" in the first place. However, that fails to address one of our central areas of misperception and false belief: That we, as individuals, have no right to take the time that is needed to become "whole."

Some Christians have declared, in effect, that "God isn't interested in wholeness, He's interested in obedience." Jesus said otherwise, however. He tells us, "Those who are well have no need of a physician, but those who are sick. Go and learn what this means, 'I desire mercy, and not sacrifice.' For I came not to call the righteous, but sinners." (Matt. 9:12-13) When He tells us, "You, therefore, must be perfect, as your heavenly Father is perfect" (Matt. 5:48), that word "perfect" could be translated just as easily as "whole" or "complete."[1]

God is not "burdened" by those of His children who need healing; rather, "Great is our Lord and mighty in power; His understanding has no limit." (Psa. 147:5) Instead of condemning us for needing help, "He heals the brokenhearted and binds up their wounds." (Psa. 147:3) Instead of withdrawing from us in our time of need, "The Lord is *close* to the brokenhearted, and saves those who are crushed in spirit." (Psa. 34:18, emphasis mine.) God does not frown upon weakness or reject those who are bruised and needy; instead, "A bruised reed He will not break, and a smoldering wick He will not snuff out..." (Matt. 12:20) Indeed, Paul tells us that God's "power is made perfect in weakness" and "Therefore I will boast all the more gladly about my weaknesses, so that Christ's power may rest on me. That is why, for Christ's sake, I delight in weaknesses, in insults, in hardships, in persecutions, in difficulties. For when I am weak, then I am strong." (2 Cor. 12:9-10)

**2) We believe there is something "wrong" with being "afflicted."** Our minister recently gave the altar call: "If you're feeling pressured, if you feel like you don't know what to do, if you're hurting inside, if you are in pain, if you feel all alone, well, then, you need to give your life to Jesus. He'll take all that away! You don't have to feel hurting and struggling and confused anymore; just give your life to Jesus!" I almost rushed down the aisle myself—and I've been saved for years!

All too often, we get the impression that if we just turn our lives over to Jesus, all the pain and hurt and confusion and anxiety we have ever felt will miraculously disappear—not only now but for all time. The implication is that if we become "born again," we will instantly be filled with joy and peace and wholeness and hope, and never have another trouble as long as we live.

Whether we have known Jesus for a short time or a long time, such a message can fill our souls with guilt. Jesus is the source of peace and hope—so why do we still feel so distraught, so filled with

[1]Strong's Concordance, #G5046.

turmoil, so hopeless? Often, we search our hearts for an answer, and come up with a very familiar one: *There must be something wrong with us.* Perhaps we aren't "walking with the Lord" the way we should. Perhaps we have "stepped out of His protection." Perhaps we have done something wrong, or perhaps there is something we *haven't* done. Perhaps we aren't praying or reading the Word enough. Perhaps we haven't surrendered our lives fully to Him. Perhaps—some Christian Adult Children fear—we aren't really "saved."

Christian Adult Children who embrace this "all your troubles will disappear" message often get caught up in what I call the "revolving door of rededication." Sunday after Sunday, we rush forward and fall on our knees, promising to *really* trust Jesus this time, to *really* "surrender all." Then the pressures and troubles of the week close around us, and we lose that sense of peace and well-being that filled us, for a few hours, after church. We suppose that, once again, we have "done something wrong" or "failed to receive deliverance." When Sunday comes again, we're up there on our knees again, tearfully offering our lives to Him yet one more time, and hoping that *this* time we'll be able to "make it stick." One young man became so guilt-ridden over the failure of his endless efforts to "rededicate" his way out of his addictive behaviors that he began to consider suicide.

Many Christians believe that if their lives are not one "non-stop victory," they are somehow failures, or worse, "failing God." We feel guilty if we are not constantly feeling, and operating in, that joy and peace that we have been told is ours in Jesus. Just as we were often taught, in our dysfunctional homes, that we must never express what we really felt, or talk about what was bothering us, we may have come to believe that we must always have a "positive confession" before God as well. We are often told that we shouldn't "talk about the problem"or that the one sure way to *prevent* God from helping us is to admit that we *need* help. We may even have come to believe that we are being "ungrateful" to God if we confess our sadness or pain or confusion.

When we believe this, we despair of ever becoming the "right kind" of Christian, of ever having the thoughts and feelings and attitudes that we are "supposed" to have. We often don't dare confess our troubles to other Christians, for fear that they will condemn us for having the "wrong attitude." Some Adult Children have been deeply wounded by well-meaning but ill-advised remarks like "Well, God must have had a reason to let you go through that, so count it all joy." Such remarks (and those who make them) are, unfortunately, no more help in time of trouble than the worldly wisdom and spiritual platitudes of Job's friends!

We may also come to believe that afflictions are a "punishment" for "sin." One young woman believed that a surgery that left a scar on her body was God's "punishment" for her "vanity." Some teach that we will not be "afflicted"—that is, that "the devil can't attack us"—unless we somehow "step out" of God's "protection" by sinning. (To add to the confusion, others teach that the devil is *more* likely to attack those who are doing God's will, and that affliction is a "good" sign!) People who believe this often demand that we "confess and repent" whatever "sin" led us out from under God's "holy umbrella," rather than offering any real comfort. Such an attitude may convince us that to have feelings of pain, or to be caught up in the issues that arose from our past, is itself a "sin."

Such teachings lead us to wonder what we are doing wrong to "feel" this way. We wonder if we were supposed to "leave it all behind" or "let go and let God," or "nail it to the cross," or if we are guilty of "unforgiveness," or if simply "praying and reading more" would "solve" the problem. We accept the blame and shame that such teachings bring to our spirit because we are *accustomed* to blame and shame, and believe that we must deserve it. The tragedy is that when we find that we just can't keep up the illusion of being completely whole, happy, triumphant Christians, we often give up altogether. We burn out, and when we give up on being "fakes" we may also, mistakenly, decide to give up on being *Christians*.

I don't know where Christians got the idea that being a Christian was synonymous with being "unafflicted," or that a close relationship with God means no more troubles, no more tears, no more grief. The Bible tells us just the opposite! Paul, for example, writes, "To keep me from becoming conceited because of these surpassingly great revelations, there was given me a thorn in my flesh, a messenger of Satan, to torment me. Three times I pleaded with the Lord to take it away from me. But He said to me, 'My grace is sufficient for you, for my power is made perfect in weakness.' " (2 Cor. 12:7-9) Jesus warns us, "If you belonged to the world, it would love you as its own. As it is, you do not belong to the world, but I have chosen you out of the world. That is why the world hates you. Remember the words I spoke to you: 'No servant is greater than his master.' If they persecuted me, they will persecute you also. If they obeyed my teaching, they will obey yours also. They will treat you this way because of my name, for they do not know the One who sent me." (John 15:19-21)

We are told, "A righteous man may have many troubles, but the Lord delivers him from them all;" (Psa. 34:19) Never are we told that troubles or afflictions are a sign of lack of faith, or of a "wrong attitude," or the result of sin. Instead, we are told that we *will* have troubles—but that God will comfort us *during* our affliction, and deliver us *from* our affliction. God promises us, "When you pass through the waters, I will be with you; and when you pass through the rivers, they will not sweep over you. When you walk through the fire, you will not be burned; the flames will not set you ablaze." (Isa. 43:2) We do not have to wear "happy faces" to please God. Instead, like David, we are permitted to pour out our feeling of brokenheartedness, trusting Him to keep His word and comfort us and be near to us and, ultimately, to heal us.

**3) We believe that recovery is "selfish."** Many Christians have criticized the "recovery movement" for its focus on "self." Unfortunately, this attitude can be carried to the point of assuming that *anything* that relates to care of "self" is "selfish" and therefore "sinful." Such an attitude simply reinforces what many Christian Adult Children already believe: That we are of "value," or "doing God's will," only when we are doing things for other people.

In dysfunctional families, the level of approval one receives is often the direct result of how much we "do" for other people, how much we give, how much we accomplish. We may have been taught to believe that we are "selfish" and "inconsiderate" whenever we aren't doing something for someone else. We may have been taught that to be "good" or "worthwhile," we must apply all our resources—including time, money, and energy—to the well-being of others, to the exclusion of our own. Otherwise, we are told, we are not givers but "takers," a burden rather than a blessing.

The assumption that recovery, or any other form of ministry to "self," is "selfish," is based upon short-term thinking. It is based upon what a person can see *today*, with no thought for what may happen tomorrow. It is much like saying that if I spend time "eating," I am "wasting" time that could have been spent "ministering." Any time that is spent maintaining one's physical (or emotional) health is time that cannot be "marked down" to "service." However, my ministry, no matter how dedicated in the short-term, would not last very long if I fail to feed myself. Nor will it be genuinely loving and caring once I become preoccupied with the pangs of hunger, or with attempting to deny that I *feel* those pangs. Ultimately, I will not only lose my ability to minister altogether, but when the effects of malnutrition catch up with me, I will *require* ministry. Others will have to "take care of me" until I recover from the effects of my short-sighted judgment!

Admittedly, this is an extreme example, but it raises a serious question: Where do you draw the line? Sadly, many Christians are able to see only the works one is performing on the *outside*, rather than the work God may be doing with us on the *inside*. If I am outwardly "unselfish" and "caring" and "giving," many will suppose that I am being a "good" Christian and that God is "pleased" with me. Inside, however, I may be dying: I may hate myself and everything that I touch; I may be so resentful of the demands upon me that I would rather tear people apart than put them back together; and I may feel so guilty about my painful feelings that I am tempted to destroy myself. Fortunately, "God does not judge by external appearance!" (Gal. 2:6)

Those who are concerned about the "selfishness" of recovery would do well to consider the long-term effects of healing. One may be able to get good work out of a starving person today, but if that person is not fed, tomorrow's work will be less, and soon that person will not be able to work at all. Similarly, we can continue to work without healing—but eventually our work, which springs from bondage and pain, will be a source of anger and despair. When we heal ourselves, we heal our ministry as well.

That is not to say that the only "purpose" of recovery is to make a person better able to "serve God." Many Christian Adult Children feel that the only way they can justify their personal healing is by arguing that it will make them better "ministers" in the long run. It will—but it is not the primary reason for recovery. Instead, this reflects the attitude we learned in dysfunctional homes: We need to *get better* so we can *do more*.

What many of us cannot imagine is that God doesn't want us to recover *just so that we can do more for Him*. God wants us to recover and heal not because of what we can do for Him, but *because* He *loves us*. He is a functional parent. He loves *all* His children. He doesn't love *you* only for what you can do for *someone else*. Such an attitude implies that you are worthwhile to God only for what you can "do" for His "more important" children.

We cannot imagine a God who loves us regardless of what we do for others. We cannot imagine a God who wants to heal us because we are His children, because He hurts for us, because He sincerely wants *each of us* to be whole and well. Though we can easily believe that God wants us to minister to others so that *they* will not hurt, we find it almost impossible to believe that God could have the same level of interest and desire in our own lives. It sounds too good to be true. We've never encountered anything like this before. No one has ever told us, "Heal, because I want you to be well."

When God assures us that "He heals the brokenhearted and binds up their wounds," and "is close to the brokenhearted, and saves those who are crushed in spirit," and "comforts us in all our troubles" (Psa. 147:3, 34:18; 2 Cor. 1:4), let no one tell you that it is "selfish" to accept that comfort, that healing, that deliverance. Let no one tell you that you don't "deserve" it, but that, instead, you should be spending your time "healing others." God does not pour love onto us just so that we can "hurry up and pass it on;" He pours His love onto us because He wants *us* to receive it. God made that promise to *you*, for *you*, not just for other people. If God says that He will heal you, then He will *not* turn around and say, "But it is *selfish* and *sinful* for you to *want* that healing!" Dysfunctional parents may claim that it is selfish for us to expect them to honor their promises, but God is not a dysfunctional parent. His promises are true, "For no matter how many promises God has made, they are 'Yes' in Christ. And so through him the 'Amen' is spoken by us to the glory of God." (2 Cor. 1:20)

**4) We believe that recovery should be instantaneous.** Most Adult Children, when they discover a problem in their lives, don't tend to say, "Oh, I should solve that." Instead, we tend to say, "I should have solved that *yesterday*!" We don't regard problems as opportunities; instead, we regard them as "evidence" that we have "failed" to do something we "should have done already."

We believe that we should be perfect—*already*. We don't see "perfection" as something to be attained in the future, but as something that we can be "blamed" or "condemned" for not being *today*. Further, we tend to perceive only two possible conditions: Either we are perfect (which we know we are not), or we are "imperfect" and "flawed." If it is at all possible to say "I could do better" or "I could be better," we consider ourselves to be "failures."

Adult Children rarely have a realistic perception of growth, change, or development. When we think of "growth," all we tend to see is "how far we have to go," and we condemn ourselves for "not being there yet." Instead of rejoicing over the fact that we have taken a step farther along the road than we were yesterday, we despair because we haven't *completed* the journey.

What we fail to realize is that God is in the growth business, not the overnight perfection business. Growth is a process that every living thing is involved in, whether it wants to be or not. Growth is not a goal, or something to be reached; it is the inevitable *process* of reaching *toward* the goal. It is not something that we should condemn ourselves for, because it is how we were divinely designed. We were *not* designed to reach some single, elusive, poorly defined goal of "perfection" and then remain unchanged from that point on; instead, we were designed to *grow* as long as we are *alive*. (And since life is eternal, it stands to reason that "growth" is eternal as well.) As long as we are capable of thinking new thoughts, learning new information, encountering new experiences and new people, we *will* grow and change—whether we want to or not!

Recovery is a matter of *freeing* areas of life so that they become capable once again of partaking of that divine process of growth. When parts of our lives are strangled by fear, our ability to grow in those areas is limited. When we are not able to experience or express our emotions, we are not able to "grow" in our ability to understand and handle emotions. When we are unable to accept who we are, we are unable to "grow" as people, because we are too busy trying to turn ourselves into something we *aren't*. When we fear a God that we perceive as possibly dangerous, certainly angry, and sometimes unreasonable, we are unable to grow in our relationship with Him.

The Bible uses many "gardening" examples to illustrate how, through Jesus, we are called to "grow." Jesus tells us, "I am the vine; you are the branches. If a man remains in me and I in him, he will bear much fruit; apart from me you can do nothing." (John 15:5) We are "like a tree planted by streams of water, which yields its fruit in season and whose leaf does not wither." (Psa. 1:3) God's people "are the shoot I have planted, the work of my hands, for the display of my splendor." (Isa. 60:21) Finally, we are told, "you are God's field, God's building." (1 Cor. 3:9) Fields do not produce crops overnight, nor do buildings spring fully formed from the ground overnight. Instead, both crops *and* buildings "grow" in God's season, "So neither he who plants nor he who waters is anything, but only God, who makes things grow." (1 Cor. 3:7)

Salvation is the beginning of our growth, not the end. It is the moment that we are planted—or rather, grafted into the living vine. "You, though a wild olive shoot, have been grafted in among the others and now share in the nourishing sap from the olive root..." (Rom. 11:17) We are advised to remember, "You do not support the root, but the root supports you." (Rom. 11:18) We do not become strong, fruit-bearing branches by condemning ourselves for not being "complete," but by partaking of the nourishment and support of that parent root, the God of all growth.

**5) We think we should be "different" already.** The final reason that Christian Adult Children tend to ask this question is that many of us have been taught to believe that salvation "should have" made us into "different people." We believe that we should have been "changed" by the miracle of salvation. We believe that we should have been "transformed." We often suppose that, as "saved Christians," we should be equipped with a completely new (and Godly) set of emotions, thoughts, attitudes, and actions. Many teachings lead us to believe that the "old man" is "dead," crucified with Christ, and that we are now completely "new" people.

When we postpone recovery by claiming, "Oh, God took care of all that," what we often mean is that we want God to miraculously (and instantly) change the way we think, feel, and behave. Most of us don't like ourselves very much, and if salvation can turn us into something "better" than what we already are, we're all for it. We want God to remove our painful feelings, our bad habits, and our "wrong thoughts." We want Him to transform us into the kind of people that *we* think we should be and the kind of people we assume *He* thinks we should be.

Many people *do* experience a profound sense of change upon salvation. We often know that *something* is different, even though we may not be quite sure what it is. We *hope* that it is *us*—but we often find that we aren't as "new" as we would like to be or think we are "supposed" to be. Old emotions surface. Old behaviors and habits reappear. Old thoughts continue to trouble us. Old memories haunt us. Old attitudes and perceptions continue to run our lives and drive our behavior. We may even begin to feel that "serving God" isn't so very different from the way our lives have always been: We still find that we are pressured to "do more and be better," and we feel guilty and condemned when we "fail" to "live up" to God's higher standards.

So we begin to ask ourselves what is wrong with *us*. We wonder what we are doing wrong. We wonder if there is something that we haven't "believed" or "received." We wonder if we have "backslid." We wonder if we are out of God's will. We wonder if we "lack faith."

The assumption that God "changes" us upon salvation, and that there is something wrong with us if we don't "feel" changed, has two major problems. The first lies in a hidden contradiction: While we joyfully thank God for accepting us "just as we are," we can't believe that He will *continue* to accept us "just as we are." We seem to believe that the moment we *are* accepted, "warts and all," it is our responsibility to get *rid* of those "warts," or God will turn around and *reject* what He has just *accepted*. We find it hard to believe that the God who loved us enough to give His life for us, sin and brokenness and hurt and all, *still* loves us even though we are *still* sinful and broken and hurt.

The second problem lies with how we suppose this "magic change" is accomplished in our lives. While we may believe that God "transformed" us, we also seem to believe that "receiving" that transformation is somehow up to us, that it somehow depends upon our actions or our faith. The reality is that if God takes care of something, *it is taken care of.* If He had removed all the effects of your past and made you into a different person, *you would be a different person.* If He had miraculously "healed" your inner brokenness and restored your spirit, *you would be healed and restored.* If it *was* "taken care of," you would know.

This perception that we should be "new and different" people is often based upon the scripture that tells us, "Therefore, if anyone is in Christ, he is a new creation; the old has gone, the new has come!" (2 Cor. 5:17) If God didn't transform us into "new people," how do we interpret this verse? Until we know the answer, this one scripture can become, not the source of joy and hope that it was intended to be, but an endless source of misery and despair.

## Meet the New Creation

How can we be "new creations" and not *feel* like new creations? How can we be "changed," yet act and think and feel so much the same? How can our old problems, the "past" that we hope has "passed away," still have so powerful an effect upon our present? Many of us suppose that the answer must be that there is something profoundly wrong with *us*. What is wrong, however, is how we interpret this scripture. It is time to take a closer look at just what *has*, and what has *not*, "passed away."

If we look closely at our lives, it soon becomes obvious that many things have *not* passed away, even though they were part of our "old" lives—and that it would be ridiculous to suppose that they *would* pass away. For example:

• **Our old bodies did not pass away.** We are still stuck with what we had before salvation. We are the same sex, race, size, general appearance, and general condition. Even if you experienced miraculous healing of a disease or injury, that healing took place in your "old" body; you didn't get a new one. We will receive new bodies as the result of *resurrection* (1 Cor. 15:35-44), but not as the result of *salvation*.

• **Our old minds did not pass away.** We still possess approximately the same mental capacities and thought processes that we had before salvation. We still have the same skills, knowledge, education level, and training; nothing was removed, and nothing was replaced. If you were an auto mechanic before salvation, you did not miraculously become a brain surgeon (or vice versa). We *did* receive "the mind of Christ" (1 Cor. 2:16), which was given to us so that we could begin to understand spiritual things—but this "mind" was not a "replacement" for our old minds, but rather, an addition to what we already have and retain.

• **Our circumstances did not instantly pass away.** Many people have been instantly delivered of some form of bondage, such as alcoholism, upon salvation; many others have not. Salvation did not instantly change your job, your lifestyle, your economic status, your residence, your family, or your friends. You may have changed some of those things, with God's help, *after* salvation—but that change involved a process of decisions, choices, and actions; old things were not instantaneously "replaced" with new things. In addition, you remain the child of the same parents and the parent of the same children. God did not magically uproot you from one "life" and plant you in another.

• **Our histories did not pass away.** You have the same "past." You grew up in the same household, with the same parents and relatives. You went to the same schools and learned the same things. You had the same experiences. There is nothing in your past that somehow "didn't happen" or "happened differently" as a result of salvation; God did not rewrite your personal history when He saved you.

From this, it is clear that much of what we call "self" did *not*, in fact, "pass away" when we got saved. God did not provide us with a replacement for our former selves. He did not magically change our personality. If God *had* replaced our "selves," there would be no reason for Him to say, "You were taught, with regard to your former way of life, to put off your old self, which is being corrupted by its deceitful desires; to be made new in the attitude of your minds; and to put on the new self, created to be like God in true righteousness and holiness." (Eph. 4:22-24, emphases mine.) He would not tell us to do something He had already done!

Yet the scripture clearly indicates that *something* passed away. If that "something" was not our minds, our personalities, our nature, or our circumstances, what was it?

The answer might surprise you. The Greek word that has been translated as "old" in this particular verse is derived directly from the word translated as "principality" in Eph. 3:10 and 6:12.[2] It does not refer to your "self" or even to your "past." It refers, not to who you are, but to *whom you belong to.*

You no longer "belong" to the "old order"—the order of shame and guilt, the powers of condemnation and blame, the principalities of worthlessness and failure. You no longer "belong" to the

[2]Strong's Concordance, #G744, G746.

world of dysfunctional perceptions, behaviors, and most of all, *destiny*, that once governed your life. You have been adopted into a new family. We are no longer, literally, "Adult Children of Dysfunctional Families," but "Children of God." We are children of a new parent, a parent who does not stand in judgment over us, who is not impatient with us, who does not condemn us for our past *or for the effects of our past*. We now have a parent who offers us the incredible bounty of His limitless resources to help us *recover* from that past and walk in the fullness of freedom and deliverance.

Many of you reading this book may have been "adopted children" in the worldly sense. Some of you may have been adopted into "better" situations and some into "worse." When I think of adoption, however, I think of a situation that occurred in the church we were attending in Germany in 1991, when the walls between "East" and "West" were crumbling. Rumania's communist government had been overthrown, and as the doors opened to Western aid, thousands of orphans became available for adoption. A family in our church adopted a 7-year-old Rumanian girl.

Try to imagine what such an adoption would be like for a child who had spent seven years of her life in an overcrowded, dirty, understaffed, state-run orphanage! She did not speak English. She had never lived in a real home. She had never had enough to eat. She had never been treated with love, attention, dignity, understanding, and most of all, an attitude of *giving*. Perhaps one of the first things this child needed to adapt to was receiving three square meals a day!

This child had many adjustments to face. Her family knew, when they adopted her, that they would have to help her overcome the effects of her "past." They did not expect that past to "make no difference" or "have no effect." They did not expect her to instantly "understand" what it meant to be a member of a Western family, or to behave as though she had always been a member of such a family. They did not *blame* her for her past, or expect her to instantly *forget* all the coping mechanisms and defenses and fears, that she had learned in a lifetime of poverty and neglect. Instead, by adopting her, they made the deliberate decision to *stand by* this child as she learned what it meant to be part of a completely new and different family. They made their resources hers, before she could ever understand what those resources meant.

This is what has happened to us. We have been adopted by a new parent, a completely functional parent. That parent, God, does not blame us for our past, expect us to instantly forget our past, or expect us to instantly "heal" from all the things that happened before we really knew Him. Instead, He adopted us, knowing full well what the effects of our past were and how long it would take us to "recover" from those effects. Instead of saying, "You're in my family now, so you should forget about everything that ever went before," He tells us, "You are in my family now, so all my resources of healing and hope and help are available to you to *help* you overcome the effects of your past."

With this adoption, we received not only a new parent but a new spirit: The "spirit of adoption" (Rom. 8:15 KJV). We are told, "We have not received the spirit of the world but the Spirit who is from God, that we may understand what God has freely given us." (1 Cor. 2:12) The "Spirit which is from God" is a spirit of love, and "the fruit of the Spirit is love, joy, peace, patience, kindness, goodness, faithfulness, gentleness and self-control." (Gal. 5:22-23) These are not only the fruits that we will one day show; they are what God shows to *us*.

Furthermore, that adoption has a legal component. If the Rumanian government were to change its mind and reach out for that child, saying, "She belongs to us; give her back," those parents have the legal right to say, "No. She is ours. She is no longer subject to your authority." This is what we have the right to say, as children of God: We are no longer under the spiritual authority of any other "agency." When the spirit of condemnation attempts to force us to live by the old rules, when the spirit of shame attempts to persuade us to believe our old identity, we have the "legal" right to say "No. I don't belong to you. You have no rights here." Paul writes, "Formerly, when you did not know God, you were slaves to those who by nature are not gods..." (Gal. 4:8) But "God sent his Son... to redeem those under law, that we might receive the full rights of sons. Because you are sons, God sent the Spirit of His Son into our hearts, the Spirit who calls out, 'Abba, Father.' So you are no longer a slave, but a son; and since you are a son, God has made you also an heir." (Gal. 4:4-7)

This means that while your parents might have blamed and condemned you for doing "wrong" or for not being "good enough," your new Father says, "Therefore, there is now no condemnation for those who are in Christ Jesus..." (Rom 8:1) While your parents may have taught you that you "deserved" abuse (verbal, emotional, physical, or sexual), your new Parent tells you, "Don't you know that you yourselves are God's temple and that God's Spirit lives in you? If anyone destroys God's temple, God will destroy him; for God's temple is sacred, and you are that temple." (1 Cor. 3:16-17) While your parents may have taught you to be ashamed of who you were or what you did, your new Father says, "And now, dear children, continue in Him, so that when He appears we may be confident and unashamed before Him at his coming." (1 John 2:28) While your parents may have accused you not only of crimes you committed but of things you had nothing to do with, Jesus assures you, "do not think I will accuse you before the Father." (John 5:45).

This is what has changed. The old ways, the old "principalities," have passed away. We have come under the authority and the blessing of a new parent, and our task now is to understand what that means in our lives. When we regard God as a bigger version of whatever parenting we have been accustomed to all our lives—as angry and vengeful, as distant and uncaring, as demanding and selfish, as impatient and critical—we are allowing ourselves to be "ruled" by the "old spirit." When we begin to see God for who and what He really is—as loving, as one who will never forsake us, as one who cares deeply about *every individual child* in His family, as one who is far more interested in blessing us than in cursing us, as the God of all hope—then we will begin to learn what it means to be a "new creation." Only then can we truly begin the process of self-transformation that God instructs us in and gives us the resources, through His spirit, to complete.

## Transformed by the Truth

Even though we are not instantly and magically turned into "new people" upon salvation, it is nonetheless true that when we enter into a relationship with God, we change. Nor does the responsibility for that change rest entirely on us. We are told, "Do not conform any longer to the pattern of this world, but be transformed by the renewing of your mind. Then you will be able to test and approve what God's will is—His good, pleasing and perfect will." (Rom. 12:2) But we are *also* told, "I am the vine; you are the branches. If a man remains in me and I in him, he will bear much fruit; apart from me you can do nothing." (John 15:5) It is clear that we are called upon to change, but we are not called upon to change "all by ourselves." Change is something that we do *with* God; He does not do it without our participation, and we cannot do it without *His* participation.

Critics of the concept of "recovery" often claim that God "changes us" (or helps us to change) *without* any reference to the "past." Many Christians claim that the past is behind us and has no influence upon us. Another scripture that is often used to support such claims is Paul's statement, "But one thing I do: Forgetting what is behind and straining toward what is ahead, I press on toward the goal to win the prize for which God has called me heavenward in Christ Jesus." (Phil. 3:13-14) Doesn't this mean that, since we *have* been adopted into God's family, we *should* forget all about what happened to us "before?"

Paul's statement is not a call for "holy amnesia." Only a few verses earlier, he provides us with a mini-autobiography that makes it quite clear that he has not, literally, "forgotten" his own history: "If anyone else thinks he has reasons to put confidence in the flesh, I have more: circumcised on the eighth day, of the people of Israel, of the tribe of Benjamin, a Hebrew of Hebrews; in regard to the law, a Pharisee; as for zeal, persecuting the church; as for legalistic righteousness, faultless. But whatever was to my profit I now consider loss for the sake of Christ." (Phi. 3:4-7)

Paul is not telling us that he has literally "forgotten" who he once was or what he once did. What he is saying is that these things are no longer the foundation of his future. Indeed, he discovered that many of the beliefs and values that he once considered important were actually lies that led him *away* from the truth of Jesus. He could not have reached this understanding, however, without first understanding what his beliefs from the past *were*.

Many Christians supopose that if we hear the truth, it will automatically change us. Some seem to regard the Bible as having magical powers—that all we have to do is read the Word and we will instantly receive it, understand it, and be changed by it. Jesus says otherwise, however. He tells us, " 'A farmer went out to sow his seed. As he was scattering the seed, some fell along the path; it was trampled on, and the birds of the air ate it up. Some fell on rock, and when it came up, the plants withered because they had no moisture. Other seed fell among thorns, which grew up with it and choked the plants. Still other seed fell on good soil. It came up and yielded a crop, a hundred times more than was sown.' When He said this, He called out, 'He who has ears to hear, let him hear.'

"His disciples asked him what this parable meant. He said, 'The knowledge of the secrets of the kingdom of God has been given to you, but to others I speak in parables, so that, "though seeing, they may not see; though hearing, they may not understand." This is the meaning of the parable: The seed is the Word of God. Those along the path are the ones who hear, and then the devil comes and takes away the word from their hearts, so that they may not believe and be saved. Those on the rock are the ones who receive the word with joy when they hear it, but they have no root. They believe for a while, but in the time of testing they fall away. The seed that fell among thorns stands for those who hear, but as they go on their way they are choked by life's worries, riches and pleasures, and they do not mature. But the seed on good soil stands for those with a noble and good heart, who hear the word, retain it, and by persevering produce a crop.' " (Luke 8:5-15)

If hearing the truth directly from the lips of the Son of God Himself was not enough to convince or change some, "reading" or "hearing" the truth may not be enough to change us today. Many Adult Children hope that if they throw enough "truth seeds" into their minds, those seeds will eventually take root and "overcome" all the "lie seeds" that were planted so long ago. We hope that truth will automatically triumph over our past, without requiring us to actually get into that "field" and dig up that "rocky soil" to make it fertile and receptive once again. The reality, however, is that you cannot get the weeds out of a field by planting a lot of wheat and hoping that it will take over. Wheat won't choke out weeds or take root in unplowed soil.

Weeds must be pulled up by the roots, and we don't want to get that close to the roots of our "weeds." We often realize that we can't confront the false assumptions in our lives without confronting *how* those lies were planted, and by *whom*. When we expose lies, we often expose liars—including people we love. We face disillusionment and grief. We face anger and resentment. We often face rejection and condemnation from our own families when we attempt to "dig" into our fields. We expose traumatic and devastating events that we would rather not remember and resolve.

We may wish to "forget" the past because we are ashamed of it—and we are afraid not only of how *we* will react to confronting it, but how *God* will react. We may believe that we really were the "black sheep" in the family, and not only responsible for the family's troubles but "deserving" of the "punishment" we experienced because of those troubles. We may feel ashamed because of who and what we have been taught to believe that we are. We may be ashamed of the things that we "got into" because of our past—drugs, promiscuity, crime, the occult. We don't want to "look" because we fear that the past will only confirm what we already believe about ourselves: That we are worthless, defiled failures.

So we often wish that God would "resolve" our past without causing us to confront it ourselves. When people declare, "I don't have to look at my past; Jesus took care of all that," the image comes into my mind of Jesus as a sort of "Holy Maid Service." It is as though we suppose that, when we get saved, Jesus creeps into our attics and basements, dustpan in hand, cleaning out all those dark corners and hidden rooms and locked closets that we have never been able to face. He doesn't "bother" us by making us aware of the dirt and debris that He sweeps out of our basements; He doesn't "bring to our attention" the years of accumulated "baggage" stowed in our attics. Instead, we hope that He will cart away anything He finds in there that is "displeasing" to Him or "unhealthy" for us, and that He will then present us with the keys to our new, refurnished, clean apartments.

If you were going to pack your household goods and move, you probably wouldn't allow a friend to come in and decide *for you* what to keep and what to throw away. You probably wouldn't let a friend come in and just take away, without your permission, those things that the friend decides you no longer need or shouldn't have. That would be stealing. You *want* to be involved in those choices, and you have a responsibility to be involved.

The same applies to the contents of your mind and heart. Jesus does not "sweep out" your house or "put it in order" with no participation on your part. It is your house. The contents of your "closets" may not be pleasing to God or healthy for you—but they are *your* closets and *your* contents. Jesus will not sneak in and cart things away without involving you in the process. He does nothing without your active permission—just as He could not even "save" you without your permission and choice.

Jesus says, instead, "I am He who searches hearts and minds..." (Rev. 2:23) David asks, "Search me, O God, and know my heart; test me and know my anxious thoughts. See if there is any offensive way in me, and lead me in the way everlasting." (Psa. 139:23-24) When Jesus "searches" us, He does not simply "remove and replace" those things that He finds that "shouldn't be there." He involves *us* in the process.

When we wish that God would simply "remove" those things that "shouldn't be there" or those things that are causing us problems today, we actually *are* feeling a lack of faith. What we are saying, in effect, is that God cannot take those things that happened to us—no matter how bad they were—and make something good out of them. We aren't sure that God can't "transform" our lives without first surgically removing those things that are "problems." We want God to change our past because we aren't certain He has the power to change our future!

The truth is that God can work with *anything* that we bring to Him. It doesn't matter how dark, how painful, how destructive, how tormented our past is; God can work with it. "And we know that in all things God works for the good of those who love Him, who have been called according to His purpose." (Rom. 8:28) There is no life so stained, so tormented, so traumatized, so "shameful," that He cannot work with it for your good.[3] With men this is impossible, but with God all things are possible." (Matt. 19:26)

God desires us to have "truth in our inward being." He does not, however, tell us to be ashamed of the truth; instead, Jesus promises us, "you will know the truth, and the truth will set you free." (John 8:32) Jesus also tells us, "So if the Son sets you free, you will be free indeed." (John 8:36) The implication, however, is that we will *not* be free if we do *not* face, and know, the truth!

When we don't want to face the truth, we often hope, literally, that God will "change" the truth. We may revert to "positive

---

[3]You may be thinking, "Oh, but she doesn't know about my past." I don't—but He does.

confession formulas," "claim healing" and "declare deliverance." We may say, over and over, "That no longer affects me; that no longer bothers me," hoping that if we "confess it with our mouths," God will make it a reality in our hearts.

All we are doing, however, is attempting to create a truth that we like *better* than the real truth, and hoping that we can actually persuade God to *change* the truth. We are saying, "God, this is what I want the truth to be. I want to be completely free of the effects of the past. I don't want to have to know what happened. I want it not to matter. I want to be completely and instantly healed. This is the 'truth' that I want. Please make it so."

God will not "make it so." God doesn't replace one truth with another. He doesn't change the past so that the truth of the past conforms with your hope for the present. Truth is truth: What happened, happened, and if it hurt, it hurt. If it still hurts, it still hurts; if it is still affecting you, it still affects you. These are truths, and nothing to be ashamed of. God will not replace those truths with something that we like better because it "looks and feels" better or seems more in line with "the victorious Christian life."

Jesus declares, "A bruised reed He will not break, and a smoldering wick He will not snuff out..." (Matt. 12:20) Neither, however, will He deny that the reed is bruised or that the wick is smoldering. Instead, He works with the reality of that bruised reed, the stink of that smoking wick, and heal us from the *effects* of that reality. He won't change the truth; instead, through the truth, He will set us "free indeed," so that we ultimately will no longer have any reason to fear or be ashamed of what is *true*.

God *can* turn anything to "good." He *can* help us overcome *every* aspect of the past and live a truly triumphant, joyful, peaceful, trusting, love-overflowing life. The incredible miracle of that victory is *not* that He takes our past away, or magically transforms us, but that He takes the building materials that we have and, through His healing grace, turns them into something we never dreamed possible. He overcomes the past not by denying it or forgetting it or telling us to ignore it, but by taking what was *really* there and turning it, with our participation, into something new. He *can* take a base vessel, a vessel of clay, and turn it into a vessel of gold that is worthy to serve at the master's table. He has done it in other lives, and He can and will do it in yours.

# - 4 -

# Discovering Your True Identity

*Fear not, for I have redeemed you; I have summoned you by name; you are mine. When you pass through the waters, I will be with you; and when you pass through the rivers they will not sweep over you. When you walk through the fire, you will not be burned; the flames will not set you ablaze... Since you are precious and honored in My sight, and because I love you, I will give men in exchange for you, and people in exchange for your life... Bring My sons from afar and My daughters from the ends of the earth—everyone who is called by My name, whom I created for My glory, whom I formed and made. (Isa. 43:2-7, excerpted.)*

THE FIRST OBSTACLE most of us run into when we attempt to "walk in love" is our own self-image. We find it hard to imagine that anyone, even God, could love *us*. Nor can we imagine how *we* could possibly learn to love *ourselves*.

"You don't deserve it," our self-talk shouts. "How can you say nice things to yourself when you *know* how rotten you are? How can you expect anyone to be patient with you when you know you aren't solving your problems quickly enough? How can you expect anyone to tolerate someone as stupid as you? How can you talk about 'being nice' to yourself or about 'doing something for your own best interest' when you are *far* too selfish and inconsiderate as it is?"

Many Adult Children say, "I don't feel *loved*," when what we *really* mean is "I don't feel *lovable*." When we can't imagine *why* anyone (including ourselves) could or would love us, we can't imagine *that* anyone loves us. We may "believe," at the "head level," that we are loved by God, but we don't *feel* it. When we look at ourselves, we don't see a person that someone as "holy" or "perfect" as God could possibly love. Indeed, many Adult Children enter recovery with a single request: "Teach me how to be a better person so that others will love me."

When asked to "describe" ourselves, we respond with a litany of self-condemnation: "I'm not good enough. I'm stupid. I'm not creative. I'm not very interesting. I could never be successful. I wish I was a better parent. I know I'm a disappointment. I'm too sensitive; I take things too personally. I'm not very organized. I'm not spiritual enough. I should be more considerate. I know I should try harder. I'd like to be a better person. I should try harder to do what people want. I should be more... I should be less..."

We define ourselves in terms of what we think we are *not*. We hobble through life with a self-image that is crippled with inaccurate negatives, and that self-image cripples *us* whenever we attempt to move forward or seek change in our lives.

"Self-image" is not the same thing as "self-worth" or "self-esteem." "Self-esteem" refers to how we *feel* about ourselves: Whether we like ourselves, whether we "feel good" about ourselves, whether we are proud of ourselves or ashamed. "Self-image," however, refers to *who and what we think we are*. Everyone has a perception of self; the question is whether or not that perception is accurate. Since we are called to have "truth in our inward being," (Psa. 51:6 RSV), that question is an important one. If our perception *about* that "being" is itself inaccurate, it affects everything else in our lives.

A self-image is like the "you are here" marker on a map. If you really *are* where the arrow says you are, you can make informed choices. You can choose to stay where you are and take advantage of the opportunities that are currently available to you—or you can

"be perfect" Matt 5:48 — can't - 2nd class citizen

not perfectionist — maintain illusion

teleios - going to completion — 1 John 4:18 → perfected in love

model = perform → approval → love
(perfect) →

quick — impatient - right away!
now — should already
fast

selfish
driven to exhaustion
what is really best for others?
dedication wins approval
fail to do ⇒ rejection
unselfish = doing what is best

deserve — unkind — criticize
abase — put down

inferior — jealous — "what others are, not who I am"
envy — "more like" "are better"

"gotten rate"
how people react — angry — kind of person who makes mistakes
not being good enough
haven't done yet

boast — "I don't mind" what we believe ... hear ... like as ... are "making"

p.p. -won't admit
-can't admit hurt
same reason { . elevate the { . dismiss the lead

proud

no problems
problem = weakness = my fault
appear problem free
pretend
to change = admit we need it
want change

rude

self talk is toxic
"stupid" "idiot"
small
worthless

plot a course to some other point on the map. If, however, you aren't where you think you are, you are literally lost. You can't take advantage of where you *are* because you don't *know* where you are. Neither can you figure out how to get anywhere else, because you don't know how your "destination" relates to your current position. It's like trying to get to Los Angeles when you *think* you are in San Francisco, but you are *actually* in San Diego: If you travel south, believing that Los Angeles lies in that direction, you will not only not end up in Los Angeles, but you are also likely to end up somewhere you neither expect nor want to be.

When we have an accurate perception of self, we can choose a course of action that is based upon our awareness of our strengths and weaknesses, of the skills we have and the skills that we may need to develop. When we *don't* have an accurate perception of self, however, we *can't* make effective plans. We are often unaware of our strengths and magnify our weaknesses; we don't trust the skills we have and doubt our ability to develop new skills.

These perceptions influence every area of our lives. They influence how we think and act and even how we feel; how we interact with others and expect others to interact with us; and how we interact with God. Without an accurate self-image, everything we do in every area of our lives is based upon a lie.

That lie can have serious consequences. It can cause us to spend our entire lives trying to disprove, "live down," or at least "cover up" flaws and imperfections that *we may not even have*. One person may spend a lifetime trying to be more "caring" and "giving"—yet believe that every time she does not meet the needs of others, she is "selfish." Another may pursue degrees and awards and promotions in a frantic desire to "prove" that he is not as "stupid" as he thinks he is—yet regard every diploma and certificate as a "fluke" rather than as evidence of intelligence. Still another may pursue relationships in a vain desire to feel "lovable and loved"—yet become increasingly convinced of her "undesirability" or "worthlessness" each time a relationship fails.

That lie can also cause us to pass up opportunities and give up our hopes and dreams. It teaches us to believe that there are certain things we "can't" do, so we decide that there is no point in trying. We may suppose that there is "no point" in pursuing educational goals because we are "too stupid" to complete them.

We may suppose that we have "no hope" in attaining promotions because we "aren't good enough"—or we may pass up promotions because we assume that if we take them, we will "fail" and be humiliated. We go through life feeling like failures, not because we have *tried* and failed, but because we have become convinced that we *will* fail before we even try. Instead of spending a lifetime pursuing our dreams, we may spend a lifetime mourning them.

An inaccurate self-image can affect how we allow *others* to treat us. If we believe that we are "inferior," for example, we may suppose that others have a *right* to treat us without respect or consideration. If we believe we are "stupid," we suppose others are justified in ignoring us, refusing to take us seriously, or laughing at us. If we believe we are "incompetent," we accept whatever criticism we receive without asking whether or not it is valid. If we believe that we are "bad" or tend to do things "wrong," we assume that we deserve blame and condemnation. If we believe that we are "unlovable," we anticipate rejection and may even bring it on ourselves. If we believe that we "should be a better person," we may allow others to dictate what we "should" do or even what we should be to become more "pleasing." We may accept abusive treatment from others because we suppose we "deserve" it or because we assume we have no right to hope for anything better.

Finally, an inaccurate self-image may cause us to simply give up. Many of us have relationships with people who are impossible to please—people who never "approve" of us no matter what we do. Or, we may find that no matter how hard we try, we can't seem to meet our own standards and expectations. But because we do not realize that these efforts, demands, and expectations are based upon a lie, we suppose that the problem is us—that we are failures, that we can't "improve," that we are hopeless. Eventually, we may become convinced that we can never become the people we (or others) think we "should" be, so we give up altogether. Ultimately, this despair can lead us to depression and even to suicide.

An inaccurate self-image can drive us to spend a lifetime trying to change who and what we *are*, when what we need to change is what we *think* we are. Until we know who we *really* are now, we have no way of changing or improving ourselves, let alone of taking advantage of the capabilities we already have. If we want to change our lives, we must first change our *perception* of our lives.

Many Adult Children are reluctant to look too closely at "self," for several reasons. One is the fear that, no matter how bad we *think* we are, if we "dig down" into ourselves, we will discover that the reality is even *worse*. Another is the concern that if we stop thinking "badly" of ourselves, we will lose our motivation to improve, and become lazy and complacent. A third is the fear that we will become "prideful" and "sinful" if we think anything "good" about ourselves. Many Christian Adult Children believe that a negative self-image is a "correct" spiritual attitude of humility.

There is nothing spiritual or scriptural, however, about believing or acting upon a lie. God tells us to "Buy the truth and do not sell it; get wisdom, discipline, and understanding." (Prov. 23:23) We are not told to "buy" a lie, but to discover truth in every area of our lives. Only in this way can you "be made new in the attitude of your minds." (Eph. 4:23)

An inaccurate self-image is an "attitude of the mind" that is false on two levels. First, it is out of line with the Word of God. If, for example, your idea of being "humble" is to believe that God made a piece of garbage when He created you, that sort of humility glorifies neither God nor the truth. Instead, the Word tells us, "For you created my inmost being; you knit me together in my mother's womb. I praise you because I am fearfully and wonderfully made; *your works are wonderful*, I know that full well." (Psa. 139:13-14, emphasis mine.) The assumption that you are a worthless, unlovable failure contradicts God's statement, "you are precious and honored in My sight, and... I love you." (Isa. 43:4)

Second, an inaccurate self-image is out of line with reality. This is more difficult for us to check: If we knew what reality *was*, we would no longer have an inaccurate self-image! Our self-image actually creates a sort of "reality screen" that *filters out* any evidence we might receive that *contradicts* what we already believe. For example, if we believe that we are "stupid," we will ignore or dismiss a thousand examples of "intelligence" in our daily lives. We think nothing of our ability to get out of bed, read the paper, accomplish our tasks, follow instructions, carry on complex conversations, run errands, balance a checkbook, read a few Bible verses, and set the alarm. Instead, we focus on the single *mistake* of the day—like burning the toast—that proves how "stupid" we are.

When our perception of self is inaccurate, we are like people who walk into a grocery store believing that apples are oranges and pears are potatoes—and refusing to accept any evidence to the contrary. When we see a sign over the apple bin that declares "ripe, delicious apples," we don't question our own perceptions; instead, we wonder what idiot mislabeled the produce.

Denying one's good qualities and focusing upon only "bad" qualities does nothing to glorify God, even though we may rationalize such an approach by saying, "I want to know what is 'displeasing to God' so that I can change those things." All you are doing is claiming that what God created is less wonderful than it really is. By the same token, if you have a mind, then no spiritual purpose is served by declaring, "I am a stupid idiot—Praise the Lord." God gave you the mind that you have, and you do not glorify Him by declaring that it is anything less than it is.

We cannot be truly humble when we simply believe that we have nothing to be "boastful" *about*. Humility arises from an understanding and appreciation of the truth. We cannot be grateful for gifts that we don't even know we have—but when we *know* what God has given us and who we are in Christ, then we can be truly thankful, and *properly* humble. Until then, our attitude is not one of humility, but of ignorance.

## Seven Deadly Lies

It would be nice to say that remedying that ignorance is "as easy as telling yourself the truth." If it *were* that easy—if we could develop an accurate self-image by reading the Word and observing reality—we would have done so already.

What keeps our inaccurate self-images locked firmly into place *in spite of* our efforts to read the Word and perceive "reality" are a series of "thought patterns" that are themselves inaccurate and dysfunctional. *What* we think is profoundly influenced by *how* we think. We cannot correct *what* we think until we change the *way* we think. However, once we learn how to recognize and change the faulty thought process that *underlie* our inaccurate self-image, that self-image will begin to virtually "correct itself."

Seven types of dysfunctional thought processes play a major role in forming and maintaining our inaccurate self-image. These processes affect how we "take in" information, how we process that information, how we interpret it, and how we "see ourselves" as a result of that information. Many of these thought processes are like family heirlooms, handed down from one generation to another. They have become so familiar to us that we don't even know they are there. They seem "right" to us because they are what we are used to—and because they are how a great many people, including our parents (and including, sadly, a great many Christians) think. Once we learn how to recognize them, however, we can choose to challenge and confront them, and ultimately to replace them with healthier, more scriptural ways of thinking.

**1) You are what you do.** Adult Children have learned that "personality" is defined by "behavior." If we *do* something stupid, we believe that we are stupid. If we *do* something clumsy, we believe that we *are* clumsy. If we do something inconsiderate, we believe that we *are* inconsiderate. Most of all, if we *do* something "bad," we believe that *we* are bad.

We have learned to believe that the words "I did..." mean the same thing as "I am..." If we can say, accurately, "I did something careless," we believe that this is the same as saying, "I am careless." Eventually, most Adult Children bypass "I did" statements altogether, and describe both their actions and their personality with direct "I am" statements. This is why a professor with a Ph.D. and a wall full of certificates can burn the toast and declare, not "I *did* something stupid" but "I *am* incredibly stupid."

We often assume that one must "be" a certain kind of person to "do" a certain thing. If we assume that "smart people" don't do stupid things, then we suppose that if we do stupid things, we can't, by definition, be "smart people." If we suppose that only "bad" people do "bad" things, then, by a sort of warped circular logic, we suppose that *we are bad people because we do bad things*, and that *we do bad things because we are bad people*.

The view that "we are what we do" is profoundly unscriptural. Though David committed adultery and murder, he is not described in the Bible as "an adulterer" or "a murderer." He is not even described as a "bad person," but simply as a person who *did* several "bad things." In addition, Paul makes a strong statement that one is *not* what one *does* when he writes: "I do not understand what I do. For what I want to do I do not do, but what I hate I do... Now if I do what I do not want to do, *it is no longer I who do it*, but it is sin living in me that does it." (Rom. 7:15, 20, emphasis mine.)

When we believe that we "are" what we "do," we do more than contradict some basic scriptural principles. We are also denying that we have any free will—and by extension, that we are even responsible for our actions.

If we "do" bad or stupid or irresponsible or selfish things because we *are* bad or stupid or irresponsible or selfish, what choice do we have? We would have no more control over responding to these "built-in character defects" than a sick person has over sneezing. At the same time, if we are *truly* bad or stupid or selfish "by nature," how is it that we are still capable of doing *good* things, or *smart* things, or *considerate* things? If you believe that you are "irresponsible," how do you manage to get out of bed, do your job, feed yourself or your family, and refrain from trashing the neighborhood or robbing the local bank?

To reach a more accurate self-image, we must begin by changing our vocabulary. We must stop turning "verbs" into "adjectives." We must stop converting our "I did's" into "I am's." This means realizing that saying "I forgot" is *not* the same as saying "I am forgetful." Saying "I failed" is *not* the same as saying "I am a failure." Saying "That was a stupid thing to do" is *not* the same as saying "I am stupid for doing it." Saying "I did something wrong" is *not* the same as saying "*I am bad.*"

When we begin to "uncouple" our "I do's" from our "I am's," we can build an "I am" that is *separate* from our perception of what we do, and therefore far more accurate. We need to be able to say, with Paul, that "If I do what I do not want to do, *it is no longer I that do it.*" (Rom. 7:20) Then, we can begin to discover who "I" really is.

**2) Only the bad things count.** Until we learn how to separate our "I do's" from our "I am's," we tend to try to change what we are by changing what we *do*. We hope that if we *do* better things, we will *become* better people. Yet it doesn't seem to work. Even when we do "good," we still think of ourselves as "bad."

The reason that changing our *behavior* doesn't change our *self-image* is that we have been taught to consider only certain actions or behaviors as "important." Anything other than those types of actions literally "doesn't count" in our perception. In a dysfunctional family, one is usually taught that the only thing that *counts* is not what you *do*, but *what you do wrong*.

Dysfunctional families focus upon those things that disrupt the family routine, that create a problem, that require "extra" attention, that are "upsetting," or that might make the family "look bad" in the eyes of others. At the same time, they generally pay little attention to those things that do *not* disrupt the routine. As long as everything is going smoothly and nobody is upset, little is said. Thus, doing what one is "supposed" to do rarely attracts comment or praise—but "problems" are sure to draw attention and criticism.

In dysfunctional families, we are not "praised" for all the times that we play quietly, but we are yelled at for the one time that we crash noisily through the house. We are not "thanked" for the times that we complete our chores quickly, but we are reprimanded for every dish we fail to wash or corner we fail to dust. We receive no comments on our satisfactory grades, yet when we receive a poor grade, we are asked, "What went wrong?"

Even the praise that we *did* receive was often "backhanded." On the day that you wash the dishes without being told, for example, you may receive "praise" that sounds something like this: "Well, for once I didn't have to remind you three times to do your job." On the day you bring home a perfect test from school, you may be told, "It's about *time* you started turning those grades around!" Instead of telling us that our good work is "admirable," such compliments tell us that it is *unusual*. We are being told that it is "abnormal" for us to do a good job, and that our "normal" behavior is unsatisfactory.

What we learn from this is that normal "good work" is meaningless. It does not attract attention, let alone praise, so it is unimportant. The only thing that is "meaningful" is what is noticed—and what is *noticed* are our mistakes and failures. In time, then, our mistakes and failures become the only things that have any meaning to *us*. We learn to ignore our *own* successes and qualities, and focus upon what went "wrong."

That doesn't mean that we stop trying to do good things, to work harder and achieve more. We have learned, however, that we cannot expect to earn praise and recognition; instead, our struggles are based on the desire to *avoid* further criticism and rejection. Our efforts to "do better" are based on our perception that we can never "do well enough."

When we live with this form of "record of wrongs," we live with a double standard that radically distorts our perception of our performance and of our self. We judge ourselves by a scale that is perpetually tilted, not because there is nothing to place on the "good" side, but because we have never learned how to add up the things that belong there. We have been taught to "see" something "bad" or "inadequate" in just about everything we do. We are like people who bake a cake, and then, instead of enjoying the dessert, condemn ourselves for having "made a mess in the kitchen." We have learned to blind ourselves to everything positive in our lives.

To correct this self-image distortion, we need to learn how to remove our blinders. We need to look at the times that we *don't* make a mistake, and give those moments in our lives "equal credit." We need to look at the times that we get up, do our daily tasks, accomplish our office assignments, handle our parenting chores, run our errands, and choose *not* to rob the local bank or mug elderly ladies in the park—and weigh those actions and choices against our desire to "beat ourselves up" over burning the toast or forgetting to turn on the dishwasher. We need to stop adding up all the things that we "didn't" do during the day, and start making lists of those things that we *did* accomplish. Instead of saying, "I didn't wash the floor," we need to learn how to say, "I *did* do the laundry." Instead of saying, "I made a mess in the kitchen," we need to learn how to say, "I baked a delicious cake."

Instead of assuming that God will only talk to us when He wants to point out something we have done wrong, we need to realize that He does not keep a record of wrongs, but delights in our achievements. We need to learn how to follow Paul's instructions when he says, "Finally, brothers, whatever is true, whatever is noble, whatever is right, whatever is pure, whatever is lovely, whatever is admirable—if anything is excellent or praiseworthy—think about such things." (Phil. 4:8)

**3) Perfectionism.** As we struggle to shift our focus from the "bad things" that we do to the "good things," we run into a new problem: How we *define* whether a characteristic or performance is "good" or "bad." Often, the process we use is "perfectionism."

Perfectionism tells us, "If it isn't 100% perfect, it is meaningless." It convinces us that the slightest flaw in an otherwise perfect performance renders the entire performance "worthless."

As a child, did you ever clean the house from top to bottom, scrubbing floors, dusting furniture, and making sure that everything was put away neatly—only to have a parent glance at your efforts and say, "You missed that spot behind the stove"? Did you ever wash the clothes, only to be asked, "Why didn't you do the ironing as well?" Did you ever bring home a school project that you had worked hard on, only to have a parent look it over and say, "My, your handwriting could certainly use some improvement"? Did you ever seek the "perfect gift" for a parent, only to be told, "You know I hate that color"? Did you ever get all dressed up in your best clothes, only to have a parent remark that your hair looked sloppy?

From comments like these, we learn that if even the *tiniest* flaw can be found in our performance, nothing else matters. The one error on a test outweighs the ninety-nine correct answers. The spot of grease behind the stove is more important than the sparkling windows and spotless counters. Your failure to pick the "right" gift outweighs your good intentions. A single imperfection in your appearance renders you "ugly." No matter how well you actually did, if you weren't *perfect*, you failed.

Eventually, we learn to judge everything in our lives by these criteria. We learn to believe that if it is possible to say "I could have done better" or "I could have done that faster" or "I could have tried harder," nothing else matters. If we can't claim perfection, then all our work is worthless and meaningless. And because we can *always* truthfully state that we could do "better," we become convinced that we are hopelessly imperfect people who do hopelessly inferior work.

We also lose the ability to prioritize, for not only do we believe that we must do things perfectly, we also believe that we must do *everything equally perfectly*. We believe that every task in our lives "deserves" the same level of perfection: The laundry, the cooking, our jobs, our parenting, our work at the church, our commitment to God. Instead of realizing that we have "100%" of time and effort to *divide* among our various tasks and commitments, we believe that *every* task and commitment deserves the *same* 100% that we think we are supposed to give to every *other* task. Naturally, we become exhausted—and convinced that the problem is our imperfection.

When we are governed by perfectionist thinking, we do not judge our work by what we do well, but what we do *badly*. We judge everything by what we missed, by what we failed to do, by what we think we *could* have done if only we had tried *harder*. We overlook or ignore what we actually accomplished, what was actually completed, and whether our work actually served the purpose that was intended. If, for example, we are caring and thoughtful parents *most* of the time, but blow up and yell at our children one day, we declare, "I am not a perfect parent; I am a failure." If we do almost all our work on time, but miss a single deadline, we believe that we are "failures" as employees. If we burn one dinner out of fifty, we say, "I am a lousy cook." We spend our days looking at what is *not* rather than at what is, and judge ourselves not by what we did but by what we *haven't done yet*.

To escape the perfectionist trap, we need to learn how to give "equal weight" to what we do. We need to change the way we "score" our work. If we have learned to believe that one error on a test "outweighs" ninety-nine correct answers, it is time to start giving every *correct* answer the *same value* that we formerly gave the single *incorrect* answer. It is time to start giving our *good* work the same value that we give our *bad* work. It is time to begin adding up "achievement points" instead of "penalty points." When we begin to look at what we have *done* rather than at what we have *not* done, our focus will sharpen, and we will begin to see things as they are rather than as we have learned to believe they *should* be.

We would do well to follow the advice given us in Ecclesiastes, which does not counsel us to strive after impossible and elusive goals of "perfection" but, instead, teaches us to become aware of what we have and to enjoy it: "This too is a grievous evil: As a man comes, so he departs, and what does he gain, since he toils for the wind? All his days he eats in darkness, with great frustration, affliction and anger. Then I realized that it is good and proper for a man to eat and drink, and to find satisfaction in his toilsome labor under the sun during the few days of life God has given him—for this is his lot. Moreover, when God gives any man wealth and possessions, and enables him to enjoy them, to accept his lot and be happy in his work—this is a gift of God. He seldom reflects on the days of his life, because God keeps him occupied with gladness of heart." (Ecc. 5:16-20) When we learn how to enjoy the toil that we *have* done, and its fruits, instead of punishing ourselves over the toil that we *think* we *should* have done, then we, too, can be "occupied with joy in our hearts," instead of becoming filled with hopelessness and exhaustion.

**4) Black-and-White Thinking.** Black-and white thinking and perfectionism go hand-in-hand. While perfectionism teaches us how to *judge* our work and personality, black-and-white thinking teaches us how to *label* them.

Perfectionism teaches us to believe that if our performance or character isn't "100%," it isn't anything. Thus, if we are not 100% good, then we cannot claim to be good at all. If we are not 100% smart (i.e., if we ever do something "stupid"), we cannot claim to be smart at all. If we are not 100% unselfish and giving, then we cannot claim to be unselfish and giving at all.

Once we have concluded that we are *not* 100% "good," we must find another way to define what we suppose we *really* are. Black-and-white thinking teaches us that we have only two possibilities: If we are not one thing, then we must be its opposite.

Thus, if we believe that we don't have the right to claim that we are "good," then by definition, we must be *bad*. If we think that we don't have the right to say that we are "smart," then the only alternative is that we must be "stupid." If we aren't caring and considerate 100% of the time, then we suppose that we *must* be "uncaring" and "inconsiderate." If we do anything that relates to self, then we can't be 100% unselfish—so we must be "selfish."

It is the *combination* of perfectionism and black-and-white thinking that is so destructive to self-image. If you believe that life is all-or-nothing, you end up with nothing every time. We see life as a two-sided coin, and in our definitions of self and our evaluations of our performance, we are always coming up "tails."

Black-and-white thinking admits no qualifiers. Even though we might *say*, "I am not as smart as I would like to be," what we *mean* is "I am stupid." Though we might say, "I didn't do that as well as I should have," what we mean is, "I failed." If we cannot have positives, we are left with nothing but negatives, and it is upon these negatives that our self-image is based.

The flaws in black-and-white thinking become apparent when we try to "reverse" the coin. If it only takes *one* selfish action to automatically make us "selfish people," why is it that one *unselfish* action doesn't automatically make us "unselfish people"? If it takes only one "stupid" action to make us believe that we are *stupid*, why doesn't one intelligent thought or deed make us believe that we are *smart*? At the same time, if one must be "100% unselfish" to qualify as an "unselfish person," then wouldn't one have to be 100% selfish to qualify as a truly *selfish* person? If one must be "100% responsible" to "qualify" as a "responsible person," shouldn't one have to be 100% irresponsible to qualify as an "irresponsible person"? If a "perfect parent" is one who *never* yells at her children, wouldn't someone have to yell at the children just about all day to qualify as a "bad" parent, by the same standards?

Black-and-white thinking is a false, inaccurate double standard. When we attempt to understand who we are *or* what we do by this standard, we are doomed. No one is 100% *anything*; in reality, every one of us is a mixture of characteristics, qualities, abilities, desires, interests, and potentials. To develop an accurate self-image, we must seek other ways to define those qualities and potentials, and see them for what they are.

To escape from black-and-white thinking, we need to build a new vocabulary. We need to begin to understand that qualifiers are valid. Life is measured on a continuum, in degrees, not in absolutes and extremes. We need to learn that even though we may not be as "smart" as we would *like* to be, that does not mean that we are *not smart*. We may be "less giving" than someone else, but we may *still* be "giving." We may be less responsible than we will be tomorrow, but we are probably *more* responsible than we were *yesterday*. We may not possess a desired skill today, but we have the opportunity to *build* that skill tomorrow. We may not have "all the information" today, but tomorrow we will learn more.

Black-and-white thinking sees the world as a set of polarized absolutes: There is the "pinnacle" of ultimate perfection, which no one can ever reach; and there is the depth of utter failure, which is where we think we are if we haven't reached the pinnacle. Life, however, is not polarized. It contains few pinnacles and few pits. Instead, it is designed as a process of continual growth, of moving toward a goal that we know we can never reach in this lifetime. Like Paul, we can understand ourselves better when we acknowledge, "Not that I have already obtained all this, or have already been made perfect, but I press on to take hold of that for which Christ Jesus took hold of me. Brothers, I do not consider myself yet to have taken hold of it. But one thing I do: Forgetting what is behind and straining toward what is ahead, I press on toward the goal to win the prize for which God has called me heavenward in

Christ Jesus. All of us who are mature should take such a view of things. And if on some point you think differently, that too God will make clear to you." (Phil. 3:12-15)

**5) Mislabeling.** Perfectionism and black-and-white thinking tell us whether to consider our actions "good" or "bad;" mislabeling tells us what to *call* those actions. "Mislabeling" is how we move from thinking of ourselves as "spillers of drinks" to thinking of ourselves as "clumsy idiots." It is the thought process that turns "verbs" into "adjectives."

This process begins when, as a toddler, you drop a cookie or knock over a drink or break something. If your parents didn't make a big deal over what is, after all, "normal" for a toddler, you probably won't think much of such behaviors today. But if someone yelled, "You klutz! Why are you always so *clumsy*?" then you just learned a definition of *self* that arose from your action. Before long, we learn to associate the *action* of spilling a drink with the supposed *characteristic* of "clumsiness." As adults, we fall victim to circular logic: We *do* clumsy things because we *are* clumsy people—and we *are* clumsy people because we *do* clumsy things. Eventually, we can no longer tell the actions and labels apart.

This association between actions and labels creates a sort of "unbalanced equation"—an equation in which the sides are not actually equal, though we have been taught to *believe* that they are. It is as though we have learned to believe that 2+2=5. Thus, we learn that bad grades "equal" stupidity, or that an unmade bed "equals" untidiness, or that failing to complete a task "equals" laziness, or that having an idea that someone doesn't agree with "equals" idiocy or foolishness. As adults, we assume that failing to meet everyone's needs 100% of the time "equals" selfishness, that failure to spend hours in prayer or Bible study "equals" lack of commitment, or that our tastes "equal" lack of sophistication.

I've encountered several Adult Children with interesting "unbalanced equations." One woman labeled herself as "disorganized" because her kitchen cupboards were not always clean. Another labeled herself a "poor hostess" (and declared that she could never have friends over to her house) because she didn't have matching china. Another was certain that she was "stupid" because she had made a poor investment.

Perhaps the most frightening example came from a young

father who was alarmed by the behavior of his two-year-old. The child was just beginning to understand the power of the word "No"—as all two-year-olds do. His father, however, was concerned about the child's "rebelliousness"—for he believed that rebellion was 'akin to witchcraft'!" (1 Sam. 15:23 KJV) To him, a rebellious two-year-old "equaled" a potential Satanist! It meant that he was a "bad parent"—for "good" parents have "good" children!

Unbalanced equations keep us cleaning cupboards, studying until we drop, and giving until we have nothing left to give, in the hope that we can change our labels by changing what we *do*. But it never works. Cleaning a cupboard will never cleanse our self-image. Instead, it traps us in the behavior of the Pharisees, to whom Jesus said, "Woe to you, teachers of the law and Pharisees, you hypocrites! You clean the outside of the cup and dish, but inside they are full of greed and self-indulgence. Blind Pharisee! First clean the inside of the cup and dish, and then the outside also will be clean." (Matt. 23:25-26) We cannot change the inside (what we believe) by trying to clean up the outside (what we do). We can become vessels of truth only when we change the false perceptions that are *causing* that compulsion to "clean the outside of the cup."

To do this, we must rebalance our equations. Instead of believing "I am a rotten parent because I yelled at my child," or "I'm a failure because I missed that deadline," we must remind ourselves that a dirty cupboard equals a dirty cupboard, and nothing more. When we clean it, it becomes a clean cupboard. When we miss a deadline, we miss a deadline; we are not *defined* by that deadline. When we yell, we are not automatic failures as parents.

We are people who are equally capable of cleaning a cupboard, or of setting our priorities elsewhere. We need to learn how to *stop* "filling the cup" with perceptions that came from hurting parents, and how to *start* filling it, instead, with the "wisdom from heaven," which is "first of all pure; then peace-loving, considerate, submissive, full of mercy and good fruit, impartial and sincere." (James 3:17) When we do this, the outside will take care of itself.

**6) Comparisons to Others.** Perhaps the quickest way to distort a self-image is to compare oneself with others. Adult Children often go through life focusing on other people and thinking, "I should be more like *that* person." We tend to believe that others, by definition, are better, smarter, kinder, more spiritual, or more lovable and loving. We suppose that others do things "more easily" and "more cheerfully," that they have the "proper attitude," feel the "right emotions," think the "right thoughts," and do the "right things."

Many of us grew up being compared to someone else: A brother or sister, or even a parent. We may have discovered that no matter what we did, we never seemed to gain as much praise and recognition as another family member—even for the same quality of work. When we had parents who asked us, "Why can't you be more like so-and-so," we become people who ask *ourselves* why we can't be more like so-and-so.

When we look at ourselves, we see the inside of the cup. We know how "ugly" it is in there, or at least how ugly we *think* it is. We know that we aren't as cheerful as we pretend to be; we know about the pain and resentment that seethes inside us; we know that when we "give until it hurts," it really *does* hurt; we know how tired, frustrated, miserable, confused, and alone we really feel.

We *know* that we are often "faking" the shiny exterior of our "cup"—but strangely enough, we *assume* that the shiny exteriors that *other people* present are reflections of *reality*. Because we can't see into the inside of another person's cup the way we can see into our own, we tend to *assume* that it doesn't *look* like ours does. We are sure that *they* don't have any of that darkness, any of that dirt, any of that doubt that lives within us. We are convinced that other people's cups are as clean on the inside as they appear to be on the outside.

This is particularly tough for Christians. When we look around on Sunday, and see the rows of smiling faces and nodding heads in the pews, we are absolutely *convinced* that everyone there is more spiritual and closer to God than we are. We are *sure* that not only does everyone else spend more time reading the Word and praying than we do, but that no one else finds it as *difficult* to "make time for God" as we seem to. We are sure that others *really enjoy* serving on countless committees and devoting endless hours to "selfless volunteering," and that there is something wrong with *us* for feeling tired and a little resentful. We are sure that everyone else feels the peace and assurance we think that we "should" feel—and we are sure that *our* "Sunday smile" is the only one that masks a heart full of doubt and pain.

When we compare our work to others, it opens up a whole new world of perceived imperfection. If we get a good grade, we look at someone else and think, "Yes, but I had to *work* for that grade; a really smart person like so-and-so gets good grades *without even trying*." If we complete a project, we think, "Yes, but a more efficient person would have done it much more quickly and easily." If we pray for an hour, we think, "Yes, but a really *spiritual* and *committed* person would have stayed on his knees much longer." If we wear ourselves out with good works, we think, "Oh, look at so-and-so; I'll bet *she* does this with *real* joy in her heart, and never complains or feels tired like I do." Whenever we perceive that someone else does something better than we do it, our perfectionist thinking tells us that we aren't doing "well enough."

The exception to that rule is "negative comparison." This, too, has its roots in childhood—only, instead of being asked, "Why can't you be *more* like so-and-so," we were asked, "Why are you *so much* like so-and-so?" "Negative comparisons" develop when we are told that we are "just like" crazy Aunt Harriet or wicked Uncle Harry. While "positive comparisons" teach us that we can never become as *good* as a better person, "negative comparisons" convince us that we will turn out just as *bad* as a the family "black sheep." While positive comparisons drive us to attempt to "live up to" someone else's performance, negative comparisons drive us to attempt to "live down" our resemblance to someone else's performance.

Whenever we compare ourselves to others, whether those comparisons are positive or negative, we are going against scripture. Paul tells us, "Each one should test his own actions. Then he can take pride in himself, without comparing himself to somebody else..." (Gal. 6:4) He reminds us that what we see on the surface may have little to do with what goes on in a person's heart: "Therefore judge nothing before the appointed time; wait till the Lord comes. He will bring to light what is hidden in darkness and will expose the motives of men's hearts. At that time each will receive his praise from God." (1 Cor. 4:5) Finally, Paul tells us, "when they measure themselves by one another, and compare themselves with one another, they are without understanding." (2 Cor. 10:12 RSV) When we learn to test our own work, and cease to worry about whether it "measures up" to another's, we will find new ways to build an accurate self-image.

**7) The Snapshot Effect.** The final "thought process" that distorts our self-image is the perception that *what we are is what we always will be.* Whenever we freeze an *action* into an "I am" statement, we are taking a snapshot of our behavior at a particular *moment* in time and claiming that it represents our personality *across* time. Our "action snapshots" are like "stills" taken from a movie. Trying to understand "self" from such a snapshot is like trying to figure out the plot of a movie by looking at a single "still."

Snapshot statements ignore the possibility of growth or change. When we say, "I did something stupid, therefore I am stupid," we overlook the possibility that tomorrow, or even a few minutes from now, we may *do* something *smart* (though we will probably ignore it). We overlook the possibility that we can *change* our behavior.

One woman, for example, described how she had made a bad investment, and went on to say, "I guess I'm just not good at investing." By turning her action into an "I am" statement, she denied any possibility that she could ever be "good at investing." She ignored the fact that, prior to making that investment, she had received no training or advice in investing—along with the fact that with that training or advice, she might very well become a "good investor."

Likewise, the woman who declared that she was "disorganized" because her cupboards were not clean did not imagine that cleaning her cupboards would turn her into an "organized" person. Instead, she felt that cleaning her cupboards would simply mean that there was less *visible evidence* of her basic "disorganized" personality. By translating her *action snapshot* into a statement of *self*, she had changed "disorganization" from a "state of cupboards," which could be corrected, into a "state of self," which she perceived as unchangeable.

When we take snapshots of self and believe that they are "representative" of our personality and capabilities, it is like looking at a class picture taken in grammar school and saying, "This is me. This is what I was then and this is what I will always be." In reality, we *know* that we have changed since that picture was taken. We don't look the same. We don't talk the same. We don't have the same thoughts or the same way of thinking. We have learned a great deal. None of us are the "same people" that we were when those school pictures were taken.

By the same token, none of us are the "same people" we were when our "action snapshots" were taken and "translated" into personality. We aren't the same people that we were *yesterday*. We will not be the same people *tomorrow*. You are not the same person now that you were when you began to read this book. I am not the same person that I was when I began to write it. Life is a process of change, and we cannot escape that process even if we wanted to.

Paul writes, "When I was a child, I talked like a child, I thought like a child, I reasoned like a child. When I became a man, I put childish ways behind me." (1 Cor. 13:11) As we mature, we can give up the childish reasoning that what we are is frozen in time, unchangeable, and worst of all, "unimprovable." Instead, we have an infinite capacity for growth, for learning, for development, for change, and for improvement. When we stop looking at what we think we *are*, we can begin, at last, to look at what we *can be*. Nor do we have to fear that we have to reach that destination alone, for we are not alone on the journey. As Paul says, we can be "confident of this, that He who began a good work in you will carry it on to completion until the day of Christ Jesus." (Phil. 1:6)

## So Who *Are* We?

I wish I could tell you who you are in reality—but the fact is that I don't know. It is my hope that by choosing healthier ways of *looking at* who you are, you will begin to discover the wonderful reality of self, and find that it doesn't match the "snapshot" you have been carrying in your mental wallet for so many years. I personally do not believe that you are stupid, or disorganized, or uncreative, or irresponsible, or worthless, or unlovable, or selfish. But only *you* can discover your real qualities and abilities that can replace those perceptions.

However, we *can* look at who the *Bible* says we are. There isn't enough space in this book to discuss *all* the scriptures that tell us, in joyful detail, who we are in Christ or how God sees us. There is room for some highlights, however. According to God, we are:

**"...A chosen people, a royal priesthood, a holy nation, a people belonging to God, that you may declare the praises of Him who called you out of darkness into His wonderful light."** (1 Pet. 2:9) We are chosen by God to be holy—not to *become* holy out of our own efforts, which is impossible, butto be *made* holy by God's selection. We are God's people, and because we are His children, we are literally "royalty." We are the brothers and sisters and children of the "king of kings." Are the king's relatives "pond-scum" or "worthless worms"? The Bible says otherwise. When we speak against ourselves and claim a false self-image, we "lie" about the chosen children of God, who are:

**"...destined in love to be His sons through Jesus Christ."** (Eph. 1:5 RSV) God did not adopt us because He had to, or because we "earned" it; He adopted us because He loves us. As His children, we have access to God's infinite love, power and resources. That access is not based upon "merit" or "hard work," but like the resources of any family, it is available to us because we are a *part* of that family. Just as we are entitled to open the family refrigerator or cupboard and take out food, we are entitled to open God's cupboard and receive what He has for us. We can do this because:

**"We have boldness and confidence of access through our faith in Him."** (Eph. 3:12 RSV) We do not need to crawl to God. We do not need to whimper and whine. We do not need to cringe away from God, hoping that He won't notice how *bad* we are and hope that He won't beat us too hard for it. Nor do we have to "become better people" so that we *can* approach God boldly; we don't have to "earn the right" to approach Him in confidence. We have that right today, as we are. And as we learn to approach Him, we will learn how to use His resources to rebuild our lives.

**"We are God's fellow workers; you are God's field, God's building."** (1 Cor. 3:9) God is the architect of your life; He designed the "blueprints" for who you are, and He is the one who supervises your "construction." He is the "farmer" who decided what to "plant" in you, He selected the seed, and He makes the field ready for it. He chose what crop you would bear, and when it will be ready for harvest. But in all this you are a co-laborer; you are not God's slave, but His partner, intimately involved in the process of building and growth but not solely responsible for it. When the crop *is* ready to harvest, we are:

**"...a kind of firstfruits of all He created."** (James 1:18) The "first fruits" are the best of the best, the cream of the crop, the part of the harvest that is considered "good enough" to offer to God. We did not, and cannot, make ourselves into "first fruits" on our own; we cannot make *ourselves* "good enough" to offer to God. However,

God has *made* us "the best of His crop," not the leavings. We will not be swept out with the chaff, but gathered into the barn—

**"For we are God's workmanship, created in Christ Jesus to do good works..."** (Eph. 2:10) We must never, ever forget that God made us. He designed us. He planned us. He made us what we are. We were made *for* good works, not *by* good works. We cannot "make ourselves" into better, more pleasing people by struggling to "do enough good works" to justify or earn God's love. We have already been made by God, and He does not make "inferior products." He puts quality first in His workmanship.

**"For everything God created is good, and nothing is to be rejected if it is received with thanksgiving, because it is consecrated by the word of God and prayer."** (1 Tim. 4:4-5) If everything created by God is good, and we are created by God and His workmanship, then we are good. We need to put aside this attitude that we are "not good enough," and, instead, learn what we are and what we have in Christ. Only then can we move forward in love and hope, instead of trying to "make up for" what we think we lack. We are not to reject the personality and characteristics that God built into us;we are to consecrate what He gave us through prayer and thanksgiving.

**"For God did not give us a spirit of timidity, but a spirit of power, of love and of self-discipline."** (2 Tim. 1:7) When we realize that God put a powerful spirit within us, a spirit of love and self-control, we no longer need to be afraid. We are not weak; we are not failures; we are not hopeless. All of those attitudes involve a "looking back" perspective; they keep us focused upon what we think we haven't done or upon what we think we have done wrong. But with a spirit of power and love and discipline, we can adopt a forward focus, and look not at what we *have* done but at what we *can do* with the tools God has given us.

**"In all these things, we are more than conquerors through Him who loved us."** (Rom. 8:37) Because of those tools, we do not need to fear defeat or anticipate failure. We are not losers in Christ. We are not failures in faith. We are *more than conquerors*; that means that we have been *assured* of victory, completion, growth, and most of all, love.

**"Now you are the body of Christ and each one of you is a part of it."** (1 Cor. 12:27) We are more than just part of a church or part of a bunch of like-minded people. We are part of *Jesus*. We are His hands, or His feet, or His eyes, or His mouth. We are told to delight in whatever "body part" we have become, for every body part of Jesus is equally important and serves a valuable purpose. Let no one tell you that you are the "wrong" part or that you need to try to become a "better" part. Instead, allow yourself to discover just what part of Jesus you are—and be confident that, as you are a part of Him, He is a part of you. No matter what we think of ourselves, Jesus values us as we value our own hands and feet. He would no more abandon us or cut us off than we would cut off our ears or rip out our tongues. We are a part of Him, and Jesus takes care of His body.

**"You are precious in my eyes, and honored, and I love you."** (Isa. 43:4 RSV) This verse speaks for itself. We are not despised in God's eyes; we are *precious*. We are not worthless failures to Him; we are *honored*. We are not unlovable, for He *loves us*. We are precious because God finds us precious; we are honored because our Parent has honor; we are loved because we are His children. If anyone tries to tell you that you are something other than this to God, remember that the Bible tells us otherwise.

**"The Lord will guide you always; He will satisfy your needs in a sun-scorched land and will strengthen your frame. You will be like a well-watered garden, like a spring whose waters never fail."** (Isa. 58:11) Because God loves us, we are like a source of refreshment to others: A spring of water that doesn't fail. Love flows into us from God, more love than we can hold, and it spills out onto those around us. We grow and flourish. We are like a garden—a place that is lovely to walk in and enjoy and rest in. Nor are we a neglected, untended garden, choked with weeds and dying for lack of water, but a garden that is lovingly taken care of, so that its flowers bloom the brightest and its fruits taste the sweetest. We need to remember, too, that a gardener does not raise flowers because the flowers have "earned" the right to be raised; instead, He raises them because the flowers delight Him with their color and beauty and perfume.

Moreover, we have the promise of God's continual guidance and direction. That guidance does not direct our attention backward to past mistakes and failures. Instead, it leads us steadily forward, leaving what we have done or haven't done or wish we had done behind, and guiding us to what we *can* be and what we *can* do. God promises to guide us in healthy, satisfying directions that will strengthen us and fulfill our needs.

**"You will be a crown of splendor in the Lord's hand, a royal diadem in the hand of your God."** (Isa. 62:3) The Bible tells us that we are jewels, not fools. How much more joyful it is to think of ourselves as sparkling diamonds or glowing rubies in a crown that pleases God, than as slimy and slithering worms whose only reason for gratitude is that God forbears from stepping on us. We do not slither; we glitter. We are not dull and plain, but sparkling. We "shine like stars in the universe" (Phil. 2:15), and when we learn to see ourselves that way, we will learn how to see ourselves as God sees us.

Perhaps the best way to answer the question, "Who are we?" is to consider the answer David gives us: "What is man that Thou art mindful of him, and the son of man that Thou dost care for him? Yet Thou hast made him little less than God, and dost crown him with glory and honor. Thou hast given him dominion over the works of Thy hands; Thou hast put all things under his feet, all sheep and oxen, and also the beasts of the field, the birds of the air, and the fish of the sea, whatever passes along the paths of the sea. O Lord, our Lord, how majestic is Thy name in all the earth!" (Psa. 8:4-9)[1]

---

[1]For additional scriptures that tell us who we are in Christ and in God's eyes, see also: Zec. 13:9; Psa. 1:3; Isa. 32:2; Isa. 44:4-5; Isa. 45:9-13; Isa. 49:2-6, 13-16; Isa. 54:10-17; Isa. 55:12-13; Isa. 58:4-12; Isa. 60:1, 8, 15; Isa. 61:7; Isa. 62:4; Matt. 10:31; Rom. 5:1; 1 Cor. 3:16; 1 Cor. 6:11; Gal .4:27-28; Gal. 5:1; Eph. 1:7-8; Eph. 2:1, 8-9, 19-22; Eph. 5:8-9; Col. 1:21-22; Col. 3:3; 1 Pet. 2:4-5.

# - 5 -

# Telling Yourself the Truth

*You were taught, with regard to your former way of life, to put off your old self, which is being corrupted by its deceitful desires; to be made new in the attitude of your minds; and to put on the new self, created to be like God in true righteousness and holiness. Therefore each of you must put off falsehood and speak truthfully to his neighbor, for we are all members of one body. (Eph. 4:22-25)*

DEEP INSIDE EVERY ADULT CHILD, there is a "voice." We all know that voice. We all dread it. We all wish it would go away. But it seems that no matter what we do, we are bound to hear it—and hear it, and hear it, and hear it.

It is the voice that says, "Oh, you stupid idiot. You really fouled up *that* time. You are *such a moron.*" (Actually, most of us hear something less printable than that.) When you want to try something new, the voice tells you, "Don't bother doing that. You couldn't do it well, so there's no point in trying. You'll just end up looking foolish." When you hope that something good will come your way, the "voice" tells you, "You don't have a chance! Nobody will notice *your* work. It isn't good enough." When you wonder how people are reacting to you, the voice tells you, "Everyone is looking at you. You shouldn't have worn that outfit. You look so stupid and out of place. Everyone is talking about you. Why did you come?" When you think about asking God for something, the "voice" tells you, "Why should He give it to you? What have you done to deserve it? Look at all the things you've done wrong. You'd better get your act together before you ask God for anything."

That voice has been a part of our lives for so long that we have learned to take it for granted; we have accepted it as an inseparable part of us. We hate it, we fear it, we want it to shut up and leave us alone—but we rarely suppose that we can *change* it.

We don't think we can *change* that voice because we *believe* what it says. No matter how much we dislike its messages, we are convinced that they are true. Moreover, the messages of that voice often become the "measure" by which we determine whether all other messages and information are true or false. The voice becomes not only our personal judge, but the method by which we judge everything else.

When we try to argue with the voice, it unleashes its ultimate weapon: "What if?" When we say, "I don't want to believe you," it whispers back, "But what if you're wrong? What if you do something *really dumb* and the *whole world* sees what a fool you are? What if you *really mess up*? What if it costs you the love of the people you care about? What if... what if... what if?"

That voice is our self-talk, and it is the mechanism by which what *other* people thought of us became *what we think of ourselves*. We were not born with it; we learned it, from the same place that we learned our self-image, our dysfunctional thought patterns, and our fears. Our self-talk keeps our families' unhealthy and inaccurate perceptions alive in us, and forms them into the foundation of our lives by telling us who we are, what other people think of us, and what we must do.

Most of us know that this "foundation" isn't very stable; instead, it feels as though we are living on an earthquake zone. Yet it is our self-talk that actually prevents us from making effective repairs. Because our self-talk *arises* from the foundational level of our thought—the level at which we no longer question what we believe to be "true"—it is very difficult for us to evaluate its messages.

Instead, self-talk continually misdirects us. When things go wrong, it tells us, "It's because you aren't trying hard enough," or "You aren't praying and reading the Word enough," or "You aren't good enough to *deserve* any better than this."

It is very difficult to change such foundational beliefs. Positive affirmations (including scriptural affirmations) don't change them; we may try to "believe" the nice things we say to ourselves, but the voice reminds us that we "know better." Praise and compliments from others don't change them; the voice simply sneers at positive feedback, asking, "What do they know? If they *really* knew you, they wouldn't say those things." Even prayer and Bible study don't change them. Instead, we often go *into* prayer and the Bible expecting to find confirmation of our "unworthiness" and proof that we aren't "doing enough"—and because we are looking for it, we will find it. Indeed, our self-talk often cloaks its familiar messages of condemnation and shame in the language of scripture, leading us to believe that our painful attitudes are "spiritually correct."

Our self-talk expresses what we believe, at the most fundamental level, about how the world works, and about how *we* fit into the world. It is upon these beliefs, and the endless commands and injunctions and requirements and fears that arise from them, that we base our actions and reactions. Frequently, when our self-talk tells us to "jump," we don't stop long enough to ask "How high?" When it says, "This is how things are," we think, "That's right."

To be "made new" in the attitude of our minds, we must be "made new" in the attitude of our self-talk. This is far from easy, however. The job of our self-talk is to protect our identity and our sense of security. It performs this mission by "keeping out" information that might threaten that identity, that security.

Recovery information is new information; it seems unfamiliar, threatening, frightening. It tells us that we must *change* many of our behaviors and ideas. Our self-talk resists these changes and ideas, and the growth that might result from them, every step of the way. We have learned to believe that "different is dangerous" and that departing from our survival skills could even be fatal. Thus when we read that "all things are possible for him who believes" (Mark 9:23), our self-talk whispers, "It isn't possible for you to become a better person." When we read that "There is no condemnation for those who are in Christ Jesus" (Rom. 8:1), it whispers,

"Wait until He (or someone else) finds out about *you.*" When we read that we are "precious in God's eyes" (Isa. 43:4), it simply laughs. Because we have spent a lifetime *believing* what our self-talk tells us, we may even believe it above scripture—and act upon its directives rather than upon God's Word.

The first step in changing that self-talk, then, is not in attempting to change what it *says*—for this is not a "level of thought" that we have direct access to. Instead, we can begin by choosing to change how we *respond* to what it says. To prove to ourselves that its message is false and ultimately destructive, we must find ways to build even the smallest of gaps between "hearing" the messages of our self-talk and "acting" upon them. Instead of "jumping" when ordered, we need to take a moment to ask "Why?" and to discover whether we have any *alternatives* to jumping.

Oddly enough, the first step in changing our response to our self-talk is to actually *listen* to that talk. Before we can analyze the messages and instructions that are being fed to us, we must discover *precisely* what those messages are. As we begin to listen to our inner voice, we are likely to discover that its messages fit into a common framework.

That framework has four basic components: Our understanding of our world and its limitations for us; our understanding of ourselves as we relate to that world; our understanding of how *others* see us and respond to us; and our understanding of *what we must do to survive.* Each of these components contains several "directives" that have the power to control our actions as long as we allow ourselves to respond to them without critical review. "Listening" to our own self-talk brings these directives to the surface. Once we learn how to listen to, and critically review, our self-talk, it loses its power to control us; instead, we become participants with choices, rather than slaves to our voices.

## How the World Works

Adult Children often have two very different pictures of the world: How we think the world works for *other* people, and how we think it works for *us.* We don't tend to believe that we live in the "same" world that other people live in; we don't believe that we have the same opportunities, chances, or benefits that are available to others. Our world seems much "smaller," with narrow boundaries, strict rules, and inescapable conditions. Our self-talk makes six important contributions to this perception:

**1) If Only.** Nearly every Adult Child has a message that says, "If only this had not happened, my life would be different." "If only" our childhood had been "healthy," we would be living a healthy, happy, fulfilled, and "perfect" life today. "If only" we had not been abused, we would have "good" relationships today. "If only" we had been praised for our efforts, we would have a more accurate self-image. One young woman declared, "If only my parents hadn't died, I would have had a personality."

The "if only" message is powerful because it contains a seed of truth: Many of our fears, troubles, and self-destructive behaviors are the result of past experiences. When we say, "If only a certain thing hadn't happened, life would be different," we are speaking the truth. Life *would* be different.

That does not mean, however, that life would be perfect, wonderful, or happy. No matter what kind of life we are living today, we can never predict *what life would have been like* if things had been "different."

When we say "if only," we are not just declaring our belief that life "would have" been different. We are actually expressing our belief that life *will never be different*. Many of us have learned to believe that our past not only put us where we are, but that it *keeps* us where we are. Many Adult Children believe that their past has permanently destroyed their chances for a "happy" future. "If only" thinking convinces us that we are helpless victims of unjust and unchangeable circumstances.

"If only" thinking is the most futile form of "wishful thinking." It fixes our eyes upon the chances and opportunities that we believe we have *missed*, and blinds us to the options that are *still available*. By focusing our attention upon the "closed" doors in our lives, "if only" thinking convinces us that there are no more "open" doors. It persuades us to spend our energy wishing that we could change the *past*, instead of allowing us to focus upon changing the *future*.

The perception that "my destiny is ruined because of my past" is a painful one—so "if only" thinking often compensates for that view by convincing us that our future *could* change... "If only."

Many Adult Children think, "*If only* I could find the perfect mate, someone who would love me, then I would feel good about myself and all my problems would go away." We think, "*If only* someone would give me a chance, I could prove myself and people would respect me." We think, "*If only* I could experience deliverance from God, all my problems would disappear and I could live the perfect Christian life."

Unfortunately, other Christians often feed this type of "if only" thinking with "if only's" of their own. Common Christian "if only's" include: "If only you would let go of all this and give it to God, you wouldn't have these problems;" "If only you would get rid of this particular sin in your life, God would be able to bless you and you would have no more trouble;" and the classic, "If only you would pray and read the Bible more, you would no longer be troubled by these issues or feelings."

"If only" thinking locks us into unforgiveness. When we believe that our future is "ruined" by people who hurt us in the past, we are holding those people responsible not only for the problems that they caused *at the time*, but for all our problems *since* (and all our problems yet to come). God's command to forgive is the first and most vital step we can take toward releasing our "if only's" and learning how to look *forward* rather than *backward*.

There are no "if only's" in the kingdom of God. Paul writes, "And we know that in all things God works for the good of those who love Him, who have been called according to His purpose." (Rom. 8:28) There is no "if only" so terrible that God cannot work with it, and with you, for good and for His ultimate purpose. No matter what others may have done to you, God has already predestined you, called you, justified you, and glorified you. (Rom. 8:30) No "if only" can stand before this! As you come to see the hope and glory of His calling, you will discover that God has transformed your life into something that you could never have imagined even *with* a healthy and wonderful childhood.

**2) I Can't, Because...** "If only" thinking convinces us that because of our past, we are "stuck" with certain limitations. We believe that, because of who and what we are, there are things that we simply "can't" do. We say, "I can't seem to keep my house in order. I can't stop yelling at my children. I can't get my act together. I can't stop drinking. I can't say nice things to myself."

When we say "I can't," what we mean is, "I am not the kind of person who is able to." Our "I can't" statements are the product of our self-image—and equally inaccurate. We believe that because we haven't succeeded in doing something today (or better yet, yesterday), it means that we are obviously "incapable" of doing it. Adult Children use "I can't" statements as declarations of permanent disability.

"I can't" statements, like "if only's," focus upon the past, not the future. They tell us that because we *haven't* done something yet, it is "proof" that we *can't* do it. We may say, "Oh, I couldn't join the choir; I can't sing." What we mean is that we have never learned how to sing, so we assume that we are *unable* to sing. We base our perception of our abilities upon what we have already achieved—or, more often, upon what we have already *failed* to achieve.

We can begin to correct "I can't" thinking when we begin to realize that what we are today (or what we *think* we are today) *is not what we will be tomorrow*. We may not know precisely what we will change *into*, but we *will change*. It is inevitable. When we begin to realize that we are capable of learning new skills, discovering new information, developing new interests, and taking on new challenges, we also begin to realize that "I can't" has no real meaning. A more accurate statement is, "I am not able to do this *yet*, but that doesn't mean that I may *not* be able to do it in the *future*." As we build time and growth into our review of our self-talk, we begin to lose that perception of "permanent disability."

God operates in the future, not the past. Our "I can't" is His "I can," for His "power is made perfect in weakness" (2 Cor. 12:9), and all things are possible for God. (Matt. 19:26)

**3) If—Then.** Another reason for our "I can't" statements is our self-talk's "if-then" messages. This message tells us that "if" we do something, "then" we will experience a terrible consequence. "If" we express our thoughts, "then" we will be criticized or humiliated. "If" we reveal our feelings, "then" we will be rejected. "If" we fail, "then" we will be shamed and condemned. "If" we do not please others, "then" they will not love us.

Because of the experiences of our past, our "if-then" messages are often traumatic. One woman believed, "If I allow myself to get angry, then I will become just like my abusive grandmother." Another believed, "If I get sick, then I will inconvenience everyone and everyone will reject me." Another believed, "If I confront my husband for abusing my child, then he will leave me."

We may also apply "if-then" statements to our self-image. We believe that "if" we do certain things, "then" we will be a certain kind of person: "*If* I take time for myself, *then* I am a selfish person." We often reverse our "if-thens" to prove what we think we are *not*: "*If* I were a good Christian, *then* I would spend more time praying and reading the Word." One woman declared, "*If* I were a good parent, *then* I would have perfect children."

"If-then" messages call our attention to bad experiences in the past, and convince us that *if* we do certain things, *then* those experiences will be repeated. We believe that our feelings will be rejected *because* our feelings have been rejected before. We believe that we will be punished for failure *because* we have been punished for failure before. "If-then" messages convince us that the only way to *avoid* the repetition of these painful consequences is to *avoid* the "risky" behavior that led to those consequences in the past. They lead us to say "I can't" when what we really mean is "I am afraid to."

The first step in turning "if-then" statements around is to realize that they represent not the *only possible outcome* of an event, but *one of many* possible outcomes. It is possible for our future to be different from our past. A different future only *becomes* possible, however, when we are willing to change the *behaviors* that we learned from the past—when we are willing to "put on the new self." As long as "if-thens" inspire us with fear of punishment, we will resist new, seemingly risky behaviors in favor of old, trusted "survival techniques." We can only overcome fear—including "fear of the consequences"—by learning how to act upon love rather than upon our "if-then" fears.

**4) What If?** Another fearful message our self-talk whispers is "what if?" Every time we approach a decision or an action, it asks us, "What if I'm wrong? What if someone gets angry? What if I end up looking stupid? What if I make a mistake? What if no one listens? What if God doesn't approve? What if I fail?"

While "if-then's" focus upon one or two *specific* consequences of a given action, "what if's" can flood our minds with *dozens* of potential consequences. Worse, they often build upon one another, threatening us with a cascade of "damages."

When confronted with an overdue bill, for example, we might think, "What if I don't get the money in on time? What if they cancel my service? What if I have to pay a huge amount to get it back?

What if a collection agency starts hassling me? What if it ruins my credit rating forever?" "What if's" transform a simple problem into the roots of a major disaster.

"What if's" tell us that we live in world with *no second chances*. They convince us that it is better not to *try*, because if we fail, we will be worse off than if we had never tried at all.

We can begin to challenge our "what-if's" in three ways. The first is to recognize that "what if's" are *always negative*. Your self-talk never asks, "What if I do well? What if everything works out OK? What if this person appreciates my efforts? What if everyone agrees with my suggestion? What if I save the day? What if I succeed? What if God is pleased with me?" We can begin to turn our self-talk around when we choose to deliberately ask ourselves those questions and explore the *positive* possibilities they present.

The second step is to confront each "what if?" with a "so what? I'll try again." The *real* answer to "what if you fail?" is "I will keep trying until I succeed." Like Scarlett O'Hara, we can declare, "Tomorrow is another day." We have a God of second chances; that is, after all, what Jesus is all about. James reminds us that "We all stumble in many ways." (Jas. 3:2) But as often as we stumble, we have the provision of forgiveness to put that "stumble" in the past, where it belongs, and move forward. Even if we need forgiveness and a second chance "seventy-seven" times, or "seven times seventy" (Matt. 18:22), it is available to us.

The third step is to realize that there are no "what if's?" in the kingdom of heaven. God doesn't ask "what if?" because He *knows* what the outcome will be. If you are hearing "what if's?" in your prayer life, you are not hearing them from God—for He does not threaten us with vague, ill-defined consequences. God knows what will be and what will not be; He doesn't waste time with "what if's." Though we may not have His complete knowledge, as we learn to put our trust in Him, we will find that we no longer wish to waste time with "what if's" either.

**5) Always/Never.** Our self-talk often tries to rationalize its messages of fear by telling us that certain things "always" happen or "never" happen. We hear, "You *always* make mistakes. You *never* do things right. You are *always* selfish. You *never* do enough for others. People *always* get angry with you. People will *never* respect you."

This form of self-talk "eternalizes" our experiences, convincing us that our "destiny" is predetermined by our past. If we believe that we always make mistakes, we believe that we will *always* make mistakes. If we believe that no one ever wants to hear our feelings, we believe that no one will *ever* want to hear them.

Once again, these statements are consistently negative. Few Adult Children tell themselves that they "always" do well or "never" fail. We still believe that "only the bad things count." It is not true that we have "never" done anything right; it may be true, however, that we have *never paid attention* to the things that we do right. It is not true that we have "always" failed; it may be true, however, that we have *always ignored* our successes.

We can begin to challenge these "eternalizations" by asking, "Is it true that no one, ever, in the entire world, has ever said anything good about me?" or "Is it true that I have never, even once, in my entire life, done *anything* right?" If you have learned how to get out of bed in the morning, if you have completed even one grade in school, if you can read this book, if you can carry on a conversation, then you can do something right.

What we often mean when we say "never" do anything "right" is that we don't do things right *all the time*. "Perfectionist" thinking teaches us to believe that failing *once* is the same as being a total *failure*. To break free from the bondage of this form of thinking, we need to learn a vocabulary that expresses concepts of change, growth, and potential. We need to learn words like "sometimes" and "occasionally." It is *true* that we "sometimes" make mistakes or that we have "some" negative qualities. In reality, though, nothing is 100% except God. When we realize that no matter what we have done in the past, we *can* and *will* change, grow, learn new skills, change our behaviors, and do new things, we will begin to see that our occasional mistakes and failures do not define us or our opportunities in the future.

**6) Denial.** The form of self-talk that has the most profound influence upon our worldview is denial. Denial is the mechanism that interferes with our efforts to change *any* of the self-talk components described in this chapter. Denial "renames" or "reframes" our experiences and perceptions; it is our way of telling ourselves that things are other than what they are. The danger of denial is that as long as we don't *recognize* what a situation really is, we can't *change* it. Instead, denial keeps us fighting the wrong battles—and losing.

Denial is the opposite of open and honest communication—and dysfunctional behavior thrives in any environment in which communication is closed. Denial grows out of secrecy, dishonesty, and "we don't talk about things like that" messages. Some Adult Children experienced so much denial in their childhoods that they have come to doubt their ability to trust their own judgment or the evidence of their own senses. Too often, they have been told that they did not see and hear what they *thought* they saw and heard; that things "didn't happen," that they "imagined it" or were "making it up," or even that they are "crazy." We were rarely told, for example, that a parent had a drinking problem; instead, we might have been told that "Daddy is sick again, so you have to be very quiet." We may have witnessed fights between our parents, only to be told the next day that "nothing ever happened." We may have experienced physical or sexual abuse, only to be told (at the time or years later), "That could never have happened. That person would never do such a thing. How can you tell such lies?" Many Adult Children are living with people today who tell them the same things—like one woman who remarked, "Whenever I ask my husband to explain something he said, he claims he never said it—so I wonder if *I'm* the one who's crazy."

When we grow up in an environment that teaches us to believe that it is "wrong" to talk about or express certain things, we learn to rename those things, repress them, or pretend that they never happened or don't exist. We deny our emotions: "I'm not unhappy. Everything's fine." We rename them: "I'm not angry, I'm just a little upset." We refuse to acknowledge that people are acting inappropriately: "He didn't really mean to hit me. It was an accident. It was my fault, really; I shouldn't have said what I did." We deny what we are doing: "I'm not an alcoholic, but I *do* need something to help me cope with stress." We deny that we are sick, that we are hurt, that someone us hurting us, that we don't like what is happening to us, that we are in a bad situation, that we don't know what to do, and most of all, that we are afraid.

When we deny or rename what is happening to us, we rob ourselves of the chance to *change* what is happening. Instead, denial shifts our focus away from the real problem and onto false problems. When we say, "I'm not angry; that doesn't bother me," we end up trying to "fix" our feelings instead resolving the situation that *causes* those feelings. When we say, "He had a right to hit me because I didn't do what he wanted," we end up struggling to change our behavior rather than addressing the other person's problem with violence. When we declare, "Oh, I've already come to terms with my past; none of that bothers me," we give up our ability to truly resolve the *results* of that past.

Change is the result of acceptance, not of denial. We cannot meet our needs until we acknowledge that we *have* needs (and have a right to have needs). We cannot fulfill our desires until we admit that we *have* desires (and a right to those as well). We cannot get rid of our fears until we confess that we are afraid. We cannot resolve issues until we are willing to face those issues. We cannot change our behavior until we recognize that we *are* behaving in a particular way. We cannot deal with our feelings until we honestly explore what our feelings are. We cannot change a difficult situation of any kind until we are willing to define the situation as *it is,* not as we wish it were or as we think it should be or *would* be if we could only "get our act together."

To some, acceptance sounds like "negative confession," or worse, "blame." There is a difference, however, between telling the truth and "placing blame." Truth is neither negative nor positive; it is simply truth, even though we may *find* it painful or unpleasant. The pain and unpleasantness is our *reaction* to the truth; it is not a component of the truth itself. Problem-solving is the direct opposite of blame; when we accept the truth, it is not to point fingers or ask "who is at fault," but to seek solutions.

God tells us to "Buy the truth and do not sell it; get wisdom, discipline and understanding." (Prov. 23:23) He does not say that truth will always bring joy— "For with much wisdom comes much sorrow; the more knowledge, the more grief." (Ecc. 1:18) Nevertheless, "I saw that wisdom is better than folly, just as light is better than darkness." (Ecc. 2:13)

## Speaking of Self...

As important as how we see the world is how we see *ourselves* in relationship to that world. Our self-talk not only helps us *form* an inaccurate self-image; it also keeps that image "alive" in our minds through five specific forms of "internal communication:"

**1) A Good Person Would...** Most Adult Children carry a set of "role inventories" in their minds and hearts. These are lists of characteristics and behaviors that we believe "good" examples of particular roles possess and practice. We have an inventory of what makes a "good mother," a "good wife," a "good Christian," or even a "good person." Those inventories may be modeled upon unrealistic media images, impossible church demands, or our memories of our own parents (we often suppose that a "good" parent is everything our parents were *not*). Most often, however, they are based upon our perceptions of our own shortcomings: We assume that a "good" person *is* whatever *we* are not.

We use these inventories as a way to prove to ourselves that our performance never "measures up." When we get angry at our children, our self-talk tells us that a "*good* parent *never* loses patience." We may suppose that a "good" wife meets the needs of every family member, and keeps a spotless house, never gets tired or angry or frustrated, and most of all, never has (or expresses) a need or feeling of her own. We may suppose that a "good" Christian spends hours in daily Bible study, gets up at 5 a.m. for prayer, is always kind and patient, never has any negative feelings, and most of all, *never does anything wrong*.

"Perfectionist" thinking convinces that whenever we fail to meet *all* these characteristics, we have *failed* to be good parents, good spouses, or good Christians *at all*. Meeting one or even most of the criteria "doesn't count." It doesn't matter how many errands we run, cookies we bake, meals we prepare, or shoelaces we tie; if we lose our temper *once* , we have "failed the test."

This kind of self-talk keeps us struggling to add behaviors and thoughts and feelings to our "perfection inventory" in the hope that we can one day make ourselves complete. The more we add, however, the more difficult perfection becomes, because we are simply adding to our burdens. We struggle to find more rules, more guidelines, more ways to "do things right"—and the more we struggle, the more we become convinced that we are failures.

When our self-talk persuades us to judge ourselves against role criteria, we become so busy trying to determine (and become) who we think we *should* be that we have no opportunity to discover who we *are*. Instead of defining ourselves by the skills that we believe we lack, we need to find ways to explore the characteristics we *possess*, not as "roles" but as *people*. Then we can discover how those characteristics *contribute* to our efforts as parents, spouses, employees, or Christians. Instead of asking, "What are the requirements of this role and how far short do I fall?" we need to learn how to ask, "Who am I, and what do I *bring* to the various tasks and relationships of my life?"

**2) It's Not Enough.** Our efforts to explore who we really are, or to change our behavior, are often sabotaged by another self-talk message: "It's not enough." No matter how hard we try, our inner voice whispers that we aren't trying "hard enough." No matter how well we do, it tells us that our work isn't "good enough."

The trouble is, we have no idea what actually *is* "enough." We measure "enough" by the same standards use we use to measure perfection: If it could be done better, then it isn't "enough." No matter how much we do, our self-talk will always say, "You could have done *more*." This has a profound impact upon our Christian walk: no matter how much time we spend in prayer or Bible study, we are always convinced that we aren't doing "enough" for God.

One way to challenge this self-talk is to begin to ask, "Enough for *what*?" What is the *goal* of our behavior? If our goal in Bible study is to learn something new from the Word, then we accomplish that goal whenever we *do* learn something new—not when we have read the Bible "enough." Learning something new is an attainable goal—but no one can ever read the Bible "enough," or be able to say, "I have now read the Bible enough to fully understand it."

When you fix dinner, is your goal to prepare an enjoyable and nutritious meal for your family—or to rival a four-star restaurant? When you write an article, are you attempting to communicate facts and ideas—or win a Pulitzer? When you clean your house, are you striving for neatness and cleanliness—or a facility in which a surgeon could comfortably operate? When you raise your children, are you attempting to raise happy and healthy "good citizens"—or the next President or Pope? When you serve in the church, are you trying to help Jesus or replace Him?

When we have no measurable or attainable goals, we can never determine what is "enough." When we determine the *purpose* of our efforts, however, we can assess those efforts more accurately.

In addition, the only way to do anything *better* is to do it in the first place. When we worry that our work won't be "good enough," we often *don't do it at all.* We leave stories unwritten, paintings unpainted, songs unsung, dreams unattempted. We fear that we will end up with a "second-best" product, so we don't try—and we end up with *nothing.*

If we *do* try, our work may not measure up to our dreams or desires (at least not right away)—but we *will* have *something.* That "something" serves three important purposes: It gives us practice and experience; it shows us the areas in which we may need to improve; and finally, it gives us *something to show for our effort.* Instead of a closet full of dreams, we can begin to build a life full of accomplishments—one "not good enough yet" step at a time.

**3) Claiming the Blame.** Besides believing that we are responsible for our own imperfections, we often believe that we are responsible for the *imperfection around us.* Adult Children tend to believe that no matter what goes wrong, it's *our fault.*

If someone doesn't like us, we assume that it is because we aren't good enough. If someone gets angry, we assume that we did something to *make* them angry. If someone is unhappy, we assume that it is our responsible to *make* them happier. If someone doesn't like our performance, we feel obligated to improve. If a situation is difficult, we assume that *we* are to blame and that it is our responsibility to remedy the situation.

When we believe this, we believe that we are responsible not only for *ourselves*, but for everything and everyone around us. Psychologists call this a "boundary" issue: We don't know where we end and other people begin. Whenever others are unhappy or upset or angry, we look at *ourselves* as the *reason* for the problem *and* as responsible for fixing it.

This creates a double standard that places a tremendous, and hopeless, burden upon us. While we believe that we have an obligation to do better and be better, to be self-disciplined and controlled, we don't believe that *others* have that same obligation. We may believe that we have no right to get angry—but others have the right to explode in fury and hit us. We may believe that *we* are responsible for keeping a home or relationship running smoothly—but no one *shares* that responsibility. If problems arise, we believe it is up to *us* to fix them; we don't believe we have the right to ask another person to look at their share of the issue.

We try to change the world by changing ourselves. We hope that if we change ourselves *enough*, people will react to us differently, approve of us, respect us, accept us, and love us. We measure our "success" at self-improvement by whether our efforts "change the world"—and when the world stubbornly refuses to change, we believe that we have failed.

We can challenge these blaming messages when we realize that God never said, "Make *other people* perfect." He didn't even say, "Make *life* perfect *for* other people." Instead, we are told, "Each one should test his own actions. Then he can take pride in himself, without comparing himself to somebody else, for each one should carry his own load." (Gal. 6:4-5)

**4) Name-calling.** Our self-talk not only helps create an inaccurate self-image, it perpetuates that self-image by reminding us who and what we think we are. Adult Children have a host of bitter names for themselves: Stupid, idiot, nitwit, numskull, twit, failure, slut, tramp, weakling, sissy, crybaby, creep, klutz. Whenever we make a mistake (or think we do), our self-talk promptly calls us a name. We think these names are accurate and deserved, and they become an easy way to "punish" ourselves for perceived mistakes and failures. We even believe that these names "keep us in line" and "motivate" us to try harder.

When we call ourselves names like these, we simply reinforce our false definitions of self. We don't use names that we don't believe—and as long as we *do* use them, we have great trouble believing anything that contradicts them.

Most of us heard the old adage, "Sticks and stones may break my bones, but names will never hurt me." To put it simply, that's a lie. When you think back to the playgrounds and backyards of your childhood, what memories stand out? Do you still remember the pain of skinning your knee? Or do you remember the pain of being taunted and called "crybaby" or "sissy" for crying over the pain of your knee? If you are like most people, the pain of the knee has long since been forgotten—but those words still "sting." The wounds of sticks and stones heal quickly; the wounds of words can hurt for a long, long time.

The Bible takes name-calling seriously: It is comparable to murder. Jesus said, "You have heard that it was said to the people long ago, 'Do not murder, and anyone who murders will be subject to judgment.' But I tell you that anyone who is angry with his brother will be subject to judgment. Again, anyone who says to his brother, 'Raca,' is answerable to the Sanhedrin. But anyone who says, 'You fool!' will be in danger of the fire of hell." (Matt. 5:22) This is a reminder that "Death and life are in the power of the tongue..." (Prov. 18:21), while "A gentle tongue is a tree of life, but perverseness in it breaks the spirit." (Prov. 15:4)

We have not been given license to speak to *ourselves* in a way that God does not permit us to speak to His *other* children. We do not have the right to call ourselves by cruel and vicious names—whether we believe that they are deserved or not. When we call ourselves names, we violate the Word of God and even call it a lie.

**5) Verbal Abuse.** Our self-talk often goes beyond name-calling, and enters areas of verbal abuse that we would never consider inflicting upon another person. We curse ourselves with profanity and obscenity. We condemn ourselves. We shame and humiliate ourselves. We are sarcastic and rude to ourselves. We threaten ourselves. We tell ourselves that we will *always* be worthless failures and that we *deserve* punishment and abuse.

We often take this form of self-talk for granted because it is the same kind of talk we hear from *others*. If we grew up in an environment that used this kind of verbal abuse, we came to expect it and think nothing of it. It hurts—but we're used to it. If we live with people who express themselves in this way, we come to believe that this is "normal" and *how we should be spoken to*.

We cannot become "imitators of God" if our self-talk is the language of fear and anger and hostility. To walk in love, we must learn how to speak in love. We are told, "Do not let any unwholesome talk come out of your mouths, but only what is helpful for building others up according to their needs, that it may benefit those who listen. And do not grieve the Holy Spirit of God, with whom you were sealed for the day of redemption. Get rid of all bitterness, rage and anger, brawling and slander, along with every form of malice." (Eph. 4:29-31) When our self-talk is filled with bitterness, rage, anger, and malice, it not only does not benefit the listener (ourselves), it actually *grieves* the Holy Spirit.

When we take active steps to change our self-talk to conform to the standards of loving communication spelled out in 1 Cor. 13, we will begin to see changes in *every* area of our lives. Eventually, we will not only learn how stop verbally abusing ourselves; we will also learn to stop accepting verbal abuse from others.

## Relating to Others

Our self-talk also tells us how *other* people relate to us. We often assume that others see us the way we see ourselves, and we expect them to behave toward us as we behave toward ourselves. If we blame ourselves, we expect others to blame us. If we are impatient with ourselves, we expect others to be impatient with us. Our self-talk *predicts* the outcome of interactions in four ways:

**1) Mindreading.** Walk into a room full of completely silent people, and your self-talk will probably provide you with a running commentary upon what everyone is "thinking." Whenever we are around others, our inner voice tells us, "Everyone is looking at you. They think you're stupid. They thought that was a dumb comment. Everyone thinks you look ridiculous. No one wants to listen to you."

We often believe that we know what others think or feel, what their intentions or motives are, and why they behave in a certain way toward us. These assumptions are invariably negative: We don't suspect that people think well of us or enjoy our company. Instead, we think that others are disappointed in us and would probably prefer it if we weren't around.

Adult Children who practice "mindreading" tend to take *everything* deeply personally. When we "read minds," we don't come up with assumptions like, "That person is enjoying the morning paper." We think, instead, "That person is reading the paper because he doesn't want to talk to me." We interpret the actions and motivations of total strangers in relation to our perception of self. When someone is rude to us, we assume it is because the person doesn't *like* us; we rarely consider that the person might be having a bad day, or that the person might be a basically unfriendly person who is *usually* rude. When someone seems upset, we assume we have "made" that person angry. When someone fails to serve us or doesn't provide what we want, we assume he did it "deliberately." When we mindread, we are often convinced that the only thing *on* other people's minds is negative thoughts about *us*.

The truth is that the only minds we are reading are our own. *We* have such negative thoughts about ourselves that we can't *imagine* anyone else having any *other* thoughts. *We* are so preoccupied with worrying about how we look or how we come across that we believe that "everyone is watching us." In reality, most people are preoccupied with the same kind of thoughts *we* are having: They are more worried about how *they* appear than about how *we* appear.

We cannot read minds or hearts; God has reserved that right to himself. We are told, "For who among men knows the thoughts of a man except the man's spirit within him? In the same way no one knows the thoughts of God except the Spirit of God." (1 Cor. 2:11) When we stop attempting to read minds, we can stop terrifying ourselves with what we suppose we will find there, and allow God (and man) to surprise us with the truth.

**2) Clairvoyance.** Once we assume that we know what people are thinking, it is easy to asssume that we know what people *will* think. Our self-talk constantly floods us with "if-then" messages relating to the reactions of others: "If you say this, then everyone will think that. If you do this, then everyone will think that." We believe that if we express our feelings, people will think we are crazy; if we express our thoughts, people will think we are wrong; if we express our opinions, people will think we are stupid.

Adult Children often apply "clairvoyance" to recovery issues. We assume that if we "admit" that we need help, everyone will think that we are "weak" or "emotional," or that we "can't handle our problems by ourselves." We assume that if we talk about our issues, we will be rejected. We assume that if we reveal incidents in our past, no one will believe us.

Clairvoyant thinking "survives" because *sometimes we are right*. We often accurately predict how people we *know well* will react to us. The trouble is, we soon assume that *everyone* , including people we don't know, will react in the same way. We suppose that our negative characteristics are "obvious to everyone," and we expect the same *reactions* from everyone.

Mindreading and clairvoyance are another way of projecting past experiences onto future expectations. Our self-talk can only "guess" at the future by "remembering" what has happened before. Our self-talk tells us that we *will* experience what we have *already* experienced; it can't "imagine" a different future, and when we listen to it, neither can we.

To counteract mindreading and clairvoyance, we need to remember that "hope" is not based upon past experiences. If it were, we would have no hope. If Abraham based his "hope" upon his experience of being childless, he would have assumed that no matter what God said, he would *always* be childless. But "against all hope, Abraham in hope believed and so became the father of many nations, just as it had been said to him, 'So shall your offspring be.' Without weakening in his faith, he faced the fact that his body was as good as dead—since he was about a hundred years old—and that Sarah's womb was also dead. Yet he did not waver through unbelief regarding the promise of God, but was strengthened in his faith and gave glory to God, being fully persuaded that God had power to do what He had promised." (Rom. 4:18-21)

**3) Rehearsing the Future.** When we attempt to read or predict the thoughts of others, we often find ourselves "scripting" conversations and situations before they happen. Our self-talk tells us, "If you say this, then he will say that, and then you will say this, and then he will say that," and before we know it, we are "rehearsing" a conversation that hasn't happened yet.

Our self-talk predicts arguments, disagreements, problems, and "hopeless situations." As we rehearse those situations, our self-talk "directs" those scripts into ever more fearful outcomes.

Our problems begin in earnest when we discover that other people "haven't read the script" and don't respond the way we expect them to. We have already planned what we want to say—and when we don't get our "cues," we may not know *what* to say. One woman finally gave up her "scripts" because, she said, "When people didn't say what I expected them to say, I was completely lost. Once I lost my script, I had no idea what to do."

The scripts that we rehearse are invariably negative. We don't expect others to compliment us or praise us or give us what we ask for. Instead, our scripts are based on what we will do when others *refuse* to do what we want. When things don't go as planned, we *might* be delightfully surprised (people usually react more positively in real life than they do in our mental "rehearsals")—but more often, we resolve to "rehearse" more carefully next time.

God does not give us scripts. He gives us life. He tells us that we would do better to experience life *as* it happens rather than to "rehearse" it (and worry about it) *before* it happens. Jesus says, "Therefore do not worry about tomorrow, for tomorrow will worry about itself. Each day has enough trouble of its own." (Matt. 6:34)

**4) What You Said vs. What I Heard.** When conversations or events don't go the way we expect, our self-talk often compensates by attempting to convince us that we really heard what we *expected* or *wanted* to hear.

One woman was going through a difficult time, and became convinced that her emotional needs were putting a strain on her relationship with her boyfriend. She was convinced that he was "tired" of her complaining, her needs, and her "weakness." Finally, she gathered the courage to ask him whether this was true. Her own description of his answer was this: "He told me that he wished I wouldn't come over just when I was upset. He said that it seemed like we never had any fun together anymore, and that he only saw me when I was having problems."

Those were the words that she quoted. But it was not exactly what she *heard*.

What she *heard* was: "He doesn't want me to come over when I'm unhappy. He doesn't want to be with me when I am upset. He only wants to see me when I'm happy. That means I have to pretend that everything is OK all the time if I want to be around him."

All-or-nothing thinking, plus a little scripting and creative mindreading, had convinced this woman that her boyfriend had *actually* told her, "Don't come over unless you're happy." What he had *told* her was that he wished to see her during happy times *as well as* unhappy times. He had not said that he didn't want to help her through her rough journey—he had simply said that he wanted some "fun times" as well. But because she *expected* rejection, she "heard" rejection, even when she repeated his actual response "word for word."

Our minds skillfully translate what we *hear* into what we *already believe*. If someone says, "I'm not sure that hairstyle suits you," we hear, "You are ugly." If someone says, "I'm not sure what you said was correct," we hear, "You are never right." If someone says, "I don't have time to talk to you right now," we hear, "I never want to talk to you again."

The only way to counteract this form of self-talk is to listen *carefully* to what we actually hear, repeating it if we have to, and to *accept it at face value*. If we're not sure what we heard, we can ask the person to repeat it, or clarify it. If we *wonder* what a person meant, we can *ask*. Asking for clarification, contrary to what we suppose, does not offend others; indeed, it can be a compliment, because it shows that we were listening. Instead of becoming clairvoyant interpreters, we need to become "human tape recorders," recording the truth rather than assuming the worst.

## Therefore I Must...

Our worldview, perceptions of self, and expectations of others combine to present us with vital "directives" for our behavior. We must find a way to cope and survive in the midst of all these negative expectations, and our self-talk is right there to remind us of the three basic "rules of the game:"

**1) I Should.** Whenever we face the need to act, our self-talk tells us what to do by reminding us of what we think we "should" do. Many of us feel driven by hundreds and even thousands of "should" statements that flood our minds daily.

"I should" is the phrase we beat ourselves over the head with. "Shoulds" remind us of our perceived responsibilities and priorities, of the "rules" that we must obey if we are to survive, and of the demands and expectations of others. We live in reaction to reminders of what we "should do" and "should be." We may even have directives about what we "should think" and "should feel."

For example, we may think that a "good wife and mother" *should* maintain a perfect home, raise perfect children, put the needs and desires of her family above her own, and be sensitive and responsive to her spouse, while never feeling angry or tired or frustrated or impatient. We may believe that a "good" Christian *should* read the Bible for a certain period of time every day, witness at every opportunity, conform to church rules and standards, volunteer for activities, never get angry, and most of all, never do anything wrong. Since we believe that we "should be" good spouses and good Christians, we assume that if we don't "do what we should do," we will never "be what we should be."

We often do not trust our own thoughts, feelings, or desires to lead us in the right direction, so we frequently rely upon the rules and expectations of others to define our "shoulds." We like specific guidelines that tell us what qualifies as "good" behavior and what doesn't. If, however, we don't *enjoy* the demands and restrictions of those guidelines, this helps convince us that if we were left to our own judgment or desires, *we wouldn't do what we should do.*

At the same time, a single "should" statement automatically classifies every other alternative as a "should not." If we "should" clean the house, anything *other* than housecleaning is an automatic "should not." We "should not" relax over a cup of coffee, read a book, watch TV, or otherwise "waste time." Then, if we *do* what our self-talk tells us we "should not" do, we are likely to condemn ourselves on two counts: We have *failed* to do what we *should* do, and we have *done* what we *should not* do.

"Should" statements are driven by the fear of guilt and condemnation. We don't obey them because we *want* to—indeed, "shoulds" are often the exact opposite of what we really want. Instead, we obey them because we are afraid of *what will happen if we don't.* If the "shoulds" are imposed by others, or by an organization, we know that "failing to do what we should" will result in condemnation and even rejection. If the "shoulds" are imposed internally, by our set of inner rules and expectations, we condemn ourselves. "Shoulds" do not motivate us; instead, they compel us. They do not offer us choices; they give us bondage.

Amazingly, the word "should" does not exist in the original Greek or Hebrew of the Bible. It has been "translated in." God does not say "should." Instead, He offers us choices—and shows us the benefits and consequences of those choices. He *also* provides us with the *right* to choose. We need to learn how to exercise that right.

It isn't easy to leave the word "should" out of our vocabulary. We can begin to let it go, however, when we learn to examine where it comes from. Whom are we attempting to please? What are the consequences that we fear? Are we obeying "shoulds" out of love, or out of "fear of punishment?" Are "shoulds" bringing us closer to God, or locking us into obedience to those who would tell us what we "should" do to "please" God? Instead of dividing our choices into a handful of "shoulds" and dozens of "should not's," we need to learn how to evaluate *every* option available to us. Maybe that cup of coffee and the rest and peace and contemplation that come with it really *are* more important than a clean sink! Perhaps we need to learn how to choose not to be like Martha, "distracted by all the preparations that had to be made" and "are worried and upset about many things," and instead learn how to choose, like Mary, "what is better [and what] will not be taken away." (Luke 10:40-42)

Since the primary force behind "should" statements is the fear of condemnation, it is important to remember that "there is now no condemnation for those who are in Christ Jesus, because through Christ Jesus the law of the Spirit of life set me free from the law of sin and death." (Rom. 8:1-2) "Shoulds" belong to the law, the law of sin and death. Choices, freedom, joy, and free will belong to the Spirit of life, to Jesus, and to us through Him.

**2) Make No Mistakes.** If there is a single prime directive in our lives, it is "make no mistakes." Mistakes are too costly. We have already learned to believe that we "are what we do" and "only the bad things count"—so we believe that the only way we can "survive" is to do nothing that can be counted against us.

We believe that a single mistake will "blow our cover." We believe that a mistake will "reveal" what we have been struggling to "conceal": Our lack of ability and worthlessness. We fear that a single mistake will cost us whatever approval and acceptance we have, and that no matter how well we do *after* the mistake, it is too late to get that approval and acceptance back. Once we make a mistake, we think it's "all over." We assume that once people "know the truth," we will never be able to "fool" them into believing that we are good or capable again.

We have also learned to believe that mistakes are a "valid reason" for condemnation and punishment. Most of us aren't familiar or even comfortable with forgiveness. When we make a mistake, we may *want* to be punished just so that we know that we have "paid" for our crime and the slate is "clean" again. Forgiveness makes us feel uncomfortable: When we *expect* to be punished, we want to get it over with. We may even punish ourselves if no one else will do it for us. Or, we may assume that any bad thing that happens to us is God's way of "punishing" us.

Thus, when we make a mistake, we expect something bad to happen to us. We expect and even demand consequences. One woman believed that if she did something wrong, it not only meant that she deserved the "consequences" of her mistake, but that she also deserved everything bad that had happened to her *before* that particular mistake. She believed that if she made a mistake, it was proof that she was a "bad" person, and if she really *was* a bad person, then her parents were justified in abusing her as a child.

Many churches teach that our "Christian walk" should be "mistake-free." Some Christians believe that the *appearance* of perfection is tremendously important, arguing that we are "examples" to the "unsaved community." We are told that if unsaved people see Christians "making mistakes," they won't take us seriously or be inspired to follow Christ.

Unfortunately, the truth is that when "unsaved people" see Christians trying to act like plaster saints, living a joyless existence hedged by lists of do's and don'ts, and trying to act perfect and "above" the rest of humanity, they are far from inspired to join us. They *do* see that we have something they don't: Lots of rules and lots of pain. How much more inspiring it would be if others could see the truth in us: That *when* Christians make mistakes, which we do (for according to 1 John 1:8, "If we claim to be without sin, we deceive ourselves and the truth is not in us"), what we *have* is a gentle and loving God who forgives us and loves us even when we do wrong.

God doesn't pay attention to us only when we "mess up." He is not the God of the Giant Flyswatter. He is the God who forgives, not just once but as many times as we need it. If mistakes were the end of the world, it would have ended by now. Instead, we need to understand that every time we make a mistake, God has made a provision for a new beginning through forgiveness. He does not "keep a record of wrongs," but "rejoices with the truth." He is much more interested in what you do well—which is more often than you realize—than in what you *haven't* done or what you have done wrong. To walk in love is to learn that we *are* loved when we make mistakes, and we can love ourselves even when we are wrong.

**3) Be Perfect.** The ultimate goal of "making no mistakes" is perfection. We have been told since childhood that if we could only manage to be perfect, we could be loved, approved, accepted, and successful. Doesn't God tell us to be perfect? For years we have been struggling to achieve that goal, believing that everything will "work out" and "be better" once we reach it. If we could become perfect, we might even learn to like *ourselves*.

Other sections of this book have discussed how we measure—or mismeasure—"perfection." If we believe that something could be done better, if it "isn't good enough," then it isn't perfect, and therefore of no value whatsoever. We believe that unless *we* are perfect, *we* are no good whatsoever. Because perfectionism keeps us focused upon what we *haven't* done yet, or what we haven't done right, or what we *aren't*, it prevents us from seeing who we are, or who we are in Christ.

But is "perfection" our responsibility? Can we really "be perfect" on our own power? Could we achieve perfection if we just tried harder and did more? Most of us might say, "I'm *supposed* to—but I can't, so there must be something wrong with *me*." That is not how the Bible answers it, however.

If we could "make ourselves perfect," by hard work or good work or by never doing anything wrong, then the law would work. We *could* justify ourselves. We *could* sanctify ourselves. All we would need to do is *try harder*.

If any human being could become perfect through his own works, then theoretically we could *all* do it if we tried. We wouldn't have any excuses; if it is possible for me, it is possible for you. But if perfection *were* possible through our own efforts, *we wouldn't need Jesus*. We wouldn't have needed His sacrifice, His atonement, His redemption. If the *law* works, we wouldn't need *grace*.

But we have grace. The Bible is quite clear on that point: "For it is by grace you have been saved, through faith—and this not from yourselves, it is the gift of God—not by works, so that no one can boast." (Eph. 2:8-9) "And if by grace, then it is no longer by works; if it were, grace would no longer be grace." (Rom. 11:6) We may feel *uncomfortable* being saved and justified by grace, because we are not *accustomed* to receiving things that we *do not deserve*. We would rather earn acceptance than be *given* it—but the fact remains that we can't.

We cannot "make ourselves perfect" *after* we have been saved any more than *before*. When we try to become perfect through works or by not making mistakes, we are once again turning to the law for justification. Paul writes, "I would like to learn just one thing from you: Did you receive the Spirit by observing the law, or by believing what you heard? Are you so foolish? After beginning with the Spirit, are you now trying to attain your goal [be made perfect] by human effort? Have you suffered so much for nothing—if it really was for nothing? Does God give you His Spirit and work miracles among you because you observe the law, or because you believe what you heard?" (Gal. 3:2-5)

Jesus is the "perfecter of our faith" (Heb. 12:2) and will "perfect that which concerns me." (Psa. 138:8 Amp.) The law can't do it;

good works can't do it; sacrifices can't do it; perfect (mistake-free) behavior can't do it. "The law is only a shadow of the good things that are coming—not the realities themselves. For this reason it *can never*, by the same sacrifices repeated endlessly year after year, *make perfect* those who draw near to worship. If it could, would they not have stopped being offered? For the worshippers would have been cleansed once for all, and would no longer have felt guilty for their sins. But those sacrifices are an annual reminder of sins, because it is impossible for the blood of bulls and goats to take away sins. Therefore, when Christ came into the world, He said: 'Sacrifice and offering You did not desire, but a body You prepared for me; with burnt offerings and sin offerings You were not pleased. Then I said, "Here I am—it is written about Me in the scroll—I have come to do Your will, O God." '... And by that will, we have been made holy through the sacrifice of the body of Jesus Christ once for all... because by one sacrifice *He has made perfect forever* those who are being made holy." (Heb. 10:1-7, 10, 14, emphases mine.)

It is Jesus who makes us perfect, not our own efforts. Our attempts to become "perfect" often just get in the way. When we allow Jesus to work in us and through us, not through "shoulds" and commands and burdens and fear and condemnation but through *love*, we will become perfect, because "when perfection comes, the imperfect disappears." (1 Cor. 13:10)

## These Three Remain...

We may wonder what we would have left if we gave up the demands, expectations, and frightening predictions of our self-talk. We fear that we would have nothing left to guide us, to tell us what is right and wrong, to keep us on the "straight and narrow." Before we are willing to give up the messages of our self-talk, or even to begin challenging and questioning those messages, we want to be sure that we have something to *exchange* them for.

We do. We have three tools that can guide us in evaluating our self-talk and its messages, and that will guide *us* when we "stop listening to ourselves." Those tools are faith, hope, and love—and they are in direct opposition to the messages of our self-talk. They are the weapons of our warfare, and the lamp unto our feet.

***Faith*** tells us that we have something beyond our predictions, our fears, and our expectations to put our trust in. We have the Word of God—and even when we don't fully understand it, we can begin to rely upon it. The Word tells us that we are beloved, even when we don't feel loved. It tells us that we are justified even when we feel like worthless failures. It tells us that we have a God who is present in time of trouble, who listens to us with love and compassion, who comforts us instead of rebuking us. It tells us that we have a place in His heart, and a place in heaven, and eternal life, even when we can't imagine why anyone would give us such things.

Faith means believing that this Word is true even though all our experiences, all our predictions, and all our fears have taught us to believe something completely different. It means that even though we are inclined to believe our inner voice above all other voices, we can at least *begin to choose* to put God's Word first. God doesn't expect us to be *finished*; instead, He asks us to start. Faith is a good place to start!

***Hope*** tells us that *things will change*. Our self-talk lives in the past; it tells us that our future experiences will be just the same as those we have already had. Our self-talk can't see the future: It doesn't have God's eyes (or His heart). When we listen to it, we listen to a guide that is literally blind. It can only look backwards, and guess at the future from what has already been seen.

When we hope, we accept that something may come that we *haven't* seen yet. "But hope that is seen is no hope at all. Who hopes for what he already has? But if we hope for what we do not yet have, we wait for it patiently." (Rom. 8:24-25) God tells us that we *will* have something that we don't have *yet*. We *will* become different people; we *will* grow; we *will* change; we *will* experience new things; and we *will* learn how to walk in love. It won't happen overnight; it won't happen next week; it may not even happen next year. "We wait for it patiently." But as long as we are *willing* to hope, instead of accepting the "doom and gloom" predictions of our self-talk, we have something *good* to hold onto instead of just something *bad* to run away from.

Hope is the ultimate outcome of suffering—and many of us have suffered deeply and are *still* suffering. You are not suffering because you *lack* character or because you *deserve* to suffer. When we learn to realize that suffering comes even to the worthy, the beloved, and the righteous, we can begin to understand that Paul means when he says, "we also rejoice in our sufferings, because we know that suffering produces perseverance; perseverance, character; and character, hope. *And hope does not disappoint us*, because God has poured out His love into our hearts by the Holy Spirit, whom He has given us." (Rom. 5:3-5, emphasis mine.)

***Love*** gives us the tools to effectively fight and change our self-talk, and to begin telling ourselves the truth. Chapter Two listed sixteen specific "love tools," and every one of those is a weapon in the battle between our perception of a hopeless, worthless life and our opportunity for a joyous victory. When we begin to apply patience and kindness and gentleness and forgiveness and truth and trust to our self-talk, we will see real change. When we accept that God *really loves us*, not for what we can do for Him and not "in spite of" our failures, we experience a freedom to grow that we may never have anticipated. When we realize that God is aware of, and interested in, what we do *right* as opposed to what we do wrong , we experience the freedom to move forward without fear. When we realize that He *forgives* mistakes, we actually become free to *make* mistakes—not because mistakes are "good" but because we no longer to fear the consequences of taking a risk or making a choice.

Of all the "love" tools in our toolkit, however, "perseverance" is perhaps the most important. Love teaches us to persevere—and Paul tells us that perseverance is one of the preliminary steps to hope. Our self-talk is bound to tell us that trying to change, or trying to think new thoughts, "won't work." We may "try it" for a short period of time, but when we don't experience "instant results," or when we begin to feel uncomfortable, we will be tempted to quit. We will be tempted to *believe* that it "isn't going to work." We may suppose that it might "work for others but not for me." We will want to seek refuge in rules and guidelines, in scripts and excuses, in directives and denial. But with *perseverance* we can overcome that temptation. We can move forward even when our self-talk threatens and argues and *pleads* with us to go back. With perseverance, even when we *do* take a step backward (and we will), we can step forward again, and again, as many times as it takes. Perseverance brings the ultimate success, and the real issue is not "how long it takes" but where it takes us.

# - 6 -

# Reclaiming Your Emotions

*Be merciful to me, Lord, for I am faint; O Lord, heal me, for my bones are in agony. My soul is in anguish. How long, O Lord, how long? Turn, O Lord, and deliver me; save me because of Your unfailing love... I am worn out from groaning; all night long I flood my bed with weeping and drench my couch with tears. My eyes grow weak with sorrow; they fail because of all my foes. Away from me, all you who do evil, for the Lord has heard my weeping. The Lord has heard my cry for mercy; the Lord accepts my prayer. (Psa. 6:2-4, 6-9)*

HOW DO YOU FEEL?

For many Adult Children, this is a frightening question. Sometimes we simply don't know the answer. Sometimes the answer fills us with fear or guilt. Sometimes we are certain that if we admit the truth, we will be punished or rejected. Sometimes we don't know how to answer, because even though we may know how we *do* feel, we wonder how we are *supposed* to feel.

Most Adult Children believe that we do not have the *right* to feel—especially if our feelings "upset" other people, distress them, or make them angry. Most of us believe that we have no right to have or express so-called "negative" feelings (such as anger or pain), but many of us believe that we don't have a right to "positive" or "happy" feelings either.

Whether we grew up in families that enforced a complete "shut-down" on feelings, or families in which feelings "ran wild" (causing damage to anyone who happened to be in the way), most of us are tremendously confused about what we "should" feel or what it is "OK" to feel. We have mixed feelings *about* our feelings: We may fear them, worry about them, feel guilty about them, or feel anxiety about what they "mean." Most of us are either convinced that we have the "wrong" feelings, or that we shouldn't have feelings at all.

In our experience, feelings can be dangerous. If we express our *own* feelings, we fear that other people will not be *pleased* by our feelings, and will reject or even punish us for *having* them. At the same time, we are often afraid of the feelings of others, because we have known other people to "take out" their negative or painful feelings on *us*.

Many of us have been taught that "feelings"—especially feelings of pain or need—are a sign of "weakness." We believe that "strong" people are people who "get over" their emotions quickly, or better yet, never experience those emotions at all. We believe that "feelings" are a sign of lack of self-control, and that if we could "control" ourselves, we could control our feelings. Because a great many Adult Children consider "weakness" to be the ultimate sin (perhaps because being "weak" and "powerless" makes us feel extremely vulnerable), we want to be "strong"—and we become very angry at ourselves for having "weak" feelings.

We often believe that we are "bad" if we have "bad feelings." We may think that something is *wrong* with us, that we actually have some mental "problem" that causes us to have "inappropriate" feelings and prevents us from having the feelings that we think we "should" have. Many Christian Adult Children are convinced that Christians "shouldn't have" certain feelings (particularly negative ones), and that if we *do* have them, it means that there is "something wrong with our walk." Many Christians interpret feelings of pain or anger as a lack of faith.

Most Adult Children have simply never been given permission to "feel." We didn't receive permission from our parents and many of us have not received it from our friends or spouses. We often don't receive it from the "body of Christ," and it only takes a few "well-meaning" comments along the lines of "You need to give those feelings to God" or "That feeling comes from the devil!" to convince us that *God* doesn't grant us "permission to feel" either.

If we didn't receive permission to feel from our parents and we don't expect to receive it from God, it is virtually impossible for us to grant that permission to *ourselves*. Instead, we are likely to suppose that we are "bad" or "sinful" whenever we experience the "wrong" feelings.

Because of what we have been taught to believe about our emotions, most of us are literally at war with our feelings. We don't know what to do with them, so we fight them. We try to control them, suppress them, ignore them, or deny them. We become so concerned about the "wrongness" of our feelings that we become trapped in feelings *about* feelings: Worry, anxiety, fear, and guilt. These "secondary" feelings misdirect our efforts, driving us to change our emotions rather than what *causes* those emotions. Our feelings, and feelings about feelings, build on one another like the layers of an onion.

As with an onion, peeling back those layers to discover what lies at the heart of our feelings generally involves tears. That onion *can* be peeled, however. The process starts by identifying what the layers are, and exploring ways to remove them.

## Why We Fear Our Feelings

Our feelings *about* our feelings are based upon what we have been *taught* about those feelings. These "lessons" make up the first "layer of the onion." As children (and as adults), we received many direct and indirect messages about our feelings, and those messages are often repeated by our own self-talk. As we explore those messages, we begin to discover *why* we feel so much anxiety or guilt or doubt about our emotions. We may not be ready to *accept* our emotions, but once we know why they "bother" us so deeply, we can begin to change how we *feel* about our emotions.

Most Adult Children had one or more of the following experiences with feelings:

**1) We were punished for our feelings.** In some dysfunctional families, feeling are simply not permitted. In others, they are a "privilege" reserved for adults. Rarely are children in such families entitled to display, or even possess, feelings that have been labeled "bad" or "inappropriate" by the family.

At the very least, we learned that when we expressed the "wrong" feelings, our parents were "displeased." We learned that if we wanted people to be happy with us, it was important to display the "right" attitudes and emotions. In some families, the "right" attitude might be one of happiness; in other, more severely dysfunctional families, that attitude might be one of meekness or submission. What we all learned, however, was that *what we felt* had a profound impact upon how *other people reacted to us.*

Expressing "unacceptable" emotions might also result in a scolding or "chewing out." We might be lectured on the "importance" of having the "right" attitude. We might have been isolated, sent to our rooms until we could be more "sociable" or until we had "learned our lesson." We might have experienced the "silent treatment" or some other form of disfavor that required us to "earn our way back" into a parent's good graces again. Some of us experienced physical punishment or even violent abuse. The line, "Stop crying or I'll give you something to cry about," is a dysfunctional family classic.

What we learned was that expressing the "wrong" feelings was dangerous. It got us into trouble. It might "cost" us the withdrawal of love and approval. If we wanted to please others and avoid punishment, it was important to *express* the *right* feelings, even if we weren't actually *feeling* them. Otherwise, we "made" people angry. Our attempts to display the "right" feelings were as much an effort to appease the feelings of *others* as to control our *own.*

It is easy to carry this lesson into our relationship with God, and suppose that He, too, will "punish" us if we express (or even have) the "wrong" feelings for a Christian. We may fear that our feelings will "cost us a blessing," or actually offend God.

At the very least, we feel guilty for having feelings we don't think we are supposed to have, and fearful of the reactions of others. When we have learned to expect punishment for "wrong" feelings, our immediate reaction upon having such a feeling is to attempt to get rid of it or change it. We may even punish *ourselves* for our feelings, in an effort to "teach" ourselves to feel the "right" things.

**2) We were told not to have certain feelings.** Parents who are not comfortable with the feelings of their children often attempt to resolve that discomfort by simply "ordering" their children not to "have" feelings the parents don't like. Many of us grew up to believe that people actually have a right to ask us (or tell us) to "have" the feelings *they prefer*.

We may have learned that certain feelings were literally "forbidden." Perhaps the most common "forbidden feeling" is anger; while many dysfunctional parents express their own anger freely, they don't want anyone to get angry at *them*. Children are often considered "subordinates," with no "right" to get angry at their "elders" or "betters."

We may also learn that certain feelings are forbidden for certain people. We may have learned that boys were not supposed to feel sad, or cry, or have feelings of tenderness or compassion. We may have learned that girls were not supposed to feel angry, or express their desires, or to resent being treated like "second-class citizens." We may have even found that feelings that were "authorized" for some children in the family were not authorized for others.

Once we have been specifically told *not* to have a particular feeling, *having* that feeling becomes the equivalent of disobedience. Eventually, we don't even have to express or display that feeling to believe that we are "doing something wrong;" just *knowing* that we have it is enough.

When we suppose that we have been literally *commanded* not to feel certain things as Christians, we assume that when we *do* feel "the wrong things," we are being disobedient to God. We know that God "searches the heart," and that He *knows* when we are "feeling wrong" even if we are able to hide those feelings from everyone else. We usually try very hard to *express* the right feelings—to wear bright Sunday smiles and sing praises and make sure that our confession is always "positive"—but inside we believe that we are "liars." Our awareness of our "wrong" feelings fills us with guilt, shame, and fear of God's displeasure.

**3) We were told that our feelings were incorrect or inappropriate.** Many of us were told by our parents, "That's no way to feel!" or "I don't see what you're so upset about!" We were told, "You have no reason to get so angry," or "You're overreacting," or "Don't be so sensitive!" or "That's nothing to cry about."

When we feel pain or anger, and are then told that we have no *reason* to feel pain or anger, we begin to wonder what is wrong with us. Why do we hurt, if nothing has "hurt" us? We quickly learn to *believe* that we are "too sensitive" or that we "overreact," and we become convinced that we actually *feel the wrong things*. We tend to assume that no one *else* feels the way we feel, and that others would think we were "crazy" if we admitted our feelings.

We may also wonder what is wrong with us if we don't feel as *good* about something as others tell us we should feel. Families often attempt to "program" their children with "acceptable" emotions, giving us messages like "You should be *happy* to have the opportunity to help out," or "You should *appreciate* what you are learning from this punishment," or "You should *want* to give your favorite toys to poor children," or "You should *love* this present." A common statement in such households is "We're really having *fun*, aren't we?"—when, in fact, we are utterly bored or miserable.

When we don't have the good feelings that we are *told* we should have, we wonder what is missing. Are we basically "ungrateful" or "uncaring" people who are "incapable" of feeling the gratitude, appreciation, or delight that we are told to feel? Why can't we having "fun" when we are being *told* that we're having fun?

As adults, the fear that we "don't know what we are supposed to feel" often robs us of the ability to judge and make choices. We often look to others to tell us what we "should" like, or not like. One woman was very confused when she found herself disliking the sermons of a particularly strident pastor; everyone she spoke with gushed over how "wonderful" the services were, and she was convinced that there must be something wrong with *her* for not "enjoying" them. When we lose the ability to trust what our feelings are telling us, we may even lose the ability to become wise consumers of religion. Instead, we end up feeling like emotional misfits, so crippled in our ability to "feel right" that we must rely on the "help" of others to "keep us straight."

Such messages keep us in a constant state of anxiety about our feelings. We worry about what we *will* feel in upcoming situations, and fear that it won't be the "right thing." We worry about what we *are* feeling, but are reluctant to ask anyone else what *they* are feeling, in case their answer simply confirms that we *aren't* feeling the "right things." Most of all, we are perpetually anxious before

God, convinced that no matter what we *are* feeling, it probably isn't what He *wants* us to feel.

**4) When something good happened, something bad happened.** Some Adult Children were forbidden to express not only "negative" feelings, but positive ones as well. Happy feelings can be noisy feelings, and many of us were punished for shouting with glee, for singing aloud, or even for laughing or giggling. After repeated demands to "be serious" or "calm down," we learned that it was safer to keep *these* emotions in check as well.

In addition, unhappy parents often aren't pleased by happy children. In dysfunctional families, misery often loves company—and misery begets misery. We learned that it was not wise to appear too "happy" when other family members were obviously in a bad mood. We learned how to "walk on eggshells," remaining quiet and unobtrusive no matter *what* we were feeling, so that we didn't upset anyone else. Most Adult Children have learned how to "align" their feelings to match the feelings of those around them.

Many of us learned that when something "good" happened, we could expect something "bad" to follow it. Good times were often followed by punishments; gifts were often followed by penalties. One woman, for example, found that whenever she visited a friend, her mother managed to find some reason to "punish" her after she got home; she soon learned that "socializing" wasn't worth the pain. Many of us believe that "good times" aren't worth the "bad times" that we expect to follow.

Some dysfunctional parents are jealous of their children's ability to feel joy or delight. One woman realized that she had been "punishing" her own daughter whenever that child was happy. On one level, she said, she had wanted to teach her daughter to understand that "life wasn't all fun and games." On a deeper level, however, she felt "left out" of her child's happiness, and expressed her resentment through punishment.

Some Adult Children have learned that it is dangerous to want something too much, because then it will be denied or taken away. Others find that it is dangerous to express a need, because needs reveal vulnerabilities that can be exploited or punished. Others learn not to care too deeply about anything, or love anything "too much," because they expect to lose it. Many of us simply prefer to avoid *good things* altogether, because we hope that by doing so, we can also avoid the *bad things* that inevitably follow. Thanks to these experiences, even our positive feelings can raise tremendous feelings of anxiety and dread.

This, too, can spill over into our relationship with God. If we are feeling "good," we are almost certain we must be doing something "wrong." If we are happy or content, we think that we must not be "doing enough for God," because we believe that a commitment to God requires pain and sacrifice. We see God not as one who gives, but as one who takes away. We may be afraid to love or take joy in anything, because we fear that this will make God jealous, and that He will actually *remove* anything we love from our lives so that we have nothing *left* to love but Him.

**5) Our families expressed feelings in harmful ways.** When other family members expressed *their* negative feelings in destructive ways, we learned new reasons to believe that feelings were dangerous. We learned to believe that there was no difference between "feelings" and "behavior"—and that if someone *felt* bad, they would *do destructive things*.

Many of us lived with parents who became abusive and even violent in their anger. Not only did we learn to be very careful never to *cause* anger if we could help it, we also learned to do our best never to *feel* it. Many Adult Children believe that if they become angry today, they will hurt someone or do something terrible.

Parents who express their feelings in destructive ways are often the same parents who *forbid* their children to express feelings. These lessons reinforce one another: We are told that we must not express our feelings, while at the same time we observe the *consequences* of expressing feelings. No matter what the dangers of *repressed* emotions may be, we are certain that they can't be as serious as the consequences of *expressed* emotions.

If it is our experience that *people* express their emotions in dangerous and destructive ways, we may expect God's anger to be even *more* dangerous. We know that people can do a great deal of harm, but God literally holds the power of life and death over us—and we are terrified of risking His wrath. We cannot imagine a God who could be angry, yet still act in loving kindness; we have no experience with people who can "feel" one way yet "act" another.

Ultimately, we come to believe that there is no "healthy" way to handle emotions. We expect to experience condemnation and rejection for our feelings, not acceptance and resolution. We expect people to be "upset" by our feelings, and often believe that people have a "right" to expect us to feel *what they want us to feel*. We tend to see feelings as the cause of problems, rather than being a key to their solution.

## What We Do About Our Feelings

We learned to build defenses against those feelings that we considered dangerous or wrong. We learned to try to "fix" them, or at least compensate for them or conceal them. If the first step in "peeling the onion" is exploring and questioning what we have learned to *believe* about our feelings, the second step lies in discovering what our *defenses* against those feelings are.

Adult Children have six primary defenses against "inappropriate" emotions:

**1) We deny them.** Once we have learned to believe that we will be rejected or punished for expressing our feelings, we stop expressing them. Instead, we pretend that we feel what we believe people *want* us to feel. Most Adult Children are experts at smiling and declaring, "I'm fine. There's no problem. Nothing bothers me!" We may be seething with pain and anger inside, and we may feel angry with ourselves for being so "false," but we are sure that this is the only safe way to live. If no one sees that our feelings are "unacceptable," no one will get upset. Often, we even deny our feelings to ourselves.

**2) We rename them.** Another way to deny feelings is to call them something else. One woman, for example, claimed that she never got "angry"—however, she was willing to admit that she sometimes became "upset." We may not be willing to admit that we are deeply hurt, but we might be willing to say that we are mildly disappointed. When things aren't going our way, we don't feel that we have the right to *ask* for what we want, so we may declare, "I'm not complaining, but…" As long as we don't call our emotions by the names we have learned to fear, we can sometimes convince ourselves that we don't *have* the emotions we "shouldn't have."

**3) We "get over" them.** Most of us believe that strong people "get over" their emotions "quickly." Even though we may experience pain or anger or loss, we think that it is important to "get over" those feelings as soon as possible, to "put it behind us and move on."

We focus upon resolving the *feeling* rather than upon resolving the situation that *causes* the feeling. One woman wondered why she hadn't "gotten over" her grief over her husband's decision to divorce her—before the papers had even been processed! We want to be able to say, "I'm not angry about that any more!" We often believe that we can "get over" feelings by declaring that we have "forgiven" someone—and then wonder why the feelings return. When feelings that we have tried to put behind us resurface, we feel guilty and wonder what is wrong with us.

**4) We blame others for them.** One way to make an "unacceptable" emotion more "acceptable" is to blame it on someone else. Thus, instead of saying, "I am angry," we may say, "You *make* me so angry." Instead of saying, "I am disappointed," we may say, "You are so *disappointing*." If we can convince ourselves that another person has "forced" us into an emotion, we feel less guilty for having it; instead, we believe that we "couldn't help it." We often apply this approach to children—and we may believe that it is a valid approach because it has been used against *us*. Many of us had parents who, instead of accepting responsibility for their emotions, chose to say, "You make me angry because you are so bad."

**5) We medicate them.** Many of us don't realize that we are "medicating" our pain because we associate that term with drugs and alcohol. "Medication," however, is whatever numbs our pain, distracts us from it, gives us no time to think about it, or makes us feel "better"—however temporarily. Many Adult Children "medicate" painful feelings by becoming workaholics, so that they have no time to "feel." Others sidestep their own problems by becoming completely involved in the problems of other people. Some turn to relationships or sex. Some take refuge in television or books. Christian Adult Children may attempt to "lose themselves" in God's work, spending hours in prayer or Bible study or "good works" to distract them from "self." The best way to identify a "medication" is to explore how we feel about "giving up" a particular behavior. If we are filled with panic at the thought, it is a good sign that we are using that behavior as a "medicator."

**6) We don't have them.** When our feelings are too painful, or when we are too frightened of the consequences of our feelings, we may choose to *stop* feeling altogether. We lock away our emotions, and hope that they never surface. Many Adult Children are capable of recounting incidents of horrific abuse—with no emotion whatsoever. This is not a sign that we have "gotten over" the feelings; it simply means that we *haven't felt them yet*. The trouble is, when we lock away the ability to feel *bad* feelings, we also lose the ability to feel *good* feelings. Our lives become neutral, with neither ups nor downs. Having "no emotions" is not a sign of being a "strong, in-control person." Instead, it is generally an indication that we have some powerful, painful emotions "locked up" inside. Unlocking those feelings may require some skilled assistance.

## A Biblical Perspective on Feelings

We don't automatically give up our emotional defenses by becoming Christians. Instead, we are likely to believe that God has no more interest in, or approval of, our negative feelings than anyone else. Adult Children are likely to add yet another "layer" to the feelings "onion" by rationalizing their defenses with spiritual arguments. Unfortunately, a great many Christians are prompt to provide us with justifications for these arguments, and to convince us that it is wiser, safer, and more spiritual to "hide" our feelings.

Is it true that some feelings are "bad" or "unacceptable?" Is it true that Christians "shouldn't have" certain feelings? Is it true that "living by faith" means to completely ignore our feelings? Is it true that some feelings are a sin? Is it true that if we "confess" painful feelings to God, this "negative confession" will block His ability to help or bless us?

The answer to all these questions is *no*.

A great many people, including a great many Christians, are every bit as uncomfortable with feelings (their own and anyone else's) as you are. Unfortunately, some of these Christians have passed along this discomfort in the form of teachings that *appear* to be scriptural. Before we accept the ideal of an "emotion-free Christian," however, it would be wise to explore what God really *does* have to say about the subject of feelings.

Whenever an Adult Child tells me, "I'm a Christian, so I know I shouldn't feel this way," I start them out in the book of Psalms. David could be speaking for us all when he writes:

"I cry aloud to the Lord; I lift up my voice to the Lord for mercy. I pour out my complaint before Him; before Him I tell my trouble. When my spirit grows faint within me, it is You who know my way.

In the path where I walk men have hidden a snare for me. Look to my right and see; no one is concerned for me. I have no refuge; no one cares for my life. I cry to you, O Lord; I say, 'You are my refuge, my portion in the land of the living.' Listen to my cry, for I am in desperate need; rescue me from those who pursue me, for they are too strong for me. Set me free from my prison, that I may praise Your name. Then the righteous will gather about me because of Your goodness to me." (Psa. 142:1-7)

Have you ever felt as though no one cared for your life, that you had nowhere to turn, that you were abandoned and without hope? Have you ever felt in desperate need, or that your spirit was "growing faint" within you? Most of us have—but many of us think that we have no "right" to "pour out our complaint" to the Lord. Yet David writes this psalm *knowing* that he has the right to express his feelings; this is part of our right to come before God "with freedom and confidence." (Eph. 3:12)

David tells us, "In my distress I called to the Lord; I cried to my God for help. From His temple He heard my voice; my cry came before Him, into His ears." (Psa. 18:6) Far from worrying about how God will react to an outpouring of "negative" emotions or a cry for help, David is confident that God will not only *hear*, but *respond*.

We often lack that confidence because we expect God to react to our emotions the way our parents did: With anger and even with "hurt feelings" of His own. Many dysfunctional parents interpret "negative emotions" as a form of criticism, a direct reflection upon *them*. It is easy to transfer this experience to God. After all, we *know* that God never makes mistakes, so how could we have the right to "complain?"

Many Christians interpret negative emotions as precisely that: A complaint, an implied criticism of God. Some believe that if we feel hurt, angry, or afraid, it is a sign that we lack faith, that we don't trust God or His plan for our lives. We are told that we "mustn't be moved by circumstances," but that we must "keep our eyes on God."

David's eyes were fixed firmly on God as he poured out his feelings about his circumstances. Through his psalms, he publicly declares to God, "My thoughts trouble me and I am distraught at the voice of the enemy, at the stares of the wicked; for they bring down suffering upon me and revile me in their anger. My heart is in anguish within me; the terrors of death assail me. Fear and trembling have beset me; horror has overwhelmed me. I said, 'Oh, that I had the wings of a dove! I would fly away and be at rest—I would flee far away and stay in the desert... I would hurry to my place of shelter, far from the tempest and storm.' " (Psa. 55:2-8)

I have yet to hear anyone accuse David of "lack of faith." The psalms of David are an affirmation that even though we *know* that God will ultimately work through our circumstances for our good, those circumstances may still hurt—and we are not "wrong" for acknowledging that pain. David knew that he would one day become king of Israel—but that did not remove the pain of Saul's decision to hunt him down and murder him! He knew that God would always be with him—but he was still hurt by the treachery of his friends and family members. David lived *on* hope and faith, even while he was living *in* extreme pain.

Hope and faith do not *replace* pain in our lives. It is not a question of having one or the other. Indeed, as David shows us, it is *when* we are in the most pain that we *need* hope and faith. We don't focus on "hope" when life is going well; we tend not to depend upon the assurance of "faith" when we already *have* the victory; we don't need the "comfort" God promises us when we don't hurt. Hope, faith, and comfort are what we have to hold onto *while* we are going through tough times *and* tough feelings.

Paul experienced persecution, rejection, hardship, and pain throughout most of his ministry. Far from supposing that he was "out of the will of God" for experiencing such things, and far from denying that they occurred, he tells us, "Praise be to the God and Father of our Lord Jesus Christ, the Father of compassion and the God of all comfort, who comforts us in all our troubles, so that we can comfort those in any trouble with the comfort we ourselves have received from God. For just as the sufferings of Christ flow over into our lives, so also through Christ our comfort overflows. If we are distressed, it is for your comfort and salvation; if we are comforted, it is for your comfort, which produces in you patient endurance of the same sufferings we suffer. And our hope for you is firm, because we know that just as you share in our sufferings, so also you share in our comfort." (2 Cor. 1:3-7)

Like Paul, we share in Christ's sufferings, and we share in His comfort. We are not condemned for feeling pain; instead, we are promised "hope and comfort" *during* our suffering.

Both David's emotional verses and Paul's calm assurances tell us that God doesn't "mind" when we come to Him with our feelings. If we did anything else, we would be lying to God. God does not honor lies, no matter how well-intentioned. He doesn't need to be "protected" from our feelings, or placated or appeased by "happy faces." God honors the truth, even when that truth seems painful to us or "offensive" to others. When we tell God, in effect, "If I could, I'd take wing and fly out of here, and find someplace safe to hide from my troubles," He understands. He tells us that when our circumstances are rough, we have the right to come to Him and be comforted. He will not condemn us for our feelings any more than He condemned David.

God does not *condemn* our feelings because He *gave* us those feelings. We are created in the image of a feeling God. He feels love and compassion—but He also feels "negative" feelings as well. "For we do not have a high priest who is unable to sympathize with our weaknesses, but we have one who has been tempted in every way, just as we are—yet was without sin. Let us then approach the throne of grace with confidence, so that we may receive mercy and find grace to help us in our time of need." (Heb. 4:15-16)

Jesus had feelings, including painful feelings. He felt anger and grief (Mark 3:5). He wept over Jerusalem (Luke 19:41). He wept for Lazarus, and when "was deeply moved in spirit and troubled" by the grief of Lazarus's sister, Mary (John 11:33, 35). We do not have to "get rid of our feelings" to be "more like" Jesus; instead, we need to learn how to *understand* them.

The first thing we need to understand is that there is a difference between "feelings" and "behavior." Many of us have been the victims of sinful behavior that has *resulted* from strong feelings. When our parents lashed out in anger, either verbally or physically, we learned to associate *actions* with *feelings*. But Paul tells us, "In your anger do not sin." (Eph. 4:26) He makes a clear distinction between the *feeling* and the *behavior*. We know that Jesus felt anger—but we also know that He was *without sin*. The Bible makes it clear that, though what we *do* with our feelings may result in sin, the feelings themselves are *not* sinful. It *is* possible to have strong, painful feelings—like David's—and yet "sin not."

Feelings are simply signals, nothing more. They do not exist by themselves; instead, they alert us to what is going on in our lives. Just as a sneeze may be a "signal" of a cold, or at least an indication that we need to get warm, feelings are a "signal" that something in our lives may require attention and resolution. When we have pain, it is because something is *causing* that pain, and we need to focus upon resolving the *cause* rather than "fixing" the pain itself. When we have anger, it is because something is *causing* that anger, and again, we need to focus upon resolving the cause rather than upon trying to "get rid of" the anger itself. If we do not focus upon causes, nothing changes, and the problems in our lives will continue to generate feelings the way an unhealed sickness continues to generate sneezes.

We have the right to feel. We have *permission* to feel—from God Himself. When we allow ourselves to feel, we allow ourselves to partake of God's grace and healing, and we come to realize that He loves us *even when we feel miserable*. The Bible tells us that "There is a time for everything, and a season for every activity under heaven: a time to be born and a time to die, a time to plant and a time to uproot, a time to kill and a time to heal, a time to tear down and a time to build, a time to weep and a time to laugh, a time to mourn and a time to dance, a time to scatter stones and a time to gather them, a time to embrace and a time to refrain, a time to search and a time to give up, a time to keep and a time to throw away, a time to tear and a time to mend, a time to be silent and a time to speak, a time to love and a time to hate, a time for war and a time for peace... He has made everything beautiful in its time." (Ecc. 3:1-8, 11)

## From Feeling to Healing

Even when we accept that God gives us permission to feel, it is not always easy to grant ourselves that same permission. Before we are willing to "feel," we still want some assurance that our feelings will not have terrible consequences. We want to be sure that our feelings are "correct," that they won't upset others, that they won't be ignored or dismissed, and that there may actually be some *benefit* to admitting and expressing feelings. Perhaps most of all, we want to be sure that our feelings won't cause us to lose control and do something terrible.

Some Adult Children *have* done harmful things to themselves or to others because of their feelings. Some of us have hurt others in our anger—perhaps our spouses, perhaps even our children. Some of us have attempted to hurt ourselves, or even to kill ourselves. Some of us have smashed things, or harmed ourselves. Those of us who *have* "lost control" are terrified of losing it again. Those of us who *haven't* are *still* terrified—because even though we may never have done something "bad" in the past, we still don't trust ourselves not to do anything destructive in the future.

There is a difference, however, between controlling our *feelings* and controlling our *behavior*. We can feel—we can have feelings so powerful that we feel torn apart by them—but we *do not have to act on those feelings*. Feelings are often not a matter of choice, but behavior *is always a matter of choice*. This is important to remember, not only in our own lives, but as we learn to understand the behavior of others. No matter what other people *feel*, even if we have genuinely *provoked* negative feelings in others, *their behavior is their choice*. Our behavior is our choice. We'll examine some *behavior* options later; first, we must examine our feelings.

One way to begin building confidence about having and expressing feelings is to have a *plan*. If we have a plan, we don't have to worry so much about what we are going to do next. We may not know precisely how to *accomplish* our goal, but at least we *have* one. The following seven-step plan can be very helpful as we seek ways to give ourselves permission to feel:

- Identify the feelings;
- Accept the feelings;
- Recognize—and avoid—our defensive reactions;
- Identify the *source* of the feelings;
- Choose a way to express the feelings in a nonharmful way;
- Seek a resolution for the *cause* of the feelings;
- Follow through on that resolution.

**1) Identifying the feelings.** Many of us have been so thoroughly trained to ignore or deny our feelings that we are no longer sure exactly *what* we feel. All we are really sure of is that our feelings, whatever they may be, are "wrong." We may have "catch-all" terms for our feelings, like "upset" or "concerned." Before we can begin to work constructively with our feelings, we must discover what they are.

One way to identify a feeling is to identify what that feeling makes us want to *do*. Feelings often appear in the form of a desire to take a particular action. This is not the feeling itself, but the reaction *triggered* by the feeling—and it is this reaction that makes us believe that the feeling *itself* is "wrong." Identifying our reactions, however, can help us identify the feelings behind them.

For example, is your "automatic reaction" a strong desire to strike out, strike back, to make someone feel the pain that you feel? Do you want to lash out with strong words or violence? Do you have the urge to smash something, or pound something with your fists?

If your reaction is to "strike out," then your *feeling* is probably ***anger***. Anger creates in us the desire to fight back, either to *stop* someone from harming us or to *punish* them for it.

This is precisely why so many Adult Children fear their anger. Because it fills us with the desire to do harm, we suppose that it is an indication of how truly *bad* we are inside. We feel guilty for even *desiring* to harm another person, even if we have never done it. We feel as though it is unforgivable to be the "kind" of person to have such thoughts.

Any feeling that makes us *want* to do something destructive seems sinful all by itself. Anger seems to be the opposite of "love," and we can't imagine how a Christian could be "entitled" to such a feeling. When we are angry, we don't feel loving—and when others are angry at us, they often do not *act* loving. Instead, we may have experienced the withdrawal of love and approval through anger, or have suffered the loss of relationships through conflict.

The Bible does not say, however, that anger and love are mutually exclusive. It says that "love is not easily angered" (1 Cor. 13:5), not that it is *never* angered. Paul writes, "In your anger do not sin" (Eph. 4:26)—so it is clearly possible to *feel* anger and yet *not* sin. Jesus felt anger, and spoke angry words to the Pharisees, yet was "without sin." Anger is allowed—and great breakthroughs in recovery come when *we* allow *ourselves* to feel anger.

Another common reaction to painful situations is the desire to *run away*. We may find ourselves filled with the desire to escape, to hide, to do whatever we can to *avoid* something—including something that may not have happened yet. We may have physical reactions such as nausea, muscle tension, and increased pulse rate. Such reactions generally indicate ***fear***. When we are afraid, we often feel helpless, lost, powerless, and vulnerable.

We often believe that *fear* is a "bad" feeling because the Bible tells us, in several places, to "fear not." We know that whimpering under the bed doesn't *solve* anything, so we regard fear as a useless emotion that leads to useless behavior. We may despise ourselves because our fear has led us to "yield" to the demands or abuse of others. Fear makes us feel weak, causes us to think of ourselves as "cowards," and seems to lead our own bodies to betray us.

Fear has its uses, however. It is not that we are never to *experience* fear, but that we are to choose not to *live* in fear. When we *are* living in fear—as many Adult Children are—it is a good sign that we are living in a situation that needs to be changed. Fear is like a signpost, telling us that something needs to be addressed and changed. When we discover fear in our lives, we discover something that needs to be *faced* rather than avoided. Even as it urges us to "run away," fear provides us with opportunities for victory.

A feeling that often *triggers* feelings of anger or fear is ***pain***. Pain is our reaction to being hurt. Whenever we are betrayed, let down, disappointed, lied to, cheated, denied, or "taken from," we feel pain. We may want to "curl up," cry, or scream out against our attacker. Most of all, we want the pain to stop. Many of us have learned to make pain stop, at least temporarily, by "giving in" to others so they will stop hurting us. Unfortunately, all this accomplishes is to convince others that they can force us to do their will by hurting us. Many of us have also learned to *conceal* pain, so that no one can discover our vulnerabilities or exploit them.

Many Adult Children associate "pain" with "weakness." We believe that if we were "stronger," we wouldn't "feel this way." We think we should have learned how to "take it" by now. We think we need to toughen up, be less sensitive, take things less seriously or personally. We may believe that we shouldn't "care" about things so that we won't "mind" if things are taken away from us.

There is nothing wrong with pain; it is simply a signal that something is wrong. Before we can get rid of pain, however, we have to decide that we aren't going to tolerate it anymore—and before we can decide not to tolerate it, we have to admit that we *have* it. Thus, it is often very important to *feel* the hurt so that we become motivated to *do* something about it.

Another common feeling among Adult Children is a sense of

***loss***. Loss tells us that something is gone from our lives and that we can never get it back.

Recovery, although it is an opportunity for tremendous gain, also involves loss. As we move forward into a new and healthier way of life, we leave behind our old life—and even though this is our choice, it involves a sense of loss. We are losing something that has been a familiar part of us for many years. We are losing ideas, perceptions, and beliefs that are like old friends, even if they aren't very "good" friends. When we begin to correct an inaccurate self-image, we "lose" our identity, even if it was an identity that we hated—and we often feel as though we have literally lost *ourselves*. We lose old, familiar, "safe-feeling" coping strategies, and feel lost when we have to confront the world "barehanded."

Perhaps one of the most painful losses in recovery is the sense of "losing our childhood." Though in reality, we lost that childhood many years ago, we may never have been aware of that loss, or felt it, until we enter recovery. For the first time, we stop "denying" the pain by declaring that "everyone has a rough time as a kid." Or, perhaps for the first time, the illusions of the "perfect" or "fairy tale" childhood are torn away, and we see our past and our parents as they really were. Many of us realize that we never had the chance to *be* children, and grieve for the joys and opportunities of childhood that we never had, though we desperately wanted them. Though some declare that it is "never too late to have a happy childhood," we know that we will never have another chance to go to the prom, or feel that thrill of innocent expectation during the holidays, or recover our innocence, or dream childish dreams uncontaminated by the awareness of adult realities.

When we recognize our losses, we often suppose that we should "accept" them and move on with no feelings of pain or grief. We argue that the past is "over" and there is no point in shedding tears over it. However, grieving for losses is a normal and important part of moving forward. The Bible does not tell us not to mourn; Jesus says, "Blessed are those who mourn, for they will be comforted." (Matt. 5:4) Through the process of mourning, we acknowledge our losses and release them. We may have to acknowledge our anger at those who *caused* our losses—which is the first step toward forgiveness. We may have to acknowledge our *fear* of loss. Most of all, we acknowledge how deeply those losses hurt.

Another feeling we need to learn how to recognize is ***stress***. Many of us live extremely stressful lives, yet we believe that we "shouldn't" be "bothered" by our situation. We suppose that we "should" be able to work a full-time job, maintain a perfect home, deal with the demands and behaviors of a dysfunctional spouse, be a perfect parent who never loses patience, and always feel perfectly calm and happy the whole time. It doesn't work—and we wonder why we feel so on edge, so ready to snap. We believe it is *our* fault, that we aren't trying hard enough, or that we aren't praying enough, or that we need to "change our attitude." The stress of "recovery" is often the last straw that causes us to snap.

Stressful situations create stress. Even *one* of the situations described above is stressful; every parent, for example, lives with stress. When we combine those situations, they overtax every reserve of energy and strength that we have—and we expect ourselves to "keep going" long after those reserves are drained dry. Stress also tends to intensify, or make us more prone to, other feelings such as anger or pain.

Stress doesn't mean that we *can't* handle our responsibilities. It simply means that those responsibilities are *difficult*. We need to accept the difficulty instead of blaming ourselves for it. Once we realize that a situation is stressful, we can stop blaming *ourselves* for being stressed. Then, we can take steps to manage or reduce stress, including steps to change the situation. Managing *stress* can help us find better ways to manage *all* our emotions.

Adult Children often feel ***hopeless***. We believe that there is nowhere left to go, nothing left to do, no way to improve our situation *or* ourselves. We feel "stuck" and "trapped." We come to believe that there is no way out of our trouble. We may not believe that even God can help us anymore. We believe that we aren't changing because we are *incapable* of changing. We see no point to our efforts, in recovery or any other area, and long to give up.

Hopelessness quite often leads to ***depression***. In depression, we often blame *ourselves* for our situation or feelings. We may decide that we really *are* as bad and worthless as we always believed ourselves to be. We may harm ourselves by passing up opportunities, because we think, "What's the point?" We may sabotage our relationships, so that we lose friends and loved ones, and then regard the loss as "proof" that no one could love us in the first place. We may provoke other people into hurting or "punishing" us. We may "purge" our lives of everything we hold dear, such as possessions or friends, because we have convinced ourselves that we don't "deserve" anything good. We may hurt ourselves in mild ways, such as by destroying a beloved possession, or cutting off our hair, or withdrawing from the world. We may cause ourselves physical injury. If depression goes unchecked, we may choose the ultimate method of self-destruction: Suicide.

Depression is a terrible feeling, and anyone who has had it dreads the thought of having it again. However, like fear, depression is a powerful signal: When we have it, we know that we need help. Something in our lives is wrong, and it needs to be resolved. Like fear, depression gives us "reverse signposts," telling us that we need to move *forward* in the exact opposite direction that our *feelings* are telling us to go. When we want to withdraw from the world, this is the time to enter it. When we want to hurt ourselves, this is the time to give ourselves treats and rewards—no matter how "undeserved" we think they are. When we want to sabotage relationships, this is the time to be honest and ask our friends for help and understanding. Most of all, it is a time to seek God, and ask His help and love in a time when we often feel the most distant from Him. Depression is not a "fate," but a message that something is wrong.

Of course, not all our emotions are so negative. We also have feelings of joy and happiness and pleasure. Unfortunately, many of us are nearly as uncomfortable with these feelings as with our negative ones. We often think that we *shouldn't* like or enjoy the things we *do* like, and that we *should* enjoy things that we *don't* like. We may not *want* to become attached to anyone or anything; we fear that if we feel love or enjoyment, we risk the pain of *losing* what we love or enjoy. We often avoid desires and pleasures because we think we shouldn't have them in the first place.

We are often concerned, as well, when we do *not* have the positive feelings that we think we *should* have. When someone declares, "Wasn't that a wonderful dinner?" or "Didn't you just love that show?" or "Wasn't that the most inspiring sermon you ever heard?" and we don't agree, we often wonder what is wrong with *us*. Why can't we "like" what other people say we *should* like? We wonder if our tastes are warped, or if we aren't capable of appreciating good things, or if our "sinful nature" causes us to "prefer bad things." Consequently, most of us spend our lives *trying* to enjoy (or at least trying to *look* like we enjoy) things that we are told that we *should* enjoy—and wondering why we are confused and miserable.

It is not a sin to have your own tastes and preferences. The fact that you do not enjoy something that another person enjoys does not mean that your tastes are "bad," or even that the thing itself is "bad"—it simply means that it doesn't suit you. I didn't enjoy a hit musical that has been running for years; that doesn't mean that the show *or* my tastes are "bad." They simply don't "mesh."

On the other hand, our dislike of a situation *may* be an indication that the situation really *is* harmful. If you are put off by a strident sermon that seems more condemning than loving, but you suppose that you "should enjoy" being condemned and yelled at, it is time to pay more attention to what your tastes are telling you. Whether a situation is bad or good, "going along with the crowd" because you are afraid of looking "stupid" or "wrong" is only going to cause you pain, and prevent you from discovering who you are or what is right for you.

**2) Accepting our feelings.** Once we have identified how we feel, our next step is to accept that feeling for what it is. We must be willing to admit, at least to ourselves and preferably to God as well, "This is how I feel."

Some of us have never done this. All our lives, we have learned to judge ourselves, condemn ourselves, and sometimes punish ourselves, not for what we have done but *for what we feel*. "Acceptance" seems the opposite of what we have learned to believe is "right" or "safe." While it sounds easy to say, "Accept your feelings," it rarely is—for we are going against a lifetime of training.

It is important to understand precisely what "acceptance" *means*. Acceptance is not a statement that our feelings are right or wrong, good or bad, appropriate or inappropriate, or even "acceptable" or "unacceptable" to others. It is simply a statement that we *have* them. It means that instead of choosing to rename our feelings, or deny them, or suppress them, we are acknowledging them. Instead of reacting to our self-talk's statements about what feelings we *should* or *shouldn't* have, we are allowing ourselves to discover what feelings we *do* have. We are not passing judgment; we are simply stating the truth.

As soon as we do, our usual *reactions* to our feelings begin to surface. We may feel guilty, or wonder how we "could" feel such a thing. We feel anxious and fearful, wondering what our feelings "mean." We may fear that someone will react negatively to us or punish us. We may be shocked. We may think that our feelings prove that we are "terrible people," especially if those feelings involved a desire to do something destructive or harmful. We may wonder what "kind" of person has that "kind" of feeling. We may wonder if we are sick, crazy, or abnormal.

We need to accept these *feelings* about our feelings. The secondary feelings are as important as the primary feelings, because they provide us clues to the lessons and attitudes that we have internalized regarding our emotions. They tell us what we think our feelings mean, or what we believe the consequences will be, and *why* we are so frightened by our own emotions.

Acceptance does not happen overnight. We often recoil from the declaration, "This is how I feel." Our secondary feelings of guilt and anxiety may be so powerful that we pull back from acceptance. However, we can return to this step as often as necessary, until we are ready to admit to ourselves how we really feel.

"Truth in our inward being" is what God desires (Psa. 51:6). He honors truth, not denial. Even though this step of "acceptance" feels almost sinful in its honesty, it is a step that God desires and requires of us. Once we realize that *He has already accepted our feelings*, long before we have, the step becomes easier. We do not have to fear His anger. God has *already* given us permission to feel; acceptance is the step we take to "receive" that permission. It is also the first *active* step we take toward finding resolutions, not only for our feelings but for their causes.

**3) Avoiding our defenses.** As soon as we feel something, and often well before we "accept" our feeling, our automatic "defense system" goes into action. We often discover that we have renamed, denied, or medicated a feeling before we were even fully aware of *having* that feeling.

The next step in "reclaiming" our feelings is to work on building a "time gap" between feeling and defense. Like acceptance, this isn't nearly as easy as it sounds. Our defenses exist because we fear traumatic consequences if we do not employ them. Laying aside those defenses makes us feel vulnerable and threatened.

When we choose *not* to turn to our normal methods of defense or escape, we often feel as though we are shut up in a box with one of our worst nightmares: Our own feelings. We may feel as though our emotions are so powerful that they will destroy us—or something that we care about. We may feel out of control, or as though we are going crazy. Everything inside us *screams* at us to return to our defensive behaviors. We are desperate to feel better (or safer), even when we know that our "defense" is actually self-destructive. The possibility of future destruction—through addiction, for example—is much less terrifying than what we are feeling *right now*.

We are also afraid that if we do not "defend" against our feelings, we may *act* upon them. We are afraid that we will "give in" to the desire to lash out at someone else, or to hurt ourselves. At the very least, we are afraid that we will do something "stupid" and humiliating. We are afraid that our feelings will be "discovered" and that we will be criticized or condemned or punished. We have never taken this step before, and we have no idea where it leads. We have given up our normal reactions—and we have nothing to replace them with.

Though we may resolve to avoid our defenses, we may find ourselves returning to them—and then feeling guilty because we think we have "failed." As with acceptance, however, we can come back to this step as often as necessary. Success will not be instantaneous. We may be more successful with some feelings than with others. The point is not to "get it right the first time," but to keep trying until we *are* able to put aside our defenses, a little at a time, and begin to deal with our feelings directly.

**4) Identifying the cause.** By the time we reach the fourth step, we have made tremendous progress against some powerful barriers. We have learned how to identify what we feel, admit what we feel, and resist our temptation to "defend" against what we feel. Now we are ready to do something we may never have done before: Discover the *real* cause of our feelings.

Often, our feelings are triggered by present events. When we are angry, something has usually happened to *make* us angry. When we are hurt, it is because something has *hurt* us. Until we could admit the feeling, we often could not acknowledge the event, or its significance. Instead, we have tended to say things like, "Oh, he didn't mean to say that, so I shouldn't be upset," or "Oh, I can't let myself be hurt by something that trivial."

When we accept our feelings, we can begin to accept that something happened to *cause* those feelings. Whether a person *meant* to hurt us or not, we were hurt. Whether a person *meant* to harm us or not, we were harmed—or at least we *perceive* that we have been harmed. We are now able to examine the actions of others in a more realistic light.

We may discover, for example, that we have allowed people to "walk all over us" for years because we didn't think that we had a "right" to feel anger or pain. We may discover that we often feel disappointed or hurt because a close friend or loved one often breaks or forgets promises to us. We may discover that we often feel "put down" or humiliated because someone frequently makes unkind remarks to us. We may discover that we often feel angry because we are often taken advantage of. We may discover that we feel left out because we *are* being ignored or disregarded. We may discover that we are feeling lonely because we are *not* being treated as though we were a valued part of a relationship. We may discover that we are feeling hopeless because we are receiving no encouragement from others. We may discover that we are feeling exhausted and resentful because others are placing unreasonable demands and requirements upon us. We may discover that we are frightened because others are actually threatening us in some way.

We may also discover that our feelings are the result of a combination of past and present experiences. What we are experiencing *today* may *remind* us of something painful that we experienced a long time ago. We may feel frightened when someone raises his voice, not because *that* person has ever hurt us, but because people have shouted at us and hurt us in the past. We may get angry at what someone says, not because that person meant any harm, but because what he said reminded us of old hurts. One woman, for example, became angry when someone said that she looked "cute"—a word that was intended as a genuine compliment. In her family, she explained, "cute meant that you didn't wear a dog collar." The present compliment was a reminder of a past insult.

Some people press these hidden "feeling triggers" by accident, and wonder why we react the way we do. Sometimes, however, people discover those triggers and manipulate them on purpose, finding them a powerful way to control us. One way to avoid being controlled in this way is to discover our hidden triggers for ourselves, and resolve them, so that we are no longer vulnerable to this kind of manipulation.

These discoveries change the way we look at life and at our problems. Until we take this step, we are often inclined to believe that the problem lies with *us*, and that it is a matter of our "perception" or "attitude." Indeed, we are often *told* that we are the problem—and if someone tells you this, that message itself is a warning flag. A person who takes responsibility for his actions, even if those actions hurt you *accidentally*, will not attempt to blame *you* for the problem. However, someone who chooses to *deliberately* cause pain or who does not wish to take responsibility for his actions, is more likely to defend his behavior by claiming that *you* caused the problem or that *you* are overreacting. We cannot rely on the honesty of others to tell us whether our feelings are justified. Instead, we must search diligently for the real cause of our feelings.

**5) Releasing our feelings.** Once we discover what the real problem is, we may find ourselves with even more emotion to deal with. When we discover, for example, that we are angry because a person is deliberately violating our rights, we may become even *more* angry. Now, too, we have a target—and it is tempting to release our feelings against that target. We feel like a bottle of champagne that has been shaken violently, and we don't know how to "uncork the bottle" without creating a damaging explosion.

Before we can deal calmly and constructively with the *cause* of our emotions, we need to find a safe way to "uncork" that bottle. We may be tempted to return to old defensive reactions, believing that these will keep us safe—but by now, the pressure has built up within us, and if we attempt to deny it or suppress it, it may explode when we least expect it to. We may lash out at an innocent target—at someone who happens to upset us at the wrong time, or at someone who is "safe" because he can't fight back. Children often fit into both of these categories; their behavior often makes us angry, and they are "safe" targets because they can't fight back. Many Adult Children discover, as they begin to explore their emotions, that they have unwittingly used their children as "venting systems" for feelings that they did not know how to "safely" express in any other way.

Whatever method we choose to safely "uncork the bottle," it needs to include "expression." While many find strenuous exercise a helpful way to "work out" feelings, that exercise is useless unless we know what feelings we are working out. It is not enough to hit a racquetball around a court, or to pound a pillow and scream, or to pummel a punching bag; we must do so with the awareness of *what* we are angry at and *why*.

Many people find that expressing their feelings on paper becomes a powerful mechanism of release. Some express their anger, pain, and resentment in a letter to the person whose behavior triggered those feelings. The letter may never be sent (and often *should* never be sent). Its purpose is not to confront, but to provide a safe outlet for our feelings so that when we *do* address the problem, we can do so constructively rather than destructively.

As we write this letter, or journal, or poem, or list of resentments, or any other form of expression we choose, we may find our feelings spilling out like never before. We may find ourselves in tears, unable to continue because we can't even see what we are writing. We may find ourselves shaking with rage, clenching our fists, wadding up the paper and throwing it across the room. We may experience physical reactions, such as stiffness, tension, and an increased heart rate. We may feel physically sick. All this can be very frightening because it is unfamiliar. We don't know what is happening and wonder if we are doing something wrong.

What is happening is that the *feelings are getting out*—perhaps for the first time. Most Adult Children have a huge backlog of unexpressed emotions, and when the cork comes out of the bottle, those emotions begin to spill out. Even the expression of feelings on paper can produce a profound emotional and physical effect, and that effect is *good*. Even though we may feel limp and "wrung out" by the time we are finished, afterward we will feel better. Furthermore, we will "feel better" not just temporarily, but *permanently*, because we have finally expressed what we formerly considered wrong, sinful, and unexpressable.

We may have to repeat this exercise several times, or for several different feelings, before we are ready to move on. As we uncork our feelings safely, however, we begin to believe that we *do* have some power and control over our lives. We begin to realize that it *is* possible to have feelings of this intensity, and yet not "sin." We may also discover for the first time in our lives what it feels like *not* to be filled with rage, fear, frustration, anger, or hopelessness, because for the first time in our lives we have *expressed* those feelings.

**6) Resolving the problem.** Now that our feelings no longer overwhelm us, now that we no longer feel quite so "out of control" or so tempted to resort to familiar defenses, we are ready to approach the problem itself. Most problems involve one of three solutions: We may need to change the *situation*, we may need to change our *reaction*, or we may need to *leave* the situation.

Changing the situation quite often means changing our *own* behavior. For example, if our coworkers have learned that they can dump their work on our desks or expect us to work extra hours without recompense or recognition, it is *our* behavior that needs to change. We have allowed this situation to develop, and as long as we continue to allow it, it will continue to occur. We cannot change the situation by asking everyone *else* to change. We can only change *our* response. We can tactfully but firmly refuse to do the work of others. We can politely stick to our decisions about work hours and vacations. We can choose to say "no." We can bring our own work to the attention of our employers. We can refuse to be frightened or intimidated by the surprised, and possibly angry, responses of coworkers who had become accustomed to manipulating us. Often, we will discover that *many* problems in our lives disappear when we cease to allow them to exist in the first place.

Sometimes, however, we may need to change our *reaction* to a situation—particularly when that reaction is based more upon past experience than upon present difficulties. If we learned, as children, to regard authority figures as dangerous and uncaring, for example, we may have a "problem" with a spouse or employer simply because that person is in a *position* of authority, *not* because that person is abusing it. We may resent our boss not because she is unreasonable, but simply because she is the *boss*, and bosses make us feel like powerless children. In this type of situation, we need to address our own reactions, seek ways to uncover the *real* issues (which have nothing to do with our current boss), and resolve *those* rather than "beating the air" over false issues.

When we cannot change the nature of a situation (either by changing our own actions or by confronting the actions of others), and the problem does not lie in our own reactions, we may have to ask why we are *remaining* in that situation. If, for example, we cannot prevent a person from abusing us, and yet we allow that abuse to continue, we are *participating in the problem.* Some situations cannot be changed *or* made acceptable or tolerable; some situations (and relationships) can only be left behind.

These "solutions" are purposely general and vague, because it would be impossible to present answers for your individual issues. One difficulty many of us face, however, is the realization that we don't know how to *find* answers for our problems. We may have the desire to find solutions, but we lack the training in social or problem-solving skills that is needed to *develop* those solutions or to make a "problem-solving plan."

In this situation, a competent counselor can be of great help. We may need to find someone who can help us rebuild the skills and insights that were not provided by our families. Going to a counselor to find help with problems is no different from going to a doctor for help with a medical concern, or going to a contractor for building advice, or going to an investment counselor for financial information. We seek what we do *not* have from those who *have* it.

**7) Following through.** Planning solutions, and developing the skills to implement those solutions, are important—but useless *unless we follow through.* The final step in resolving emotional issues is to *carry out* the resolution.

Adult Children are plagued by procrastination. We put off our plans because we are afraid of what might happen if "it doesn't work" or "others get upset." We think that we will really put our foot down—tomorrow. We will definitely change how we handle a situation—next week. We will discuss the problem—when it seems like a good time.

We must not allow ourselves to become the slaves of our good intentions. Good intentions are worthwhile only when they become the foundation of *action.* Sooner or later, if we truly wish to resolve the *causes* of our emotions, we must "tune out" our self-talk, "tune in" our courage, and take the first step in our problem-solving plan. If the plan doesn't work—and it may not—then we rethink our options and select a new plan. We need to remember that the *only way to fail is to fail to try.*

When we give ourselves "permission to feel," we set in motion a chain of events that goes far beyond the feelings themselves. Recognizing and accepting our feelings are the first step on the road to changing our lives. Until we learn how to feel, until we learn that it is OK to feel, the tragic reality is that we *cannot* change our lives, or resolve the situations that bring us so much grief and pain. Our feelings provide us with the motivation to change, and the key to understanding what *needs* to be changed.

As we rediscover our feelings, we rediscover what it means to be human, and to be created in the image of a "feeling" God. Something else often begins to happen when we do this: We not only learn how to feel anger and pain, but we *also* rediscover our feelings of *joy* and *wonder* and *delight*. The mind does not distinguish between "signals;" when it is required to shut down "some" signals, it shuts down *all* of them. When we reopen these signalling channels, we reopen our ability to receive joy.

We rediscover our ability to enjoy today's sunset without worrying about what we should be doing tomorrow. We rediscover our ability to smell the flowers without wondering what we need to do to become better gardeners. We rediscover our wonder in the incredibly beautiful world God created for us and gave to us. We rediscover our childlike delight in simple things—in glittering dewdrops and the kiss of rain and the excitement of a wrapped package. We remember how to kick off our shoes, splash in puddles, play games, and paint pictures without supposing that they have to be *perfect*. We relearn how to take pleasure in *doing* instead of in *doing right*, in *feeling* rather than in *feeling correctly*, in *being* rather than in *being better*. We rediscover delight, freedom, enthusiasm, passion, energy, and even innocence, as we rediscover who and what we are in God.

# - 7 -

# Forgiveness: Passport to Freedom

*Then Peter came to Jesus and asked, "Lord, how many times shall I forgive my brother when he sins against me? Up to seven times?" Jesus answered, "I tell you, not seven times, but seventy-seven times." (Matt. 18:21-22)*

THE REDISCOVERY AND EXPLORATION of our emotions sets something new in motion in our lives. For the first time in years, perhaps, we are not simply *thinking* about what is happening to us, but *feeling* it. We are no longer intellectualizing our problems, holding them at arm's length and reviewing them with the detachment we might feel for a newspaper article. No longer do we feel as though those disasters happened to "someone else." All at once, we become keenly aware of what happened—and what may still be happening—to *us*.

The intensity of these emotions can be frightening, even overwhelming. We are astonished by the power of the feelings we experience *today* over events that happened *decades* ago. All at once, emotions that have been repressed for most of our lives—anger, pain, shame, and fear—demand our immediate attention.

Reclaiming our emotions often means reclaiming our memories. For some, the memories have always been there—but we have numbed ourselves to them, regarding them as distant and meaningless events, part of the past that we want to leave behind. For others, the memories don't even begin to surface until the emotions surface; then our repressed anger and pain comes bubbling up like a geyser, bringing with it the events that *caused* all that pain.

When we begin to remember, and to feel, and remember even more, it is often as though we are not merely *reliving* our past experiences, but actually *living* them for the first time. When we went through them the first time, we may not have been allowed to express our feelings (or even "have" them), so we may have shut them down, or denied to ourselves that we felt *anything*. Now, with those restrictions removed, we are often not only *recalling* pain, but *feeling* it for the first time.

At the same time, we may suddenly discover what we actually feel about what is happening in our lives right now. For the first time, we realize that the emotional abuse and put-downs and lack of love we may be experiencing today *really hurts*. When we stop "rationalizing away" the inappropriate behavior of others, we tend to become very *angry* about that behavior. We may discover that we are being taken advantage of, misused, and even physically or sexually abused. We may begin to realize that we have been in an intolerable situation for years, that we have felt trapped and desperate and powerless, and that our life is a misery to us.

As these feelings burst into our awareness, we may think that they are "running wild" and have no idea how to control them. We are startled by the "negativity" of those feelings: It isn't joy and delight that have been repressed for decades, but anger and bitterness and hurt. For the first time, we *feel* the helpless anger and hurt of a child whose trust is betrayed, who is trapped and abused by those whom she most loves and needs. We feel the stinging humiliation of harsh words, sarcasm, and unfair accusations and punishments. We feel the loss of our self-image, our sense of worth, our sense of lovability. We feel robbed, cheated, misused, and ashamed. We feel *very angry*. Often, we want to strike back.

We are often shocked by the intensity of these feelings, whether they are directed at people in our present or people in our past. We didn't realize that we had so much locked up inside us—and we may feel guilty for having such powerful anger and hate, and such a burning desire for revenge. As Christians, we are certain that we "shouldn't" have feelings like these, and that something is terribly wrong with us for having them.

Many Adult Children wish, at this point, that they could stuff all those feelings "back in the bottle." Life was much simpler when those feelings weren't there. It wasn't that life was painless—but at least we didn't feel the pain! It is easy for us to suppose that the "Christian" thing to do is simply "get rid of" those feelings—that is, to stop "feeling" them.

Feelings, like champagne foam, are not that easy to put "back in the bottle," however. Once they are released, they are released. Even if we ignore them, we can no longer pretend that we never knew they were there. We know that even if we *do* manage to "cork them up," they are waiting, ready to burst out again when we least expect them. We can no longer "lie" to ourselves about what we feel.

Christian Adult Children now face a new dilemma. The very intensity of our feelings tells us that we haven't *forgiven* the people who hurt us. Yet that same intensity makes us wonder how we possibly *can*. We wonder how we can ever forgive our parents for what they did to us—and we may wonder how we can forgive people who are still hurting us *today*. We may even wonder how *God* could possibly forgive some of the things that were done to us, let alone how He could ask *us* to do so.

Most of us have an invisible "forgiveness line" in our minds. Often, we "forgive" things that we can "understand," even a little bit—even if we would never do such things ourselves. But there are things that we can't understand, abuses we can't imagine how a human could commit. We can't imagine how even God could forgive things that fall on the other side of that line. How, we wonder, can God forgive a parent who sexually abuses a child? How can He forgive a parent who tortures a child, breaks bones, inflicts burns, and worse? How can He forgive a parent who keeps a naked and starving child locked in a closet, or chained to a bed? How can He forgive a parent who subjects a child to ritual abuse? How can He forgive a parent who "sells" a child to perverts or pornographers for money or drugs? We know that, scripturally, we are "required" to forgive. Jesus says, "For if you forgive men when they sin against you, your heavenly Father will also forgive you. But if you do not forgive men their sins, your Father will not forgive your sins." (Matt. 6:14-15) But could Jesus possibly expect us to "forgive" sins like these—especially if they were committed against *us*?

Ironically, it is when we feel *least* able to forgive that we are actually moving closer to *genuine* forgiveness. The reason that we feel so unable to forgive is because, for the first time, we are becoming fully aware of *what was actually done to us*. We are no longer able to apply a superficial "lip service" of forgiveness to people and events of the past. Instead, we are discovering the extent of what we *need* to forgive. Our former glib statements like "Oh, it really didn't matter; they didn't mean to hurt me; I forgave all that years ago" suddenly appear shallow and meaningless. For the first time, we are counting the cost, assessing the damage, and feeling the pain.

Though these discoveries may seem to drive us *away* from forgiveness, they are actually bringing us closer to a point at which we can offer *genuine*, rather than superficial, forgiveness. We cannot truly forgive a person *until we know what we are forgiving*. Superficial forgiveness, however, is simply a form of denial in spiritual guise. Now that we have broken through the denial, we can explore not only what *happened* to us but what it *meant* to us.

One woman, for example, was concerned about the feelings she was having toward her husband, who, she had discovered, had been unfaithful to her throughout nearly twenty years of marriage. The couple had gone to counseling, he had promised to reform (and apparently had), and she thought that she had "forgiven" him. Yet she still felt anger and resentment toward him, and found it impossible to trust him. She wondered why these feelings hadn't "gone away" once she forgave her husband.

Though this woman had forgiven her husband for the *action* of infidelity, she had never examined what his unfaithfulness had meant to *her*, personally. As she explored the issue more thoroughly, she discovered how deeply she had been wounded. Her self-esteem had been low to begin with, but this event had "confirmed" to her that she was a worthless person, unable to win or hold her husband's love and faithfulness. She felt betrayed, cheated, and of no "value" to her husband. Worse, she felt utterly "stupid" for having trusted the man she loved for so many years, and she feared that if she trusted him again, she would be even more "stupid."

Ultimately, she was able to forgive her husband, not simply for what he had *done*, but for what he had done to *her*. When she addressed these issues, she was able to discuss them with him, and they were able to reach a new level of understanding in the relationship.

We may have known for years that we were mistreated or abused by our parents—and we may have "forgiven" that abuse because we knew it was the "Christian" thing to do. Until we "bring home" those experiences and understand what they meant to us, however, such "forgiveness" has no more meaning than "forgiving" some total stranger for a crime we read about in the newspaper. When we reclaim our emotions, we reclaim our experiences—and ultimately, we face the need to *forgive* those experiences. This is not easy, and we may wonder how we can ever achieve it.

## What Forgiveness Isn't...

One of the primary barriers many of us have to forgiveness is a set of misperceptions about what forgiveness really means. Before we can come to terms with God's command to "Love your enemies, do good to those who hate you, bless those who curse you, pray for those who mistreat you," (Luke 6:27-28) we need to clear up those misperceptions.

• **Forgiveness does not require understanding.** Adult Children often try to use "understanding" as a basis for forgiveness. We believe that if we could just understand *why* a person does something, we will find it easier to "forgive" them. One woman, for example, declared that she was "able to forgive" her father for sexually abusing her because she had discovered that he had been sexually abused as a child himself.

When we seek to "understand" a person's behavior, we may be seeking a way to justify or excuse that behavior. Perhaps because we love the person who hurt us, and we don't want to "think badly" of them if we can help it. Finding a way to "excuse" that person's actions as somehow "understandable" may help us preserve our illusions about that person. Many Adult Children declare that their parents "did the best they could" or "were just under a lot of stress" or "didn't know any better because they were abused by their own parents."

While understanding is an important part of a relationship, it is *not* a prerequisite for forgiveness. If we cannot forgive until we find something "forgivable," then we are not practicing genuine forgiveness in the first place. In addition, as long as we base "forgiveness" upon "understanding," we remain unable to forgive actions that fall *outside* our ability to "understand."

Forgiveness has nothing to do with understanding or justification. We do not forgive crimes because they are "justified," but crimes that are *unjustified*—for this is what God has forgiven us. If we could be "justified," even a little bit, in our sins, then we would not have needed sacrificial redemption from those sins. Forgiveness is powerful because it *replaces* justification or rationalization.

Forgiveness does not depend upon the nature of the crime, or upon the nature of the person who committed it—but upon *us*. God has given us the power and authority to forgive in the name of Jesus. Forgiveness depends upon our conscious decision to *exercise* that authority in *obedience* to God's command. When we forgive, we are making a decision based upon our will, not upon another's merit. Forgiveness cannot be earned; it can only be granted.

• **Forgiveness does not require repentance.** We often want someone to "change their ways" before we are willing to forgive them. At the very least, we want a person to come to us and apologize, *admitting* that they have wronged us, before we grant them a "pardon." We often feel as though we are "wasting our time" if we forgive someone who hasn't changed, or who commits the same crime over again.

The idea that repentance must precede forgiveness seems scriptural. We know that *we* are required to repent of our sins so that we can receive forgiveness. Jesus says, "If your brother sins, rebuke him, and if he repents, forgive him. If he sins against you seven times in a day, and seven times comes back to you and says, 'I repent,' forgive him." (Luke 17:3-4) Doesn't that mean that someone must repent before we are required to forgive?

If that were true, it would shift the burden of obligation onto the recipient of forgiveness, rather than upon the forgiver. We would not be "obligated" to forgive until someone "earns" forgiveness by changing his actions or by apologizing. Forgiveness would no longer be a gift; it would be a reward that we could withhold or dispense as we chose.

The Bible, however, puts the burden of forgiveness squarely

upon *us*, not upon those that we are called to forgive. Jesus says nothing in Matt. 6:14-15 about waiting for other people to "repent" before we "forgive" them. He tells us, "And when you stand praying, if you hold anything against anyone, forgive him, so that your Father in heaven may forgive you your sins." (Mark 11:25) Nor did He wait for our "repentance" before He offered His life to redeem us from sin. His forgiveness was not a "reward" for our repentance or good behavior, but a free gift from God. Even as He offered the gift of His life, He asked of the unrepentant soldiers and Pharisees who had condemned and crucified Him, "Father, forgive them, for they do not know what they are doing." (Luke 23:34)

Forgiveness is not based upon repentance. Our obligation to forgive is not diminished just because those that we *need* to forgive have not changed, apologized, or even realized that they did anything wrong. Once again, forgiveness is a decision based upon *our* will, not upon someone else's behavior.

• **Forgiveness is not "condoning" the crime.** Many Adult Children believe that "forgiving" is virtually the same as saying that what happened was "OK." One woman declared, "I would be stupid to forgive my mother for what she did to me. It would be like telling her that she had a right to do it." We may feel as though we would be granting a sort of "retroactive permission" for our abusers. We may think that "forgiveness" is the same as telling someone that she had a "right" to hurt us in the first place.

When we forgive, we do not forgive *crimes*, we forgive *people*. Jesus teaches us to pray, "Forgive *us* our debts, as we also have forgiven our debtors." (Matt. 6:12, emphasis mine.) It is not our "debt" that is forgiven; it is we who *owe* that debt who receive forgiveness. Crimes are usually "unacceptable"—but one *can* accept a person *without* accepting that person's behavior. We may have been deeply wounded by what was done to us, but it is the *person* we are angry at—and it is the *person* that we need to forgive.

Forgiveness is not a statement that what happened was "OK" or "acceptable." In fact, it is just the opposite. If what happened *was* "OK," there would be nothing to forgive. When we decide to forgive, we are declaring that what happened was *wrong*. Thus it is important for *us* to decide, in our own minds, that what happened was wrong, instead of trying to excuse or rationalize it as "understandable." Forgiveness is not saying, "You really didn't do anything bad." It is saying, "You *did* do something bad—and I forgive you for it." We are stating the truth, like Joseph, who said to the brothers who had sold him into slavery, "You intended to harm me, but God intended it for good to accomplish what is now being done, the saving of many lives." (Gen. 50:20)

When we forgive, we are saying that what happened was *wrong*, but that we are no longer holding that person accountable to *us* for what happened. Joseph says, "Don't be afraid. Am I in the place of God?" (Gen. 50:19) When we don't forgive, we are attempting to put ourselves in the place of God, so that we can act as judge and jury (and perhaps executioner) over those who hurt us. When we forgive, we turn our enemies *over* to God, and accept that they are accountable only to Him, not to us.

• **Forgiveness doesn't mean it didn't hurt.** Often, we attempt to forgive by minimizing the seriousness of what happened—especially if we are forgiving a person directly. We may try to say, "Oh, it wasn't that serious; I know you really didn't mean to hurt me; it doesn't matter now; I've resolved all that." We often believe that we aren't supposed to feel any painful emotions about the events, or toward those who caused those events. We may also believe that when we forgive, all our pain is supposed to disappear.

The truth is that many of us *were* hurt, and some of us were hurt traumatically. We do not serve truth by denying the existence or the intensity of that pain. When we forgive, we do not need to pretend that it didn't happen, or that it didn't matter, or even that it doesn't affect us anymore. Indeed, when we *do* attempt to pretend these things, it may be because we are trying to use "quick and easy forgiveness" as a way to *avoid* dealing with our hurts.

When we forgive, we are admitting to ourselves and, if appropriate, to the recipient of our forgiveness, that what happened to us *did* hurt and that it *did* have significant effects upon our lives. We are admitting that we *are* upset and angry and grieved over what happened—and that in spite of our feelings, which may not be resolved yet, we are still choosing to obey God and forgive. Even after we forgive, we may have to deal with the long-term events of those hurts in our lives.

• **Forgiveness is not forgetfulness.** While "forgive and forget" is a popular phrase, it is not a scriptural one. We often suppose that if we "forgive" people, then we are supposed to "forget" what happened, or at least pretend that we don't remember. Forgiveness, however, is not a call for holy amnesia.

If we have to "put something out of our minds" before we can forgive it, we are not practicing true forgiveness. We are simply putting a painful event "away," where it won't hurt us. Forgiveness does not mean "stuffing" the past into a closet where we can't see it or be hurt by it. Forgiveness is the end product of *resolving* the hurts of the past, so that even when we *do* recall them, they no longer have power over us.

Forgiveness, in fact, is just the opposite of forgetting. Forgiveness gives us the power to *remember*—safely. When we forgive, our memories will no longer be traumatic or bitterly painful. Forgiveness does not *remove* the past, but it *does* take the "sting" out.

Think back to some injury that you experienced in your childhood—such as a time when you skinned your knees on the playground. Can you remember the details of that event? Chances are that you can—vividly. You can even remember that your knee hurt, at the time. But as you think of that experience, does your knee hurt now? Not likely—not even a twinge.

What you *may* remember is the *emotional* consequences of your injury—the psychological aftermath. Perhaps someone tripped you, and laughed when you tumbled to the ground—and you remember that mocking laughter, that deliberate attack upon you. Perhaps when you began to cry from the pain, your playmates gathered around and made fun of you, calling you "sissy" or "crybaby." Perhaps you were scolded by your parents for being "clumsy" or for getting your clothes dirty. If anything like this happened, chances are good that these memories carry a far greater burden pain than the memory of the injury itself.

Even though you can "remember" the pain of your skinned knee, you can't feel it. That injury has healed. You can talk about it, describe it, even draw pictures—but you don't feel it. In a very real sense, your body has "forgiven" that injury against it.

It is possible to heal the pain of emotional injuries in the same way. The memories of someone tripping you, of people laughing at you, of your parents criticizing you, still hurt *because they have not healed*. Most of us were given at least minimal treatment for our *physical* injuries—but where offered no means of healing emotional pain. We couldn't talk about it, release it, or even let anyone know we *had* it. So we locked it up inside, where it wouldn't get us into even *more* trouble, and it never went away. When we "remember" those emotional traumas, we hurt—perhaps as much or more than when the events occurred.

Forgiveness is a process that enables our emotions and minds to heal in much the same way that our bodies have healed. By "treating" the wounds that we have received—by expressing the pain and allowing ourselves to receive comfort and healing—those wounds gradually scab over. They don't vanish overnight, but the process of healing has begun, and it usually *begins* with the decision to forgive. One day, we will be able to "remember" the traumas of our past, as vividly as ever, yet without the burden of anguish and grief that we may feel as we recall them today. When we reach that point, we will know that real forgiveness has taken root in our hearts, and brought the healing power of God's love and comfort into our lives.

• **Forgiveness does not necessarily mean reconciliation.** One of the most confusing aspects of forgiveness is the question of what it means to a relationship. Does this mean that we are "friends" again, and that everything is supposed to be wonderful? Does it mean that we will now go on as though nothing had happened? Do we have to *tell* a person that we have forgiven them for our forgiveness to count?

It is important to remember that while *forgiveness* involves the will of *one* person (you), a *relationship* involves the will of *two* people. Each of us has an individual responsibility to forgive, a responsibility that does not depend upon another person's behavior or repentance or worthiness. However, for a healthy relationship to result from forgiveness, it is necessary for *both* people involved to assume responsibility.

The person you are forgiving may not be ready, able, or even interested in doing that. That person's behavior may not have changed; she may still be doing the same thing that you are forgiving her for. He may be unaware that he is doing anything wrong, or unwilling to accept that his behavior is a problem. She may be unable to have a healthy relationship with *anyone*. He may be prepared to hurt you all over again if you "get close."

Reconciliation involves two people. God forgives *us*—but it is necessary for *us* to repent and turn to Him in order to be reconciled to Him. Joseph may have forgiven his brothers long before they ever arrived in Egypt (we don't know, one way or the other) but it was necessary for them to come to *him* and acknowledge their crimes against him before they could have a relationship again. If another person is not able to have a healthy relationship, or is not interested in changing her behavior, our forgiveness will not change that. It only changes *us*.

Sometimes it can be helpful to go to another person and forgive them directly. Joseph's brothers had lived in guilt and fear for nearly twenty years. Before they even knew that they were standing before Joseph, they assumed that their current troubles were the result of that ancient crime. "They said to one another, 'Surely we are being punished because of our brother. We saw how distressed he was when he pleaded with us for his life, but we would not listen; that's why this distress has come upon us.'" (Gen. 42:21) Similarly, people who know that they have caused us harm may be living in bondage to shame, guilt, and fear—and our forgiveness can free them from this and clear the way for a better relationship.

In other cases, however, direct forgiveness may *not* be called for. If a person has no idea that he caused us harm, or refuses to acknowledge any wrongdoing, direct forgiveness may simply make the relationship worse. If a person isn't aware of our anger, and we suddenly declare, "I have been very bitter toward you for years, but now I forgive you," we may cause more pain than healing. Our "forgiveness" may sound like condemnation—and we must take care not to use "forgiveness" as a sneaky form of confrontation.

Whether forgiveness will involve reconciliation is a highly individual matter. Only you know how others will react to your forgiveness, or whether family members or friends are able to form healthy relationships. Forgiveness can be a powerful stepping-stone toward reconciliation, but it is not an iron-clad guarantee. However, if reconciliation is our ultimate goal, it is important to remember that while forgiveness does not *guarantee* it, *unforgiveness* almost certainly guarantees that it *won't* happen.

## What's In It For Me?

Forgiveness often seems to be a nice, caring, "Christian" thing that we do for *other* people. But when we are in the throes of pain and anger, being sweet and caring isn't always our highest priority.

At such times, we may wonder what forgiveness does for *us*. How does it contribute to recovery and healing?

Until we choose to forgive (and it is a choice), we tend to spend our time and energy wishing that we *weren't* in the situation that we are in. We *regret* our problems, we are *angry* about our circumstances, and we *wish we were somewhere else.*

We may feel trapped in a painful, destructive relationship. We may be addicted—or married to an addict. We may have seen the failure of one relationship after another, until we have come to believe that we can never *have* a good, loving, healthy relationship. We may be bewildered by the behavior of our children, or we may have discovered that we have been practicing or permitting abusive behaviors in our homes. We may find ourselves turning again and again to self-destructive behaviors in an effort to build feelings of self-worth or medicate our pain. We may be struggling with profound feelings of worthlessness and hopelessness. We may believe that we have no hope for a better future. We may feel that we do not deserve the love of God, and we may not know how to receive it. We may feel trapped by the rules and requirements that we assume we must meet in order to be a "good" (or "better") person. We may be tired, frustrated, bitter, and miserable.

In the past, we blamed ourselves for these circumstances. We assumed that we were not trying hard enough, or that we were not good enough, or that we were somehow incapable of being "normal" or "functional." Though we spent years struggling to "improve" ourselves, nothing ever seemed to change, so we blamed ourselves even more. But as we entered the process of recovery, we began to learn that we were *not* "responsible" for all our painful circumstances, though we may have contributed to them. We began to learn that these "circumstances" are common to those who grew up with dysfunctional family teachings and behaviors. We learned that the past *had* a profound effect upon our lives.

We found someone else to blame.

At first, finding someone *else* to blame for the problems that we have hitherto blamed *ourselves* for is a truly exhilarating and liberating experience. For the first time in our lives, we stop thinking that everything is "our fault." For once, we can think of things as being "someone else's fault." We realize that we are "here" because someone else *put* us "here." We realize that we *were* hurt, lied to, and misled. We were *not* "trained in the way that we should go," and if we never "departed" from our way, it was because we never realized that any other way was possible.

We learned that we weren't crazy, abnormal, or hopelessly dysfunctional. We learned that we were not alone—that others had experienced the same traumas, and the same consequences, that we have experienced. We may have found support, companionship, and acceptance in groups of Adult Children like ourselves. This new discovery is exciting, delightful, and freeing. At the same time, it may fill us with rage and bitterness against those who "caused" the problems that we have lived with for so long.

This step is normal and healthy—for a time. It is the natural reaction to discovering the truth. It is wonderful to realize that we aren't crazy or "to blame" for everything that ever went wrong in our lives. However, it is only a step, not a final destination.

Some Adult Children reach this stage and find that it feels so "good"—at least compared to what has gone before—that they decide to "move in." They treat what is actually the *beginning* of recovery as though it were the *end*, the final goal. Some move from group to group, telling and retelling their histories of woe, explaining why they can "never" do this and "never" be that because their parents "ruined their lives forever." They live in the anger that they have rediscovered, and bring up that rage over and over again as though it were a precious possession rather than something to be resolved. They lament the fact that they "shouldn't be where they are"—but they refuse to move on to anyplace else.

When we get stuck in this stage, we are like travelers who discover that we are lost, and then *stay* lost while we try to figure out *what went wrong*. We try to figure out who is to be blamed for giving us the wrong directions, who is responsible for taking the wrong turn miles back, and why we *wouldn't* be here if only *someone* had put us on the right path. We spend our days studying the *wrong part of the map*—the part that shows us the ground that we have *already* covered. It may be emotionally satisfying to point out the "exits" that we "could" have taken, and fixing the blame on those who "steered us wrong"—but in the meantime, we aren't *getting* anywhere.

This does not mean that exploring the past has no value. Its value, however, depends upon how that exploration is applied to the present and the future. It is not a goal in itself, but a tool that we can apply toward understanding ourselves, our misperceptions, and our choices. "Looking back" is valuable only when it is used as a *part* of "moving forward."

Forgiveness is like refolding the map of our lives. It is our way of deciding that instead of spending the rest of our lives reexploring *old* territory, we will look ahead to something new. Instead of trying to figure out who is to blame for where we *are*, we begin to chart new routes, and attempt to discover a way to get to where we would *like* to be. It is our declaration that, even though our parents or our past may be "responsible" for where we are *today*, *we* are responsible for where we will be *tomorrow*.

No matter what form of abuse you experienced, and no matter what circumstances you are in today, you are not "stuck" there. It is true that what we learned from our dysfunctional families may be "responsible" for the pain we have experienced thus far in our lives. We are where we are because we learned to operate out of a system of lies and fears. But once we *realize* this, something new happens. We may be where we *are* because we didn't know the truth—but now we do. And once we *know* the truth, or at least know where the truth can be found, our parents are no longer responsible for our lives. We are.

This is often not a pleasant decision to make. We grew up with far more experience with *blame* than with forgiveness *or* with responsibility. The purpose of blame is to determine who is "at fault" for a situation, so that we can discover who is "responsible" for "fixing" it. In our own homes, if we did something wrong, we were usually held responsible for "fixing" the problem, even if that was beyond our capabilities. "Blame" was our parents' way of washing their hands of the situation: "You got into this mess, you get out of it." In addition, we were often blamed for problems that we had nothing to do with, such as our parents' alcoholism or abusive behaviors. We learned to believe that we had no right to expect our parents to "fix" their behavior, because we were told that their behavior was "our fault."

If we couldn't "fix" a problem, at the very least, we could "pay" for it. We learned that one could not "move on" from something until one had been sufficiently "punished" for it. Even after we were punished, we knew that our "crimes" usually became a part of our "permanent record," and that we could be "reminded" of past mistakes long after they occurred. We may still be in a relationship with someone who "fights dirty" by saying, "Yes, maybe I did that yesterday, but it's not nearly as bad as what *you* did a *year* ago!" What most of us have learned is that a "problem" must *always* be followed by "blame" and then by "punishment."

Responsibility is exactly the opposite of blame. Responsibility says, "There is a problem here. It doesn't really matter how it got here or who 'caused' it. What matters is finding a solution. I choose to become part of that solution."

We aren't accustomed to this approach to life. If our families had used this approach, they would not have been dysfunctional in the first place, and we wouldn't be in "recovery." We often don't expect this sort of approach from God, either. Instead, we expect God to "blame" us for our mistakes and sins, and to require that we "get our act together." Many Christians teach that even though God "forgives" sin, He "removes His hand of protection from us when we sin, and allows us to experience the consequences of our actions." We believe that God may forgive us, but He still expects us to "clean up the mess," because the "mess" is "our fault."

God actually did just the opposite. God didn't cause our sinful condition, our lost state; He wasn't "responsible" for it. He could have easily pointed a finger at us, and said, "Look, you got yourselves into this mess, it's up to you to get yourselves out of it." In fact, this attitude *is* the teaching of most other religions—and sometimes the teaching of legalism.

But God didn't do that. Instead, even though *He wasn't to blame for our sin, He made Himself responsible for it*—literally. Instead of blaming us for the problem, He made Himself responsible for the solution. In fact, He made *Himself* the solution. Jesus died to free us from a problem of our own making. Paul tells us:

"Therefore, since we have been justified through faith, we have peace with God through our Lord Jesus Christ, through whom we have gained access by faith into this grace in which we now stand. And we rejoice in the hope of the glory of God. Not only so, but we also rejoice in our sufferings, because we know that suffering produces perseverance; perseverance, character; and character, hope. And hope does not disappoint us, because God has poured out His love into our hearts by the Holy Spirit, whom He has given us.

Very rarely will anyone die for a righteous man, though for a good man someone might possibly dare to die. But God demonstrates His own love for us in this: While we were still sinners, Christ died for us. Since we have now been justified by His blood, how much more shall we be saved from God's wrath through Him! For if, when we were God's enemies, we were reconciled to Him through the death of His Son, how much more, having been reconciled, shall we be saved through His life!" (Rom. 5:1-10)

This is what forgiveness and "responsibility" are all about. It is what Jesus did for us, and modeled for us, when He took our problems upon Himself and solved them. Forgiveness is saying, "Regardless of who *caused* this problem, I am now assuming responsibility for *fixing* it."

Forgiveness is the cancellation of a debt. Jesus used examples of financial indebtedness to illustrate His teachings on forgiveness (Matt. 18:23-35). It is not a statement that no one "owes" us anything; instead, it is a statement that in spite of what we are *owed*, we renounce our *claim* on that debt.

Most Adult Children, once they discover what parental dysfunction has *cost* them, tend to believe that their parents "owe" them something. At the very least, we want our parents to apologize to us, to admit that they did something wrong, to acknowledge that they hurt us. We may want them to "make up" for their neglect in the past in some way, such as by telling us, at last, that they approve of us or love us or are proud of us. Yet most of us discover that our parents have no intention of doing that, and no awareness that they did anything wrong. This only tends to increase our anger, to make us more determined that "someone needs to pay."

Yet we realize that it is impossible for our parents to "pay us back" for what their behavior cost us. We can't live our childhood over again, without the traumas and misperceptions that we endured the first time. We can't "go on" as though nothing ever happened. Our parents can't "give us back" the self-image that we "should" have had. They can't restore our innocence, rebuild our trust, or "make up" for the years that we felt unloved and unlovable.

When we realize that our parents can't repay what was stolen, we often want to make them "pay" in the only other way possible: By punishing them. We don't want to "forgive" our parents until we are satisfied that they have "hurt" as much as we have hurt. If we can't get "recompense," we at least want "satisfaction."

Most of us would never follow through on our fantasies or desires of revenge. However, we are also unwilling to give them up. We want to have someone else to blame—perhaps because we fear that if we *do* take responsibility, we will "make a mess of it." It is frightening to forgive, when we realize that "forgiveness" means that we are now taking responsibility for our destiny, instead of "blaming" that destiny on someone else.

Until we forgive, however, our focus remains upon the past, not upon the future. It remains fixed upon those things that we *cannot* change (no matter how much we wish they had been "different"), instead of upon those things that we *can* change. It keeps us trapped in anger and bitterness. Those emotions are the result of *past* experiences; it is impossible to feel "angry" or "bitter" over a future that hasn't happened yet! Until we forgive, we are saying that we would rather *hit* the person who "brought us here" than get behind the wheel of our lives and drive someplace else.

Forgiveness is the single most powerful decision we can make about our future. It is the step through which we reclaim personal responsibility for our lives by releasing others from blame. It is not a way of saying that nothing happened. Instead, it is our way of saying, "No matter what you did, no matter what happened, I am no longer holding *you* responsible for *my* future." We are choosing to trust God and follow His guidance. We are choosing to believe that "in everything God works for good with those who love Him, who are called according to His purpose." (Rom. 8:28) Instead of believing that our lives are forever "ruined" by the past, we are choosing to believe that "with God all things are possible." (Matt. 19:26) We don't have to *like* where we are, but by taking the step of forgiveness, we *accept* where we are, so that we can move on.

As we do this, we say goodbye to bitterness and hate, because however justified these emotions may be, they keep us focused upon the past. We realize that whenever these emotions surface (and they will), they are showing us new areas of our lives that need to be forgiven. Forgiveness is not a one-time event, but something that we will do over and over again, each time that we identify new events and new people that we need to forgive. Each time we forgive, we take more control over our own destiny.

When God forgave us and died for us, He was not telling us to fixate upon the past (even though some churches do precisely that). He wasn't telling us to focus upon how *bad* we were to *need* such a tremendous sacrifice. He was telling us, not to look back, but to look forward, to the "hope of glory," which is "Christ in you." (Col. 1:27) When we practice this same forgiveness, we put its healing and redeeming power into effect in our own lives, declaring our acceptance of God's love, freedom, and forgiveness. When we make the choice of forgiveness, we become able at last to say, with Paul, "...one thing I do, forgetting what lies behind and straining forward to what lies ahead, I press on toward the goal for the prize of the upward call of God in Christ Jesus." (Phil. 3:14)

## Who Needs Our Forgiveness Most?

Whether or not you are ready to declare your "independence" from the past, whether you are ready to "forgive" the abuses of your parents, whether you are ready to "get in the driver's seat" of your life, there is *one* person that you desperately *need* to forgive if you are to make progress in recovery.

No matter how "bad" or "undeserving" you think that person is, you need to forgive. No matter what that person has done—or hasn't done—you need to forgive. Even though that person may have done things that were deeply destructive to you, that got you into considerable trouble, that created long-term consequences in your life that you are *still* dealing with, you need to forgive. Even if that person is committing dysfunctional actions *today* against you or your loved ones, you need to forgive. Even though you hate that person more than anyone else in your life, you need to forgive.

That person is you.

Adult Children who wrestle their way through an uphill battle to forgive violently abusive parents often never even approach the battle to forgive *themselves*. Yet we are often the people that we blame the *most* for the difficulties that we have experienced. We don't think that *we* have any "excuses." We *know* what we did wrong, and why. We *know* that we "knew better." We *know* that we could have chosen other behaviors, other directions. We know that if we forgive ourselves today, we may go right back out tomorrow and make another mistake. We "know" how "bad" we are. We can't imagine what self-forgiveness would accomplish. We are the last person we imagine we could ever be "reconciled" to.

Many of us learned to believe that we were "disappointments" to our parents and even to our spouses. We learned that we never did "well enough" or tried "hard enough" or managed to be "good enough." But most of all, we were a disappointment to ourselves. We kept hoping that we could do better and be better—but because we never succeeded in "earning" the approval of those we loved, we became convinced that we were failures. We blamed ourselves for everything that we failed to receive—including love, acceptance, and approval—and for everything that went wrong in our lives.

We may also have blamed ourselves for our families' problems. We may have believed that if only we had worked harder, or tried to be more considerate or responsible, our alcoholic parents would have stopped drinking or our violent parents would have stopped abusing. We may have believed that if we hadn't "asked for it," or if we hadn't been "pretty," or if we had "fought back," we wouldn't have experienced sexual abuse. Those who found themselves enjoying the contact, the illusion of love and acceptance, or the physical pleasure that may have accompanied sexual abuse, feel even more guilty and worthless: They suppose that they have no right to "complain" or that they were "to blame" because they "willingly participated."

Many of us still condemn ourselves for our "acting out," our rebellion against the unreasonable or impossible demands and standards of home. Sometimes our rebellion involved nothing more than bizarre clothes and loud music. Sometimes, however, it was not so innocent, and had destructive consequences. Many Adult Children turned to drugs or alcohol to numb the pain of family dysfunction, or to promiscuous sexual relationships in their search for the love that was not to be found at home. Many became pregnant, and struggle today with their resentment of an unwanted child, or their guilt over a teenage abortion. Some turned to same-sex relationships. Some turned to crime to get their parents' attention, to express their anger at life, to strike back at an uncaring society, or to find some excitement.

Many of us are terrified that our friends, family, or church will "discover" what we were like or what we once did. Many fear that they will be rejected if their past is revealed—and some Adult Children *have* been rejected by other Christians for their "sinful past." Some of us struggle today with the same temptations and compulsions that "drove" us into those behaviors in the past, and we feel guilt over our "double lives." We cannot "forgive" ourselves for what we did "back then" because we may still be doing it, or aware that we still *want* to do it.

Many of us haven't forgiven ourselves for the "kind" of person that we think we are. It isn't just that we "did" bad things—we are convinced that we must have been "terrible people" to do such things. Many of us have never forgiven ourselves for being "stupid" or "selfish" or "inconsiderate" or "irresponsible." Many of us feel worthless and unlovable, and blame ourselves for *being* worthless and unlovable.

When someone tells us that something is our fault, we believe it. Instead of taking responsibility for our *own* lives and feelings, we have accepted responsibility for everyone *else's* problems and emotions. When a spouse says, "I would be able to love you if you just tried harder to be more responsible and pleasing," we accept that demand and struggle to fulfill it. When the "love" that was promised as the "reward" for a "better performance" never comes, we assume that our performance must not have been good enough, blame ourselves, and try harder. When someone declares that we "make him so angry," we assume that *we* are responsible for that person's feelings—*and* for that person's reactions to those feelings. If someone reacts to anger with violence, we suppose that the violence was "our fault."

We may blame ourselves for ongoing problems. We blame ourselves every time we make a mistake, do something wrong, or fall back upon an "emotional medicator." We may have trouble keeping a job or earning promotions because we don't know how to call attention to our good work, or because we have trouble taking orders from authority figures. We may find it difficult to finish what we start or follow through with plans. We may procrastinate and avoid. We may have discovered that we are perpetuating dysfunctional patterns in our *own* families: That we are yelling at the kids, calling them names, neglecting their physical or emotional needs, and teaching them the same negative messages that caused us so much pain. All this simply confirms to us that we really *are* as bad as we thought we were.

Most of us have spent our lives trying to "live down" or "repay" the debt we believe that we owe others, or God, or ourselves. We try to "do better" so that we can redeem ourselves from our failures of the past. We try to "be better" so that we can redeem ourselves from our *identity* of the past. We struggle from task to task, achievement to achievement, yet never stop to take pride or pleasure in our accomplishments. Instead, we simply hope that they will somehow "compensate" for all the things that we have done wrong before. We believe that we are obligated to "make up for" the disappointment we were to others, for our mistakes, our bad behavior, our "worthlessness." We don't see how we can "forgive" ourselves until we prove that we are "worth" forgiving.

We may even believe that self-forgiveness is bad, that it "condones" our sinful nature. We believe that we need to "crucify" the flesh, not forgive its mistakes. We fear that we will "slack off" if we start *forgiving* our errors instead of struggling to "make up for them." Our Christian walk often deteriorates into a "dirt quest," in which we assume that we are called upon to hunt out and expose every little flaw, every mistake, every error in our lives—and eliminate them. But because we never run out of flaws and mistakes, we never "finish" our quest. And because our "dirt" is the only thing we focus on, it is the only thing we ever *see*.

God does not call us to a "dirt quest," no matter how "spiritual" it seems or whether it reflects the teachings of your church. God does not tell us to focus on *sin* but on *Him*. We won't find Christ in us by focusing on the *dirt* in us. He tells us to "seek first His kingdom and His righteousness, and all these things will be given to you as well." (Matt. 6:33)

"All these things" includes ourselves. We cannot find ourselves, or discover who we are, by focusing upon the mistakes, the problems, the flaws. We can find *ourselves* only when we focus upon God *first*. When we seek God's presence in our lives, when we focus on Christ in us rather than dirt in us, we can begin to move forward.

God's presence in us means that His forgiveness is also in us. We are to forgive ourselves just as we are to forgive everyone else in our lives, because God has forgiven *our* sins along with everyone else's. We must come to terms with what we find so bad and unforgivable about ourselves,and *forgive* those things. We must forgive our past mistakes—accepting them as mistakes, but declaring that they are no longer the foundation of our future.

We must realize that since God has forgiven us, we can no longer hold against *ourselves* a debt that He has already paid. When God says our debt is canceled, it is *canceled.* We cannot "refuse" payment because we think we don't "deserve" payment; instead, it is our very unworthiness that makes this payment so valuable and powerful.

When God says you are forgiven, you are *forgiven.* When God says you are free, you are *free.* When God says you no longer "owe" anything for the past, you no longer *owe* anything. You no longer have to work hard to "make up" for past mistakes. You no longer have to "keep yourself in line" by "kicking yourself" for things that happened years ago (or even hours ago). Nothing more is desired, required, or owed.

If we attempt to believe, or act upon, any other "reality," we are calling God's Word a lie, and counteracting the power and redemption of His gift in our lives. When we choose to become "imitators of God," we choose to walk in His forgiveness: Not just the forgiveness we know He calls us to show to others, but the forgiveness that He has already provided in our own lives.

# - 8 -

# "God's Guide to Healthy Relationships"

*If anyone says, "I love God," yet hates his brother, he is a liar. For anyone who does not love his brother, whom he has seen, cannot love God, whom he has not seen. And He has given us this command: Whoever loves God must also love his brother. Everyone who believes that Jesus is the Christ is born of God, and everyone who loves the Father loves His child as well. This is how we know that we love the children of God: by loving God and carrying out His commands. (1 John 4:20-5:2)*

OUR RECOVERY PROCESS often *begins* with the discovery that we grew up in unhealthy families that taught us dysfunctional beliefs and coping strategies. As we seek ways to undo the effects of what we experienced and what we were taught, we often discover that some of our *current* relationships are unhealthy as well. Once we learn how to recognize "loving" behaviors vs. "unloving" behaviors, we often find—to our shock and dismay—that many of the latter are very present in our closest relationships.

We may find that unloving behaviors have been practiced against us, and we *may* find that we are practicing them in our families.

We *want* "healthy" relationships. But we never learned how to "do" healthy relationships. Relationships rich in love, communication, honesty, and acceptance were not "modeled" in our homes. Nor are they taught in school, and we aren't likely to find that many "role models" of healthy relationships in the world or in the media. We want things to get better—in our relationships with our spouses, our friends, our parents, our children—but we don't know *how to make them better*.

Fortunately for us, the Bible has plenty to say on the subject of healthy relationships. It is, after all, the instruction book for "love"—and God does not simply tell us to *love* our neighbor without also telling us *how*.

There isn't enough room in this book to explore *all* the scriptures that apply to building and maintaining healthy, loving relationships. The book of Colossians, however, contains a chapter that reads almost like a course outline for "Relationships 101." When we put the skills described in these verses to use in our own lives, our relationships will heal and prosper. In addition, as we become more familiar with these patterns and characteristics of "healthy" relationships, we will become better able to recognize when *others* are not acting in a loving or healthy fashion toward *us*.

• **"But now you must rid yourselves of all such things as these: anger, rage, malice, slander, and filthy language from your lips."** (Col. 3:8) Most of us grew up with an unhealthy dose of *all* of these elements in our home life. We often learned to take anger, rage, malice, slander, and filthy language *for granted* as "normal" elements of a relationship. We aren't surprised when people talk to us in this way or treat us in this way; we have come to *expect* it.

Yet these are the elements that poison a relationship. Love does not survive intact when these elements are present. The more we experience anger or malice or slander, the more we hurt, the more we pull away from the person who is practicing them, and the more our love dies and is replaced with emptiness and pain.

Anger is the result of unresolved problems and hurts that linger beneath the surface of a relationship. Rage is the result of anger that has been allowed to build up until the original causes are forgotten; all that is left is a burning desire to lash out, perhaps violently. Slander is the same as name-calling and labeling; it is a lie about who and what you are, and brings nothing but hurt feelings (and sometimes the desire to "hurt back"). Malice is the result of unforgiveness; instead of *working out* a problem, malice is a way of deliberately *taking out* problems on another, in a way that is calculated to hurt. Filthy language, when used against us, makes us feel worthless and contaminated—and when we use it ourselves, we feel dirty and guilty.

It is no coincidence that "anger" is listed first in this scripture, because *anger* is the *root* of all the other "proscribed" behaviors. Anger leads to rage, malice, slander, and filthy language. When we do not deal with the anger, we will ultimately have to deal with its various unpleasant "children."

This does not mean that one can *never* get angry in a healthy relationship. In fact, it means just the opposite. Paul writes, " 'In your anger do not sin': Do not let the sun go down while you are still angry, and do not give the devil a foothold." (Eph. 4:26-27) When we repress anger, "stuff it," or pretend it isn't there, we let the sun "go down" on that anger many times—because we aren't doing anything to *get rid of it*. If anger cannot be *expressed* in a relationship, or expressed *safely*, then it will simply build up—and ultimately lead to the consequences described above. When we begin by dealing with anger, we "cut off" the opportunity for all of those other things to grow and "choke" our relationship.

We can resolve anger by applying the seven-step plan described in Chapter Six. This includes recognizing that we are angry, accepting that anger, and finding a way to resolve the problems that *cause* it. As long as we "sleep" on anger, we give the devil a foothold: We stew and simmer and remind ourselves of our hurts, until anger gives birth to all those other things.

In a healthy relationship, both parties must be able to express their anger without fear of reprisal or rejection. If one or both parties are "forbidden" to express, or even to *have*, anger, the relationship will suffer. For a relationship to thrive, anger must be dealt with, not as a way to control another person, but as a key to underlying issues.

While children are expected to "honor their parents," they, too, have a right to feel anger—and to express it in a healthy fashion.

Many of our own troubles were the result of being denied the right to have or express feelings. One way that we can ensure that our children learn healthier coping skills—and to actually *reduce* the amount of anger they experience—is to make sure that they are given the right that was taken away from us.

It is also important for *us* to realize that there is no such thing as an "anger-free parent." Children arouse anger in even the most mild-mannered of parents. When our children become irritable and irritating, break our favorite possessions, spill grape juice on the white carpet, and rub Ben-Gay on the cat, we are going to get angry. This is normal. The danger is allowing that anger to accumulate, until it is likely to explode as rage, or emerge as name-calling and "slander." Our children do *not* have a responsibility to "control" our anger *for* us—as we may have learned to "manage" the feelings of our *own* parents. When we grant our children the opportunity to grow up "healthy," we assume the responsibility of resolving our feelings.

Many Adult Children wonder whether it is a form of "slander" to "accuse" one's parents of being dysfunctional. In this situation, it is important to remember that "slander" is a form of "lying." We can express the truth without accusing our families of being "parents from the pit." We are told, "Do not rebuke an older man harshly, but exhort him as if he were your father." (1 Tim. 5:1) We can discuss our issues without resorting to slander, name-calling, or filthy language. Only the truth brings honor—to our parents, ourselves, or God.

- **"Do not lie to each other..."** (Col. 3:9) This instruction is more complex than it sounds. While we may already realize that it is better not to "lie" about where we are going or what we are doing, or about how much money we spent or how the car got dented, there are other areas in which "lying" has become almost second nature.

Most of us have learned that it is safer *not* to be "honest" about our opinions, feelings, needs, desires, interests, and even our personality. We have been rejected or condemned in the past for revealing "who we are." Yet a *healthy* relationship *requires* honesty in these areas—no matter how threatening that honesty seems.

When we attempt to "deceive" another about who we are or what we think, that person does not actually have a relationship with *us*. He has a relationship with an *image*—with an unreal person. We are, in a sense, defrauding others of the right to associate with *us* rather than with our *masks*. Though we may believe, especially in the early stages of recovery, that "to know us is to hate us," until we *allow* people to know us, we can never fully experience the joy and support of a genuinely healthy relationship. It is a risk—but it is a necessary risk.

Honesty also means being able to admit that we are wrong, that we made a mistake, that we are at fault, or that we don't know the answer. These are also areas in which we may have experienced condemnation in the past. We have not learned to expect *forgiveness* for our mistakes, so we are afraid to *admit* them. Yet a truly healthy relationship is one in which both parties are free to *make* mistakes without having to live in the fear that a mistake may destroy the relationship.

It is also important to be able to tell the truth about our past. Some of us have found that our friends and loved ones "don't want to hear" about the wounds of our childhood. They want us to "put it all behind us and move on." Some of us are afraid to reveal some of the things that we did as teenagers, or even in later years, for fear that we will be condemned for our past even today. We fear that our friends will leave us if they discover that we are "that kind of person," or that our spouse will lose respect for us. Yet "honesty" must be applied retroactively: If we have to lie about who we *were*, then a part of us is being excluded from the relationship.

We must be equally willing to *accept* honesty from our friends, family members, and partners. Sometimes we want to *be* honest, but we don't really want to hear how the other person is *reacting* to that honesty. If a relationship is to be healthy, we must also give our partners the opportunity to express *their* feelings, reactions, opinions, and thoughts. We must give them a chance to tell us their dreams and goals, as well as their fears and concerns. When both parties in a relationship realize that they do not have to "lie," the truth sets them "free" to *have* a relationship.

Children deserve our honesty as well. Some parents believe that they must never admit that they made a mistake, or that they were wrong, to their children. Some believe that they must be "pillars of strength," never revealing their emotions to their children. Generally, however, an honest apology can do far more for a relationship than attempting to con a child into believing that you are "God." When we are honest about *our* feelings, our children feel more free to express *theirs*. When we can admit a mistake, our children feel safer in coming to us with *their* problems. When we reveal to our children that we are human, like they are, they begin to realize that they don't have to become "perfect" to please us.

Honesty is an important part of Christian fellowship. You are not only *entitled*, but *encouraged* to express your true feelings and thoughts to God. He will never condemn us for being truthful.

Being honest with God, however, is sometimes easier than being honest with other Christians. All too often, we believe that we must keep a "Sunday smile" on our face, and never reveal that we are troubled or that we have difficulties in our lives. We often believe that we must display the "right" emotions, the right degree of joy and enthusiasm, and the right shade of "holiness" when we are around other Christians. If we cannot cry without having five people rush up to "cast out" our "negative emotions," if we cannot grieve without being accused of "lack of faith," if we are rejected when we confess a sin, or if we cannot express a concern about a service or sermon, we are in the wrong place. Many fellowships are more concerned with presenting a surface illusion of perfection than with dealing with the real hurts of real people. If honesty is not possible in your fellowship, you are *not* being offered a healthy relationship by that particular portion of the "body of Christ."

• **"Here there is no Greek or Jew, circumcised or uncircumcised, barbarian, Scythian, slave or free, but Christ is all, and is in all."** (Col. 3:11) There may not be any "uncircumcised barbarians" in your family—or you may feel as though there are. What this verse tells us, however, is that there is no place in a relationship for divisions. Relationships are sustained by equality, not by hierarchies based upon as race, sex, age, education, income, family connections, or any other factor.

This means that a bank executive is not "superior" to an auto mechanic. Wage earners are not "better" than homemakers. A partner with a Ph.D. does not have the right to treat a partner without as an "intellectual inferior." The person who earns more money does not earn more "privileges" along with it.

God deals with us as individuals, not in terms of "roles." When we deal with one another in the same way, our relationships will be significantly strengthened. When we perceive ourselves (and our friends and loved ones and children) as individuals rather than "husband" or "daughter" or "mother," we become able to take advantage of *all* our resources. We stop worrying about what a "good parent" or "good spouse" would do, and begin to explore what each of us is best *able* to do.

The most successful relationships are those in which tasks, interests, and interactions are based not upon artificial distinctions, but upon the strengths, weaknesses, and interests of everyone involved. Relationships work when everyone has an equal share of responsibility *and* freedom, when people are not divided between "givers" and "takers" but share the "give and take" instead. In such a relationship, people begin to mesh like the pieces of a puzzle, finding ways to fit together according to their Creator's design, rather than being "forced" to fit, awkwardly, into an artificial pattern of man's making. Everyone has the opportunity to be appreciated for what they *contribute* rather than condemned for *not* doing what someone *thinks* they should do.

In a healthy relationship, if a husband loves to cook and a wife loves to tinker with cars, these strengths and interests are seen as part of God's design rather than "contrary to nature." What matters is that the cooking and the car repairs get *done*, not by *whom* they get done. The Bible doesn't tell us whether the Scythians or the barbarians are "responsible" for "kitchen duty" or "lawn patrol;" it tells us that in God's eyes, there are no distinctions.

• **"Therefore, as God's chosen people, holy and dearly loved, clothe yourselves with compassion, kindness, humility, gentleness and patience."** (Col. 3:12) Many of us have never been treated as though we were "holy" or "dearly loved." When we realize that every member of a relationship is "chosen," "holy," and "dearly loved" by *God*, it can make a tremendous difference in our *own* perspective. When we realize that we *also* fit into that category, it can make an even greater difference in the behavior that we are willing to *accept* from others.

Some of us have never experienced the aspects of a relationship listed in this verse. We may even wonder what, exactly, they *are*.

"Compassion" means a genuine, sincere concern about what is going on in the life of another person. When we have compassion, the needs and feelings of another are as important to us *as our own*.

This is an important distinction. Compassion does *not* mean "codependency." It does not mean that we put *aside* all our needs, feelings, and desires so that we can be the slaves of another. Jesus was compassionate, but He was not "mastered" by any man. Compassion has the well-being of others at heart, but it does not exclude our *own* well-being. When we have compassion, we "serve"—but out of love, not out of fear or obligation. We have the *best* interests of another at heart, but we do not jump to respond to *selfish* interests. Indeed, when we are moved by compassion, we may act in ways that an *unhealthy* person would prefer that we did *not* act: We may arrange an intervention for an alcoholic family member, for example, or make sure that a family member gets help for a problem that he would prefer to ignore.

"Kindness" means a desire to choose actions and words that are helpful and uplifting, rather than discouraging or hurtful. I have seen many relationships in which this simple quality is completely lacking—and the atmosphere of the home is filled with tension and strife. All too often, partners in a dysfunctional relationship become involved in a sort of competition to see how much kindness they can *extract* from the other person, and how *little* they will be forced to offer in return.

Kindness is a choice. It means that we *choose* to speak kindly, act considerately, and treat our friends and loved ones with respect—*even if we are not receiving kindness in return*. It means doing the little things, like bringing your spouse a cup of tea or offering him a backrub after a long day, or baking your friend a cake, or driving an elderly parent to the doctor. Once again, it does not mean slavery; it means making wise, considerate choices. It means refraining from saying the angry, hurtful words that may automatically spring to your lips, and finding a more caring way to express your feelings. Kindness becomes a habit as we learn how to make kind choices rather than angry or defensive ones.

"Humility" is also a rarity in relationships. Many of us have been treated as though we were the inferior partner in all our relationships—even our relationships with our children. Many relationships turn into power struggles when "humility" is confused with "humiliation." Genuine humility, however, does not "put us down" or denigrate our actions or feelings. It is simply the choice, on both sides of the relationship, of not trying to be "first" or "on top" in all things. It means listening instead of insisting upon being heard, hearing the other person's side of an issue, accepting another person's feelings and opinions, and not worrying about being "right" all the time. It means being able to admit a mistake, being able to apologize for hurting someone's feelings, being able to say that one was wrong. It means not competing for attention—but it does *not* mean turning oneself into a self-effacing mouse.

"Gentleness" applies to every word or action we bring to a relationship. It applies to what we say: Gentle words bring healing and promote change in a relationship, while bitter words tend to cause others to "dig in" and defend their position. A gentle tone of voice tells another that we are willing to listen—even though we also have a right to be heard. A gentle touch tells another that we respect their body, their physical feelings. A gentle silence (as opposed to a cold silence) can tell others that they can express their emotions without fear of rejection or reprisal. We can even "rebuke" gently; gentle words of correction go farther with children than harsh shouts of anger. Indeed, we may discover surprising results when we try the "gentle" approach to children who have become "mother-deaf" to reprimands and threats.

"Patience" is a vital ingredient in any relationship. Patience means realizing that others may not do what we want them to do, or be what we want them to be, *when we want it*. It is tempting to ask the world to change at our command—but in reality, people change in God's season, not our own. Many of us have been the victims of impatience in others who want *us* to change according to *their* schedule—and some of us pass this expectation along.

One woman was "impatient" to find the "right man" and get married. As she got older, she felt the years slipping by. At last she "found" him. He was not a Christian, which worried her, but to her delight, he got "saved" a few weeks before the wedding.

A few months later she was ready to walk out. Her new husband wasn't "walking with the Lord" as strongly as she thought he should be. He hadn't "changed" as quickly as she expected him to. She had hoped that salvation would miraculously turn her "right man" into the "perfect man"—and it wasn't happening. She was out of patience.

Patience doesn't mean that we don't have the right to express our concerns and feelings. When we turn those concerns into *expectations*, however, and then blame others for not *fulfilling* those expectations, we are practicing unhealthy relationship behaviors. Patience means that we choose not to continually nag, remind, demand, fuss, pressure, and complain. It does not mean that we accept unhealthy *behaviors* from another, only that we must realize that we cannot change others according to our desires and our schedule.

- **"Bear with each other and forgive whatever grievances you may have against one another. Forgive as the Lord forgave you."** (Col. 3:13) People are not perfect; if they were, the Bible wouldn't tell us to "bear with" one another. When we accept the imperfections and "quirks" of those we care about—just as we want them to accept our own—we are fulfilling the command to "bear with each other."

To keep our relationships healthy, we may have to "bear with" our spouse's desire to watch sports events or soap operas. We may have to "bear with" a child's attempts to "cook breakfast for Mommy" that turn the kitchen into a disaster zone. We may have to "bear with" a friend's taste in reading or movies. We may have to "bear with" our parents' conviction that they know everything about everything. "Bearing with" does not mean putting up with unhealthy, inappropriate, or abusive behavior. It means accepting (or at least tolerating) the differences, foibles, and flaws that make each of us unique and human.

Sometimes issues arise that we can't "bear with"—and these blossom into "grievances." Grievances, conflicts, and disagreements arise in every relationship. People disappoint one another, let each other down, and hurt one another—even when they are doing their best *not* to. No one can be "all" that we need, and we can never be "everything" to another. These are not signs that a relationship is *unhealthy*. The health of a relationship depends upon how those grievances are *resolved*.

We may keep quiet about grievances because we are afraid of how others will react if we bring them up. We may not be open to the grievances of others. Or, we may have drawn "lines" in a relationship that define what *can* be discussed and what "*can't*."

Some couples, for example, believe firmly that they should never "bring work home." All too often, however, this simply means that neither partner has any way of discussing or relieving the tensions of the office in a safe, loving environment. A compassionate partner *cares* about *every* aspect of your life; you are still that person's partner even when you are at work. The stress of the office affect us as *people*, not as "workers." As *people*, we bring those effects home. When our relationships include the opportunity to express what is going on in *every* area of our lives, we will gain strength and healing *for* every area of our lives.

Our relationships suffer when we attempt to "compartmentalize" our problems. We may consider some issues "personal problems" that need to be resolved individually. We may consider others "office problems" that need to be resolved elsewhere. We may expect one member of the relationship to be exclusively responsible for "financial matters" and another to be exclusively responsible for "child discipline." When we remove these barriers and find ways within the relationship to handle *all* "grievances" and problems and issues *together*, we will discover that those grievances begin to disappear.

Many of us haven't had much practice at resolving grievances—perhaps because we don't know how, or perhaps because our partner has never been willing to do so. Resolution can only be accomplished when bitterness, malice, defensiveness, and condemnation are put aside. It is important not to attempt to "deflect" a grievance by bringing up a "counter" grievance. Sometimes, a partner will *deliberately* use these techniques to *avoid* having to deal with the real issue; the key to success is refusing to be discouraged by "delaying tactics."

Forgiveness is a vital part of grievance resolution. Grievances cannot be resolved by placing blame or making accusations. It doesn't matter who is "wrong;" all that matters is finding a way to *solve the problem*. To solve a grievance, both parties must decide that the relationship itself is more important than pride, than being right, or than being the "victim." Sometimes all that is needed is a partner's willingness to listen, to let the other person's feelings be heard and accepted. Sometimes a grievance can *only* be resolved through forgiveness—as when we have grievances against parents whose dysfunctional behavior caused us harm. We cannot change the past, and our parents may be unwilling to address or change their dysfunctional behavior. We *can* choose to forgive our parents for old grievances. If, however, parents who are still *unhealthy* persist in creating *new* grievances, we may also have to choose to put some *healthy distance* in that relationship.

Grievances are not "resolved" if they can be brought up over and over again. Resolving grievances means "tearing up" that record of wrongs—including your own. Few things are as destructive to a relationship as unforgiven issues and buried resentments—and few things are as healing as unconditional forgiveness.

- **"And over all these virtues put on love, which binds them all together in perfect unity."** (Col. 3:14) All of the relationship skills described in these verses are *based* on the actions of love. Love is the *foundation* of any healthy relationship. When we learn to walk in love, the rest becomes much easier.

While we are *learning* to walk in love, however, we can sometimes be susceptible to "emotional blackmail." "Emotional blackmail" is anything that *takes advantage* of our efforts to be loving.

A warning sign of "emotional blackmail" is any statement that sounds remotely like, "If you loved me, then you would..." In the earlier stages of recovery, we are still vulnerable to demands that we "prove" our love, or accusations that we are *not* "loving enough." We often encounter "emotional blackmail" from family members who are accustomed to manipulating us through guilt and intimidation, and who don't approve of any recovery process that makes us less susceptible to these forms of unhealthy control.

When we walk in *genuine* love, we will be less likely to respond to someone's stated *desires* and *demands*, and more likely to pay attention to their actual *needs*. Sometimes, what a person *needs* is the last thing that he actually *wants*. When we learn to walk in love, we will begin to learn how to *stop* "giving in" to desires that actually *conflict* with a person's genuine *needs*.

This may be easier to understand when we think about the best way to "love" a child. Suppose, for example, that your child angrily declares, "Mom, if you really love me—and if you want me to *love you*—you'll give me chocolate ice cream for dinner, and you won't make me eat those nasty vegetables." Most of us would not yield to that child's request (though a few of us might!). We know that the child's *desire* or *demand* for ice cream is in direct conflict with that child's *need* for healthy food—and also with the child's need to understand that he is not always going to get what he wants just because he yells for it.

Nor would we be "acting in love" if we chose to allow a child to watch television all night while we completed that child's homework. While the child might enjoy being indulged (though overly indulged children are rarely truly happy children), we know that the child *needs* to have the experience of learning, and of learning *how* to learn. We know that learning responsibility and handling his own tasks is an important part of growing up, and we know that we would not be truly "loving" if we robbed our children of that opportunity—no matter how much our children might prefer it.

While we can clearly see the negative effects of yielding to a child's "emotional blackmail," we often give in to the same types of requests from adults. Perhaps we believe that adults "know" what is good for them—but the sad truth is that many do not. Many adults, instead, deliberately seek relationships with people who can be coaxed, coerced, or bullied into doing what they *want* rather than what they *need*. We may experience this kind of blackmail from our friends, parents or other family members, and spouses.

We do not "act in love" when we enable an alcoholic to drink, or when we call a spouse's boss with an "excuse" for why the spouse can't make it to work that day. We do not "act in love" when we allow a spouse to shift *all* the responsibilities and burdens of running a home and raising children onto *us*. We do not "act in love" when we allow a partner or friend to avoid taking responsibility for his own feelings or actions. We do not "act in love" when we allow a person to commit inappropriate or abusive actions against us. Instead, we are literally "spoiling" that person, removing that person's need to take personal responsibility for his or her life, and ruining our *own* lives in the process.

When we learn to act in love, we will also learn to recognize whether or not we are *receiving* love. If someone says, "I will love you if..." or "I *would* love you more if only *you* could be a better person," that person is not acting in love. Love is not a "reward" for good behavior. If someone says, "If you loved me, you would..." that person is not acting in love; instead, that person is asking us to "buy" his or her affections. If someone attempts to manipulate or intimidate us "in the name of love," that person is not acting in love—for love does not manipulate, intimidate, accuse, control, or condemn. Love is responsible, beneficial, and healing. Anything else is a counterfeit that destroys the unity of a relationship.

• **"Let the peace of Christ rule in your hearts, since as members of one body you were called to peace. And be thankful."** (Col. 3:15) One of the meanings of "peace" is an absence of warfare, a cease-fire, a lack of hostilities. A peaceful relationship is one in which both parties consider *resolution* more important than *victory*.

"Peace" often means the decision to yield to another. I once knew a couple whose lives were filled with "bickering"—not fights or open warfare, but an endless exchange of "sniping." The game in this household was to see how much one could get the *other* person to do, and how little one could be "forced" to do oneself. The wife might "win" the first round—persuading her husband to get up from the table and fetch her a bottle of soda from the storage room downstairs. Then her husband would retaliate with "round two"—scolding his wife for failing to offer her guests something to drink. As these exchanges flew back and forth one evening, with each "side" smirking a little over every victory and sulking over every defeat, my husband and I began to understand the meaning of the verse, "Better a dry crust with peace and quiet than a house full of feasting, with strife." (Prov. 17:1)

There can be no peace in a relationship that is a struggle for power or control. There can be no *real* peace in a relationship in which each side has marked off personal "territory"—the TV for the husband and the kitchen for the wife, for example. There may be no "hostility" as long as everyone "respects the lines," but this is not peace, it is only "detente." There can be no real peace in a relationship that involves a "ruler" and a "servant;" this is subjugation. There can be no real peace in a relationship that is not based upon equality.

Peace is not easy to achieve or maintain, but it is possible. It involves the destruction of artificial barriers, boundaries, and rules. It involves the ability of all parties to communicate freely and honestly. It involves the decision of *all* parties to put the *relationship* ahead of *self*—not in an unhealthy way, but out of a sincere desire to make the relationship *functional*. Peace can't be achieved "unilaterally;" it is the result of people working *together*.

Another kind of peace is "lack of anxiety." We are told, "Do not be anxious about anything, but in everything, by prayer and petition, with thanksgiving, present your requests to God. And the peace of God, which transcends all understanding, will guard your hearts and your minds in Christ Jesus." (Phil. 4:6-7)

Relationships often involve many worries, concerns, and fears. We worry over money, over what to say to one another, about what the other person is thinking, about how the children are doing, about how external problems will affect the relationship. Some of us actually *worry* when everything is going *well*, because it seems "too good to be true."

We often confuse "worry" with "concern." Concern is justified; problems *do* exist, and we may not know how to resolve them. "Worry" and "anxiety," however, are habits; they are the results of "what if's" and "if-then's" that have no answers, and therefore no resolution. "Worry" is not an emotion, it is a *choice*, a decision to "fixate" on a problem instead of trusting God for the solution.

In a relationship filled with fussing and fretting, peace cannot prevail. When we worry, we cannot experience the peace of God that "guards our hearts." Peace comes only when we acknowledge our concerns, acknowledge our helplessness in some cases and our responsibility in others, and allow God to guide us to the solution.

This verse concludes with the "throwaway" line, "And be thankful!" A great deal of health is restored to relationships when we restore *thankfulness* to those relationships.

All too often, we become caught up in the habit of focusing upon what is wrong, upon what irritates us about another person, upon the problems and difficulties, upon the disappointments and disagreements. We lose sight of what we originally "liked" about the other person in the first place. We lose sight of his or her positive qualities and contributions. As the troubles accumulate, they soon consume all our time and energy, and we wonder what we have to be thankful *about*.

Relationships grow strong when we begin to seek out and focus upon what we are *thankful* for—in the relationship, in the other person, and in life in general. Instead of being upset that our friend was ten minutes late to pick us up, we may be thankful that she came at all. Instead of being irritated at our husband's love of sports, we may be thankful that he is willing to help around the house when he is *not* watching the game. Instead of being upset by our children's taste in music or clothes, we may be thankful that they are healthy and happy.

As we "practice" thankfulness, we will begin to discover more and more things in our lives to be thankful *for*. We learn to seek out the benefits instead of the difficulties, the opportunities instead of the constraints. We may even learn how to focus upon the things in *ourselves* that we are thankful for, instead of only those things that we consider "in need of improvement." As we focus upon thanks, we often discover that while our problems don't necessarily go away, they start to look much smaller.

• **"Let the word of Christ dwell in you richly as you teach and admonish one another with all wisdom..."** (Col. 3:16) I have encountered more than one person who at least *thought* that the Word of Christ "dwelt" in him—because he (or she) could recite that Word, chapter and verse, in response to any circumstance or situation. These people often took to heart the command to "admonish one another," and "admonished" at any opportunity.

For some reason, no one really wanted to be around them for very long. These people generally interpreted the rejection they received as "being persecuted for their faith," but I think something different was involved.

When the Word truly "dwells in us richly," we don't become walking "recordings" of the Bible. James tells us, "Do not merely listen to the word, and so deceive yourselves. Do what it says. Anyone who listens to the word but does not do what it says is like a man who looks at his face in a mirror and, after looking at himself, goes away and immediately forgets what he looks like. But the man who looks intently into the perfect law that gives freedom, and continues to do this, not forgetting what he has heard, but doing it—he will be blessed in what he does. If anyone considers himself religious and yet does not keep a tight rein on his tongue, he deceives himself and his religion is worthless." (James 1:22-26)

The Bible is not a device that was given to *some* people so that they could control *others*. When we "admonish," we need to remember to keep a tight rein on our tongue, and be sure that we admonish *with wisdom*. This means that one can't simply rush around waving a Bible and telling everyone, "Well, you *know* that this is what you are supposed to do, because this is what the Bible says, and if you don't do it, you are sinning and God won't protect you from the consequences." That is not admonishing *or* wisdom; it is simply a religious way to hurt people and to act self-righteous.

If you have been *experiencing* this sort of treatment from others, you are not being admonished "wisely." You are being controlled.

One woman was told by her church that all her problems would "go away" if she would just "stop sinning." Her *sin* was that of having a sexual relationship with a boyfriend. Her *problems*, however, including issues of severe physical abuse from a parent, a traumatically distorted self-image, an eating disorder that she had developed years before becoming involved with her boyfriend, and a desire to commit suicide that had been with her since adolescence. It was highly unlikely that these problems would "go away" if she simply "gave up the sin." Wisdom, however, might have helped this woman (and those around her) understand that her sin was the *result* of her problems rather than the other way around. When we admonish, we need to be sure that we have the wisdom of God instead of a handful of quotations.

When the Word dwells in our hearts, our hearts will be filled, not with "chapter and verse," but with love, compassion, truth, and the desire to encourage. We will seek the freedom of others rather than their bondage. We will choose kindness over an approach that may bring pain; we will choose tenderness over anger; we will choose forgiveness over condemnation. We will, eventually, find ourselves doing these things more or less *automatically*, because the more we know and understand the truth, the more that truth becomes *part of us*. It is no longer something that we "obey" or "act on" but something that we *are*. The Word, dwelling richly in us, becomes a basic part of our character. We don't need "scripture references" to "back up" what we say, because we will desire to *speak the truth*, and say nothing that *contradicts* God's Word.

- **"And whatever you do, whether in word or deed, do it all in the name of the Lord Jesus, giving thanks to God the Father through Him."** (Col. 3:17) It is difficult to imagine shouting, "You are a stupid idiot—in the name of Jesus." It is difficult to imagine acting maliciously toward another "in the name of Jesus." When we commit *all* our actions to the Lord, and consciously think of doing them "in His name," we will take a close look at *everything* we do.

We will also take a closer look at what is done to *us*. If we are being abused, we need to ask ourselves if abuse can be justified through the name of Jesus. Can someone strike another "in God's name"? Not according to scripture! God does not condone unkindness, criticism, accusations, condemnations, unforgiveness, or any form of abuse. If it cannot be committed "in His name," it has no place in any relationship.

God does not "bless" sinful behaviors under any circumstances. He does not condone violence or abuse, even when it is committed in the name of "discipline." He does not condone rape, even when it is committed in the marriage bed. He does not condone robbery—whether one is stealing a person's material goods or their hope, confidence, or self-esteem. He does not say that some behaviors are "OK" just because they occur within a marriage or family.

On the other hand, it is encouraging to know that God *does* look with approval upon our compassion, our understanding, our loving kindness. We often suppose that God only "notices" those things that we do *wrong*—but He *also* notices those things that we do *right*. When we do "all" in the name of Jesus, we will "then... be able to test and approve what God's will is—His good, pleasing and perfect will." (Rom. 12:2)

- **"Wives, submit to your husbands, as is fitting in the Lord."** (Col. 3:18) Like many Adult Children, this verse has been grievously abused. It has been used to "justify" immoral, sinful, intimidating and abusive behaviors, by rationalizing that it is a wife's duty to "submit" to such behaviors. It has been used by husbands who forget that they are God's *representatives* and start acting as though they were His *substitutes* instead. It has also been used by wives who don't want to confront or change abusive behaviors, including the abuse of their own children.

If this verse is taken out of context, as though the verses that precede it don't exist or have no meaning, it *could* be misinterpreted. It could be used to imply that a wife is "property," with no rights or will of her own. It could be used to imply that a husband is "God," and that his will is "law," no matter how abusive that will may be. These implications have been drawn, and used against people, but they are wrong. We can *only* reach this sort of conclusion if we decide to *ignore all the rest of the Bible*, including the scriptures that directly surround this verse. This verse does *not* stand alone; it stands in relationship to the rest of the chapter.

Paul has just given us, in this chapter alone, nine verses emphasizing the importance of love, patience, kindness, humility, and holiness. It is hardly likely that he is *now* declaring that these instructions somehow "don't apply" in the husband/wife relationship. If they *do* apply, then the dreaded "submission" verse must be interpreted *in the context* of the rest of Paul's instructions about loving and godly relationships.

Paul provides more explicit instructions on this topic in his letter to the Ephesians, which authorities believe was written at about the same time. He writes, "Submit to one another out of reverence for Christ. Wives, submit to your husbands as to the Lord. For the husband is the head of the wife as Christ is the head of the church, His body, of which He is the Savior. Now as the church submits to Christ, so also wives should submit to their husbands in everything. Husbands, love your wives, just as Christ loved the church and gave Himself up for her to make her holy, cleansing her by the washing with water through the word, and to present her to Himself as a radiant church, without stain or wrinkle or any other blemish, but holy and blameless. In this same way, husbands ought to love their wives as their own bodies. He who loves his wife loves himself. After all, no one ever hated his own body, but he feeds and cares for it, just as Christ does the church..." (Eph. 5:21-29)

A closer examination of these scriptures shows that while the wife is told, twice, to "submit" to her husband "as to the Lord," the bulk of the admonishment is given to the *husband*. In fact, the wife appears to have the easier "burden" in this relationship. While she is called upon to "submit," the husband is given a detailed list of his responsibilities as an *imitator of Christ*. He is called upon to be like Jesus, to be God's representative in the home as Jesus is God's representative to the church. That is an awesome responsibility.

Jesus does not "bully" the church. He does not impose unreasonable or impossible demands. He does not control the church through intimidation or manipulation. He does not threaten. He does not condemn or accuse. He does not use words of sarcasm or insult. He does not call His church names, like "worthless" or "stupid." He does not keep His church locked in bondage, but promises freedom and peace. He does not ask the church to "earn" His love by "doing more." He does not tell the church that He "might" love it if it could only do what was required of it. He does not withhold love or communication as a form of punishment. Most of all, He does not abuse—nor does He require the church to "submit" to abusive behaviors that destroy relationships, such as gambling or drinking or pornography or infidelity.

Instead, Jesus is faithful. He acts in love 100% of the time—which means that He brings *all* of the components of love described in 1 Cor. 13 into that relationship. He speaks words of comfort and encouragement. He uplifts and supports. He protects and defends. He forgives and redeems. He sanctifies and saves. He shares His peace, provides His authority and power, and washes us with His own blood. Because of this, His church is radiant.

This is what a husband is called upon to do for his wife.

A husband cannot "present a wife to himself as radiant" if he abuses her, puts her down, demoralizes her, discourages her, hurts her, controls her, manipulates her, or terrorizes her. Jesus does not treat the church as "second-class citizens," and a wife is not a second-class citizen in her own home.

If a woman wonders whether she ought to "submit" to abusive behaviors, one question to consider is whether one can abuse "in the name of Jesus." Wives are called to submit "as to the Lord." This does *not* mean submitting to sin; it means just the opposite. God will *never* call you to sin; thus, He will never ask you to *submit* to sin, no matter what. Submission to abuse is submission to sin. Most of us realize that it would be "wrong" to agree to rob a bank for our husband just because we are supposed to "submit." Neither are we called to submit to any other behavior that God condemns.

Jesus is the head of the church, and the head brings life. The husband is to be the head of the household in the same way. If there is no life in the head, there will be no life in the relationship. The "head" of a body is physically connected to that body; what the body experiences, the head experiences. The head is not some sort of detached "boss" member, separate from the consequences of its own commands. If the head commands the hand to thrust itself into the fire, the head is going to feel the pain. Husband and wife are "one flesh," and the Bible makes it clear that anyone who abuses that flesh abuses himself.

"Submission," then, is not a master/slave relationship. Indeed, the word translated as "submit" is *not* the same word used to instruct slaves to "obey" their masters or children to "obey" their parents. The relationship implied in this verse is very different. It does not imply that one person has no will or rights. It does not mean that wives are not entitled to have needs or desires—or to have those needs and desires fulfilled.

What it *does* mean is that each partner seeks to do what is in the best interest of the *relationship*, for the relationship is a "shared body." Both partners have a responsibility to contribute to and maintain the health of that body—by seeking what the will of God *is* for our "relationship bodies" and by *submitting* to that will. If we submit to any *other* will—including the destructive will of sin and the devil—we destroy the body with unhealthy behaviors.

• **"Husbands, love your wives and do not be harsh with them."** (Col. 3:19) Husbands have a tremendous responsibility in a relationship, not to be a boss or a master, but to operate in love and everything love means.

The "loving husband" is patient and kind. He is not envious or jealous of his wife's interests, friends, or individuality. He does not boast of his achievements or put down his wife's work; he does not claim to be superior out of pride. He is not rude, in word or deed. He is not self-seeking, but puts the priorities of the relationship over his desires. He does not get angry easily, and when he *is* angry, he finds healthy ways to express and resolve that anger. He keeps no records of his wife's wrongs, and does not bring up past mistakes to use against her. He does not pursue evil activities, but pursues the truth. He always protects his wife—and is never himself a source of harm or danger to her. He trusts his wife and gives her freedom; he is not jealous or suspicious, and he does not try to control her every action. He does not tear down his wife's hopes, but builds them and helps bring them to pass, nor does he give up hope on her. He perseveres through problems and tough times, standing by his wife and the relationship even when that relationship seems to be in trouble. He does his best never to fail her, let her down, or betray her. (In other words, he is a lot like God!)

It's a tough job. I doubt that *any* husband does all of these things 100% of the time. However, a husband who *tries and fails* will have a far healthier relationship than one who *fails to try*.

This burden does not rest on husbands alone, however. Wives, too, have a tremendous responsibility. One way to look at "submission" is to view a wife's behavior in the *context* of a husband's duty to "love." If a husband is called to be patient, for example, a wife has an equal responsibility to avoid deliberately *taxing* that patience. If a husband is called to be polite and gentle in his speech, a wife has an equal responsibility to avoid rudeness. If a husband is to be slow to anger, a wife has a responsibility to do her best not to *provoke* anger deliberately. If a husband is to trust, a wife has a responsibility to be *trustworthy*. Part of the wife's job of "submission" is to *help* her husband perform his job of "love." The best way to do *that*, of course, is to operate in love as well!

If one party "violates" this contract, it does not give the other party a license to do the same. If a wife fails to "submit," for example, this does not give a husband an "excuse" to "be harsh" with his wife or abuse her. Wives are not to be "beaten into submission." At the same time, a wife is not entitled to give up all attempts to be loving and kind in a relationship simply because the husband is making *no* attempt to do so. While "peace" is the result of the actions of *two* sides, it also takes two to "make a war."

• **"Children, obey your parents in everything, for this pleases the Lord."** (Col. 3:20) While wives are called to "submit," children are called to "obey." The words are not the same, because the relationship is not the same. While wives can be expected to perceive and pursue the actions that are best for the relationship (which is why marriage is a partnership), children aren't able to make those decisions. Thus they are called to *obey* those who *can*.

One way in which dysfunctional family patterns are sometimes perpetuated is by forgetting the proper relationship between parent and child. Sometimes, parents who are starved for love by their mates seek to gain love from their children. Children are often called upon to play the role of "surrogate spouse," providing Mom or Dad the love, comfort, support, and emotional sustenance that is not offered by a spouse.

When a parent "needs" the love of a child, that parent often becomes afraid of "alienating" a child's affections through discipline or normal parental demands. The parent may become unable to insist that a child complete his chores, do his homework, or show an appropriate degree of respect and good behavior in the home. While the child runs wild, disrupting the household, the parent feels helpless and powerless—and the longer the situation remains *out of control*, the more the child becomes the controlling member of the relationship.

Sometimes we are afraid to discipline or control our children because we don't want to be as unfair and abusive as our own parents were. Many Adult Children determine that they will *never* treat their children the way *they* were treated. However, because we often *have* no healthy model of child-rearing, we don't know how much "niceness" is healthy and how much is extreme. We often don't know when, or how, to say "no"—and we may feel very guilty about saying no. We often feel as though *any* form of disciplinary action is "abusive." Many Adult Children who were *over-controlled* as children become *under-controlling* as parents. It helps to realize that "discipline" (which comes from the same root as "disciple") does not mean to *punish*, but to *teach*.

Children are not supposed to "control" their parents. Obedience is the keynote of this relationship, according to the Bible. Children are not yet able to run their own lives—and when we permit them to run *ours*, everyone suffers. Ultimately, the child suffers—for the child has not learned how to have a healthy relationship or how to submit to the responsibilities and requirements of life.

This does not mean that we are to treat our children like slaves, or to rob them of all freedom, including freedom of expression. There is a fine line between requiring *obedience* and imposing *domination*. We are called upon to act in love, and in accordance with the relationship instructions described above, to our children as well as to everyone else. The primary difference in this relationship is that here, like nowhere else, the children are "subordinate." No home will be healthy if it is run by a child (or by an adult who still acts like a child, for that matter).

- **"Fathers, do not embitter your children, or they will become discouraged."** (Col. 3:21) This final instruction is the one that will interrupt the Adult Child cycle once and for all—at least in *your* household. Discouragement and fear are legacies that have been handed down from one generation to the next—but we can choose *not* to hand them on to our own children.

Some of us discover, upon entering recovery, that we have *already* been practicing dysfunctional behaviors and passing along unhealthy messages in our own families. Some Adult Children have become abusers themselves. Some have entered into dysfunction through the route of alcohol or other compulsions. When we discover that dysfunctional family issues apply not only to what we experienced but to what we *do*, we feel terribly guilty.

We may feel as though we have "ruined" our children, and fear that they have no hope of leading healthy lives because of what we have done. We may fear that they will never forgive us. We may fear that they will never be able to have healthy relationships of their own. We may condemn ourselves and punish ourselves for our mistakes. But none of this solves the problem.

What matters is not what we *have* done. That is covered by God's forgiveness. What matters is what we *choose* to do once we know *what* to do.

At any point, we can begin to practice encouragement rather than discouragement. We can begin to practice praise rather than criticism. We can begin to reward good behavior, making sure that our children see that we "notice" it, instead of recognizing and condemning only the *bad* behavior. We can respond to a "B-" with the same enthusiasm we once reserved for an "A+." We can begin to recognize progress rather than expecting overnight perfection. We can begin to employ alternatives to black-and-white and all-or-nothing thinking. We can find new ways to handle our anger, instead of exploding whenever our children do something that upsets us. We can begin to participate in our children's vibrant joy (even when it is noisy), instead of expecting our children to act like solemn "mini-adults" around the house.

We can begin to understand our children's developmental stages, and not expect more of them than they are capable of providing at their age. We can, for example, stop expecting a two-year-old to have the understanding and restraint of a child in grammar school—and we can stop treating an adolescent like a toddler. We can begin to explore what constitutes a *reasonable* level of responsibility for a child, instead of regarding our children as our maids or our therapists.

It is up to *us* to learn how to be parents. It is not up to our children to find ways to defuse our anger or comfort us in our pain. Only *we* can control how we feel—and how we *express* our feelings. It is up to us to learn, and practice, healthy relationship practices—not up to our children to "deserve" them. In this relationship, there is only *one* responsible party: You.

If you have discovered that you have practiced unhealthy parenting in the past, your task is not to try to "make up for" all the things that you have *already* done wrong. You don't have to try to be "super-good" or "super-caring" to make up for the times that you were angry (and wrong) in the past. We often suppose that we are required to "undo" all the damage that we have already done. In reality, however, it is our responsibility not to look *backward* but to move *forward*. As we learn new, healthy ways to parent, much of the damage will "undo" itself.

If we get stuck in guilt for the past, we may give our children a "weapon" to use against us. Once they know that we want to "make up" for past mistakes, they will be sure to remind us of those mistakes whenever they want something from us. We must also realize that it will take time for our children to trust, believe in, and respond to our changes in parenting style. They may not expect it to last. They may not want to give up some of the habits and behaviors that *they* have learned as a response to our parenting techniques. Change will take time, not only on our part, but on the part of our children.

It is no shame to seek out parenting classes and advice to help improve this relationship. Parenting classes are not just for "bad" parents. "Bad" parents don't *go* to that sort of class because they don't *care*. They see no reason to improve or change their behavior. Instead, parenting classes are for "good," *caring* parents who can admit, in loving humility, that they do *not* know all there is to know about parenting, and that they have a sincere desire to learn. If you choose to find such a class, you will find yourself in good and often supportive company. Think of it as choosing to *prevent* your children (or even your grandchildren) from having to shell out money for a book like this!

## Counting the Cost

As we begin to practice healthy relationship behaviors in our lives, we often hope for a miracle. We have often begun to see remarkable and wonderful changes in our own lives through recovery, and we want to share those changes with others. We want to share the joy of being *able* to interact in a healthy and loving manner, as opposed to a dysfunctional and fearful one. We want to share the "new" person that we are becoming with the people that we love.

We are often disappointed. I would like to conclude this chapter by declaring that "if you just learn how to walk in love and practice these relationship skills, the world will turn around," but it simply isn't true. As you may have guessed already from reading this chapter, it takes *two people* to make a *healthy relationship*.

Your relationships *will* change as you choose to practice these skills. In many cases, they will improve. Sometimes all it takes is for *one* person to begin to *model* loving behaviors, as well as to practice them, to create a dramatic change in a relationship. But sometimes it takes more than that.

It is very difficult to have a "healthy" relationship with an "unhealthy" person. Many of us are involved with unhealthy people—with unhealthy friends, unhealthy parents, and unhealthy spouses. If our parents were abusive, they may *still* be abusive. If our spouse is alcoholic, he or she may *still* be alcoholic. If our "friends" stayed with us only because they could get us to do whatever they wanted, they may not "like" us anymore.

When Adult Children face the fact that *other* unhealthy people may not *want* to change, they are often very discouraged. We wonder what we are doing all this *for*, if it isn't going to miraculously "transform" all our relationships. The sad truth is, God never called us to transform *other people*. He only called us to transform *ourselves*.

Others may resist that transformation. Our families have become accustomed to dealing with us as we were, not as we are becoming. We may no longer be so easy to manipulate, intimidate, or control. *Our* changes mean that our families must also learn a new set of coping skills, because the old ones no longer "work" with us. Even though the change is for the better, people tend to automatically *resist* change.

Thus you may experience pressure to "do things like you used to." If you have given up an addiction in your quest for recovery, you may be pressured to return to it—especially if it was something your friends or loved ones associated with "fun," like going out to the bar for a few beers. If you have given up "taking care of" everyone around you in an unhealthy, rescuing way, others may moan and complain and act helpless and hurt, in an effort to persuade you that they "need" you. If you have begun to express your feelings and thoughts in a healthy way, you may find that those around you aren't yet ready to listen.

When certain behaviors *work* —when they "get us what we want"—we don't give them up easily. Your friends and loved ones have developed "behaviors" that "work" with you—behaviors that get you to do what they want. When those behaviors *stop* working, people don't instantly abandon them. Instead, they tend to do *more* of the same behavior: They try harder. If a child learned to get his way by throwing temper tantrums, for example, that child isn't going to "give up" temper tantrums the first time you don't respond to them in the old way. Instead, in the beginning he is likely to throw *more* temper tantrums, and bigger ones. Those around you are likely to "press harder" at whatever they have already been doing, in the hopes that your newfound "changes" will disappear and you will be your "good old self" once again.

This is perhaps the ultimate test we face in recovery: Will we stand firm, or will we give in? We know what the *Bible* tells us to do: "Do not conform any longer to the pattern of this world, but be transformed by the renewing of your mind. Then you will be able to test and approve what God's will is—his good, pleasing and perfect will." (Rom. 12:2) But it is not always so easy to resist "conforming" to the pattern of the world, when you fear that you will *lose* those you *love* otherwise.

The Bible also makes another promise: " 'I tell you the truth,' Jesus replied, 'no one who has left home or brothers or sisters or mother or father or children or fields for me and the gospel will fail to receive a hundred times as much in this present age (homes, brothers, sisters, mothers, children and fields—and with them, persecutions) and in the age to come, eternal life.' " (Mark 10:29-30)

God *knows* that becoming "transformed" has a cost—and that cost may be people that we love. It is little consolation to realize that if those we love do *not* want us to be healthy, free, whole, or joyful, it is an indication that *they* do not genuinely love *us*. The truth is that it *hurts*—but God promises us a "return" for that pain.

The alternative is to stay where we are—but once we have begun the journey of recovery, it is very hard to step aside from that road. It is hard to turn away from freedom, peace, joy, and health once we have had a taste. Once we have *tasted* recovery—once we have "tasted God" and found Him a "good" parent instead of a "dysfunctional" one (Psa. 34:8)—it is very difficult to turn back to our "former selves." Formerly, we did not know what we were doing or what we were missing. Once we *do* know, it is hard to *choose* that unhappy, fearful life for ourselves.

When we become healthy and begin to practice healthy skills, we cannot guarantee that those around us will respond in the same way. But if we do *not* practice these skills, we guarantee that they *won't*. We guarantee that *nothing will change*—including ourselves. We are not called by God to practice these skills "only if" others practice them as well. We are called, instead, to trust God and act on His Word, regardless of what others do. Jesus tells us:

"Why do you call me, 'Lord, Lord,' and do not do what I say? I will show you what he is like who comes to me and hears my words and puts them into practice. He is like a man building a house, who dug down deep and laid the foundation on rock. When a flood came, the torrent struck that house but could not shake it, because it was well built. But the one who hears my words and does not put them into practice is like a man who built a house on the ground without a foundation. The moment the torrent struck that house, it collapsed and its destruction was complete." (Luke 6:46-49)

When we obey the Word of God, we may find pain and loss. We may find that our loved ones don't approve of the changes in us or in our behavior. But in spite of the struggles we may face, the house we are building will stand, because we are digging deep. We will never lose what God has given us. And when we see the houses of others crashing around us, we will be glad that ours is securely founded upon the Rock.

# - 9 -

# Free to Choose

---

*It is for freedom that Christ has set us free. Stand firm, then, and do not let yourselves be burdened again by a yoke of slavery." (Gal. 5:1)*

RECOVERY BRINGS US face to face with the need to make a number of new decisions and choices in our lives. This "need" becomes one of our last, and sometimes greatest, obstacles.

Until we entered recovery, decision-making might have been an alarming process, but at least we had some "rules and guidelines" to make it easier. We had certain boundaries that we "knew" we could never cross, certain assumptions that we could not violate. Our perceptions of ourselves, others, and the world around us provided us with additional guidelines. We might not have known precisely what we *could* choose, but we had some definite ideas about what we could *not* choose.

As we begin the journey of recovery, however, many of these certainties, boundaries, and assumptions begin to disappear. We begin to question the guidelines that have governed our lives thus far, and to learn that many of our perceptions are false. As we do so, we recognize the need to make better, more informed, healthy decisions—but at the same time, we have lost much of the decision-making framework that we once relied upon. Many of us simply did not learn effective decision-making skills, and now we are likely to feel rather lost and adrift in a sea of unfamiliar choices.

The various perceptions described in this book often dominated our decision-making process. For example, our self-image taught us to believe that no matter what choices we faced, we had to be sure to make the *right* one—or we would be "stupid failures." We often made decisions that we hoped would make us *look* better or *be* better. We made the decisions that we thought would please others and cause them to "like us" better.

Our self-talk warned us away from many choices, filling our minds with "what if's" and "if-then's" that made many choices look terrifying and impossible. Its "shoulds" and "musts" told us what we thought we were "expected" to do—and what we might be condemned for doing or not doing. Our self-talk told us what we thought we were capable of and incapable of.

Our concerns about our emotions often led us to make choices that we hoped would help us control or avoid "negative" emotions. When we felt pain, we often made choices that would help alleviate that pain—rather than resolve the *cause* of pain. We also tried to avoid arousing the negative, angry emotions of *other* people: In our decision-making process, we often made ourselves responsible for everyone *else's* feelings as well as our own.

Our sense of unforgiveness, especially toward self, made us determined to avoid any decision that might bring *more* blame and condemnation down upon us. We did not know how to "forgive" ourselves for making the wrong decision, or for being the "kind of person" who made "bad decisions."

Our relationships also had a powerful influence upon our choices. We made the choices that we hoped would please, placate, and win approval. We made choices to avoid the anger and condemnation of others. We made choices that reflected the choices of others, assuming that others were more likely to choose "correctly" than we were. We made whatever choices we thought were necessary to "hold onto" unhealthy, fragile relationships.

As these misperceptions begin to give way to truth, love, and healing, we suddenly find ourselves much more "free" to make choices and decisions. At the same time, that freedom can be frightening, because we no longer have a built-in set of guidelines that tell us what the "right" choices are, or what the consequences of making the "wrong" choice may be. Many of our fears about "choosing incorrectly" are still with us. We may wish for the security of having our choices "prepackaged" by dysfunctional rules and assumptions, even when we know that this "prepackaging" kept us in a virtual bondage to the beliefs of the past.

It is time to learn new decision-making skills. As we learn them, we will find new ways to address and resolve issues in every *other* area of our lives—and as we resolve *those* issues, our decision-making skills will continue to improve. Each step toward healing moves us forward in *every* area of recovery—and this is one of the most important steps.

## Ten Obstacles to Free Choice

The first step in improving our decision-making skills is to identify those fears and misperceptions that still *hinder* our ability to choose. Many of these fears are based upon painful experience, so it is no surprise that we haven't "already gotten rid of them." When we discover what we *believe* about choices and options, however, we are well on our way to *changing* those beliefs and *walking* in genuine freedom and recovery.

**1) We are afraid of making the *wrong* choice.** Most of us believe that if we make the "wrong" decision, it proves that we are "stupid." This fear often leads us to "stick to" a bad decision, even after we discover that it was wrong, because we believe that if we change our mind, we will reveal to *other* people that we were "stupid" in the first place. We often feel as though the only thing worse than *being* so "stupid" is to have everyone *discover* our "stupidity," and that fear often keeps us locked into bad decisions that we could otherwise easily change.

We have also experienced condemnation, punishment, and rejection for making the "wrong" choice. We often believe that this is an unforgivable mistake, almost as serious as a sin or deliberate disobedience. We may believe that we are "expected" or even "commanded" to choose correctly, and that there is "no excuse" for "failure." We are often reluctant to make *any* choice because we are so afraid of making "the wrong one."

**2) We believe there is no turning back.** One reason that we fear making the wrong choice is that we often assume that we are "stuck" with whatever choice we make—perhaps forever. We tend to regard choices as one-way roads, with no exits and no chance to turn around. We don't believe we can "unchoose" something we have chosen. Sometimes we believe that a single decision will be with us for the rest of our lives. We don't know how to "choose again" when we receive more information, or we discover that we are traveling in the wrong direction, or when the circumstances have changed so that our original decision is no longer workable. We suppose that "we picked it and we must stick with it."

**3) We look for the "single right choice."** We often believe that out of all the *options* available to us, only one is "right." Therefore, all of the others, no matter how good they may appear, must be "wrong." Our task, we believe, is to single out that one "correct choice" from all the possibilities—and heaven help us if we are wrong. This is often like looking for the needle in the haystack, and can create a great deal of anxiety in us when we aren't sure *which* choice is "right."

**4) We want permission.** One of the greatest problems we face is the overwhelming feeling that we need "permission" from some external agency for any course of action we want to undertake. We want to be sure that our choice is "correct"—and we usually don't believe that we can trust our own judgment. We want to know, in advance, that we won't be penalized for doing "wrong." We want our decisions to be "pre-approved" before we feel safe in making them. The concept that it might be "better to ask forgiveness than permission" is unthinkable to us; we can't imagine going ahead with something until we have been *told* that we *may* go ahead. Most of us had to be sure that we got permission from our parents for *everything* that we wanted to do, and some of us are living in a similar situation with our spouses. Often, we transfer this desire for permission to God, and are virtually unable to do *anything* without being sure that we have "a clear word from the Lord" on it.

**5) We have little experience in making choices.** Many of us were not granted the right to make choices when we were growing up. We weren't able to choose what to eat, what to wear, how to schedule our time, where to go, or even how to "have fun." Often, even our tastes in music, books, entertainment, or friends had to be "pre-approved" by our parents. Many of us were *told* what to like instead of being allowed to discover and *choose* what we liked. One woman, for example, was not able to choose her own wardrobe until she had nearly completed high-school—when she got a job and was able to purchase her own clothes. Our parents may even attempt to choose the directions of our adult lives as well. They may want to have the final word on our studies, our interests, our career, where and how we choose to live, and even whom we date or marry. While our parents often believed, and declared, that they "only wanted what was best for us," the result was that we never had the opportunity to *practice*, and therefore develop, good decision-making skills.

**6) We base our choices upon the rules and requirements of others.** When we are deeply concerned about "doing" and "being" the right thing, we often look for others to tell us *how*. Many of us grew up in households in which the "rules" were never clearly spelled out; instead, we only discovered what the unspoken rules were when we broke one. Thus we often feel much safer in an environment that is very structured, and in which the "rules of conduct" are clear. School provides that sort of environment, and so does the military. Many churches have long lists of "do's and don'ts" that tell us "how to be good" and the consequences of being "bad." We may find ourselves in *relationships* that are rule-based rather than love-based. We may not *enjoy* being fenced in with rules, but we often feel much safer when we *know* what will bring approval and what will bring condemnation.

**7) We do what other people *want*.** Our first criteria in making *any* decision is often *what other people want from us*. Many of us live with people who do not hesitate to make their demands, desires, and expectations known—and these become the foundations of the majority of our decisions. When someone says, "I wish you'd do *this*," or "I'd really appreciate it if you'd do *that*," or even, "If you really loved me, you would do *such-and-such*," we respond. We want love and approval—and we have learned that the way to *get* love and approval is to *choose* those actions and behaviors that "make others happy." We often allow others to dictate how we spend our resources, including time, energy, and money. We often allow others to dictate how we spend our *lives*, what we should be "interested in," and how to spend our free time. We go where others want us to go and do what others want us to do. When someone asks us what we want, we are likely to respond with something like, "I don't know, what do *you* want?"

**8) We are governed by "shoulds."** Most of us experience an automatic "should" response to any situation that presents itself. No matter what the occasion, our self-talk will tell us, "You *should* do this" and "You *shouldn't* do that." We usually believe that we *should* choose whatever makes another person happy or seems to help them, and we *shouldn't* do anything that seems to benefit only ourselves. Our shoulds are designed to protect us from perceived danger or anticipated condemnation. Whenever we have "shoulds" in our minds, however, everything that falls outside of our perceived "should" becomes an automatic "should not"—and whenever we do a "should not," we believe that we have deliberately sinned. "Shoulds" are simply modified rules that remove our ability to perceive our options.

**9) We know how things are "supposed" to be.** Many Adult Children have strongly held notions about how the world is "supposed" to work. Our range of tastes, choices, and ideas is often predefined by those that our parents had selected as "acceptable" or "appropriate." Our ideas of "right" and "wrong" may involve something as major as whether or not a woman "should" work outside the home, or whether it is OK to bake a cake from a mix. When our world is predefined in this way, we experience stress over whether someone hangs the toilet paper "in the wrong direction," or squeezes the toothpaste tube from the middle. We have learned to believe that there is a "right way" and a "wrong way" to do everything, including things that are tremendously unimportant.

**10) We choose what others choose.** We often do not trust our own taste or judgement as "guides" in making choices, so we look around to see what choices *others* are making. We often feel very out of place if our tastes do not conform to the "prevailing" tastes of our church, our profession, our social standing, or our educational group. We often assume that if something is "popular," it must be good—and if we don't like it, there is something wrong with *us*. We may follow this procedure in attempting to determine what form of "ministry" we ought to follow. When those around us preach "missions," we think we ought to become missionaries; when those around us preach "nursery volunteers," we think the best way we can serve God is to diaper babies. We may also suppose that if we don't *like* what we have chosen, this is all the more reason to "stick with it," because we clearly need to "learn how to follow the demands of *God* rather than the desires of the *flesh*." When we are told that "everyone ought to make this their highest priority," we believe—because we assume that others "know better than we do" about what is important for us or to God.

## Breaking the Decision-Barrier

Making healthy choices is not as difficult as it seems. As we build a better understanding of what choices *really* are, and how to go about the process of *selecting* a decision, we will feel much less threatened when we are confronted with a range of options. We can begin by counteracting the ten misperceptions listed above with ten *new* and *healthy* perceptions about decision-making.

**1) Choices are a beginning, not an end.** Often, we look at choices as door-closers rather than door-openers. Whenever we "pick one" from a range of options, we may believe that all the rest of those options are now "forever closed" to us. We believe that opening the door on *one* opportunity *slams* the door on every *other* opportunity—and if we picked the wrong one, we are out of luck.

In reality, choices are an end to some things and a beginning to others. Choices are interrelated, not isolated. If life is a journey, a road, then choices are like the exits, intersections, and junctions that we encounter on that road. As we come to each new intersection, we have a decision to make, and that decision may lead us in a new direction. But as long as we keep traveling, we will always encounter *new* opportunities, *new* branches, and the opportunity to *change* the direction that we have chosen if we find that we don't like it. There is rarely only *one* way to get to a desired destination, and few choices are "irreversible."

When we *choose*, we need to know what we are choosing *from*—and the action of making a decision usually concludes the process of gathering and interpreting this information. Sometimes the information-gathering stage can go on for a long time, and sometimes it is very short. "Spontaneity" is simply accelerated decision-making. When we develop the ability to make wise decisions, the wisdom of those decisions will not necessarily be based upon the amount of *time* we spend "weighing the alternatives;" instead, we become more efficient at spotting advantages and disadvantages.

The information-gathering process, however, often doesn't end when we make an initial decision. Often, it is necessary to *make* a decision so that we can discover *more* information. New information may come to us *after* we have made a choice, presenting us with the need to make *another* and perhaps *different* choice. Suppose, for example, that you have purchased a new blouse for a party. You may think that decision is "final." But then you discover that the party has been canceled, or that the skirt you planned to wear with the blouse is torn. Now you have new information—and the need to make a new decision. Do you take the blouse back? Do you exchange it for something that you can wear with a different skirt? This new information doesn't mean that you made a *bad* choice the *first* time; it means that you now have the information you need to make a *better* choice the *second* time.

Choices lead to choices. While a "choice" may be equivalent to the "off-ramp" to the road that we have already been traveling, it is also an "on-ramp" to a new road. That road will have its *own* set of options, choices, and decisions. Each choice leads us to an entirely *new* set of intersections, freeways, paths, and choices. Every choice sets in motion the options for more choices.

That may seem frightening, but it can also be encouraging. We often think that decisions are the equivalent of setting our future in concrete. We suppose that if we choose a career, we must *stay* with that career "for the rest of our lives"—so we become terrified of choosing the "wrong one." We may suppose that choosing a particular course of study will determine how we spend the rest of our lives, so we become desperate to find the "right" topic, the topic that will hold our interest for the next forty or fifty years.

The truth is that our interests, tastes, skills, and desires will change as *we* grow and change. The choice that may have been right for you *yesterday* may not be right *today*. The choice that you make *today* is not going to be right, perhaps, ten years from now—but at the same time, the choice that will be right in the future is *not* going to be right for you *today*. Many choices will not be right for *you* until you are ready for *them*.

Unless a choice involves something like marriage, we can rarely "choose" for "eternity." Few choices have this level of "life-time commitment;" in most cases, we can only choose for the present and immediate future. As we change and grow, our options change, and we can only *continue* to grow if we make new choices that take our changing selves and circumstances into account.

We can't *get* to tomorrow's choices, however, without *making* today's choices. Before we can *discover* what we would like to do *tomorrow*, we have to *start* doing something *today*. Only then can we determine if this path is "right" for us, or if it is leading us to something different. When we start to learn one thing, it may lead us to information that is far more interesting and inspiring, but that leads us in a totally unexpected direction. We would never have gotten to that information if we hadn't *started* down the road of our *first* choice. Choices don't set our future in concrete; they set our future in *motion*.

**2) There is nothing wrong with making the wrong decision.** We all *do*. We all *will*. Wrong decisions are a part of life. Sometimes we simply don't know enough about the situation to make the *right* decision. Sometimes our interests pull us in a direction that we later discover wasn't the best for us. Sometimes others *push* us in a direction that isn't the best for us. No matter how hard we try to choose "right," sometimes we choose *wrong*.

What matters is not whether or not we *made* the wrong decision but what we decide to *do* about it. If we decide to punish ourselves for it, blame ourselves, call ourselves "stupid," and add it to our "permanent record" of wrongdoing, we have made a choice to *allow* that decision to hurt us and haunt us. If we decide to *stick* to that decision once we *know* it is wrong, because we are afraid of "revealing our stupidity" to others, we are now responsible for all the *consequences* of that decision. Living with the momentary shame of having to change one's mind can be a lot less painful than living with the long-term problems involved in *staying* with a course of action that is useless or harmful.

On the other hand, we could decide to *forgive* ourselves for that "wrong decision," and choose not to hold that mistake against ourselves. We could decide to *move on* from that decision, and do our best to make new, better decisions that will change our direction into a more helpful and beneficial one. We could decide that what *others* think, either about our original decision or about our decision to *change our minds*, really isn't all that important. We could decide that *all that really matters is moving forward and doing our best*.

Sometimes a "wrong" decision is not necessarily a "bad" decision. We make decisions based upon the information available to us, and upon our ability to *interpret* that information. Quite often, we simply don't know enough to make the best choice. Sometimes, we need to make *some* choice so that we can *find out* what we need to make a *better* choice. For example, if you were "shopping" for a new church, you would have to make a decision, each Sunday, about where to go. None of these decisions may become "final;" they are efforts to gather information. You may find each decision is the "wrong" decision in that none of the churches you visit are churches that you want to become a part of. But you will never *know* that the church is "wrong" for you until you make the decision to visit in the first place.

You may not have married the first person you dated. You may not still hold the first job you ever applied for, or still pursue the first career choice you ever made. That doesn't mean that your career choice was "wrong" *then*—but it may mean that it is wrong for you *now*. Most of us have made *series* of choices in our lives, each based upon what we have learned from *previous* choices. Some choices show us that we need to make *new* choices, not because the original choice itself was "bad," but because it *would* be harmful to *stick* with that choice.

**3) You can change your mind.** As we gather new information, including information that shows us that the road we are traveling is not the best, we have two options. We can keep doing what we hate to do, and be miserable and ruin our lives, or we can *change* what we are doing. We can find an exit. We can make a U-turn. We can pick a different road. We can *change our minds*.

Very few things are "final." We build freedom and flexibility into our lives when we learn how to change our plans, even if those plans seemed "perfect" to start with. Plans are not the equivalent of the Ten Commandments, etched by God into stone. Instead, God often offers us new opportunities and possibilities—opportunities that we *miss* if we are incapable of changing the plans that we ourselves have made. Since we cannot see the future, we cannot plan for the future in such a way that we take all "possibilities" into account. Instead, we can only plan to travel a particular road until we discover a good reason to change directions.

Plans are not important in themselves. They are important only for their ability to help guide us to a goal, a destination. The point is not "following the plan," it is "reaching the destination." Often, we don't know exactly how to *get* to particular destination, such as "a healthy marriage" or "a joyful life." Sometimes the "destination" changes—we might have thought that "buying a home" was the most important goal in life, only to decide later that our fervent passion is to travel around the world as a missionary. We can only make plans based upon our knowledge *today*; as our knowledge and our perception of our destination change, our former plans will only get in the way.

Sometimes we need to change a plan because the original plan isn't working. We can only find out whether or not a plan will *work* by *trying it out*. If we don't test a plan, we will never know whether it is the right one—and once we *have* tested the plan, we can choose whether to stick with it or formulate a new one. But if we want to be sure that we get everything *absolutely right the first time*, we will get very little done at all.

One man was decorating his apartment, but he couldn't decide where to hang his paintings. He had spent a great deal of money on fine artwork, but he wanted to be sure that he hung that art in "the best place." He spent months looking at the paintings and looking at the walls—but the two never came together. He wanted to get it right "the first time."

Once we *try* something, we gain one of two important pieces of information. We may discover that our decision was *right*—in which case we have already accomplished what we set out to do. Or, we may discover that our decision was *wrong*—and we now know that this option is no longer available. If the man had hung a painting and decided that it looked nice where it was, he could go on to the next painting. If he had decided that he *didn't* like it in that location, he would *still* have had an *answer* instead of a *question*. Until he made the decision to *hang* a painting, however, he had nothing but questions—and bare walls.

Every time we make a choice, we come closer to our destination, either by finding the right option or ruling out the wrong one. Each time we avoid a choice, we postpone the completion of our journey.

**4) All choices involve tradeoffs.** Once we learn to stop worrying about making the right choice the first time, and once we realize that we can change our mind, we begin to realize that choices are not so much a question of "this" vs. "that," but a question of *tradeoffs*. Every option that we consider has advantages and disadvantages. Of course, we *also* have options that offer *no* advantages—but we usually eliminate those from our range of choices automatically. For example, when considering a career, you *could* choose the option of taking *no* job, making no money, and starving. That, however, is the option we are usually trying to *avoid*.

We choose among the options that we *perceive* to have advantages. And this is where the process becomes complicated, because all the options that we are considering seem to have *some* advantages. The difficulty lies in deciding which option is *best*. When we select an option, we often agonize over the advantages that we may have "missed" by *not* choosing something else.

One woman had dreamed of living in Europe. So she got her nursing degree through the Army, and her dream came true: She was stationed in Europe. Yet later she began to wonder if she had made the "right choice": Should she have "worked her way" to Europe rather than going with the Army.

Each option had its advantages and disadvantages. Finding an independent job in Europe might have meant more personal freedom and flexibility; she could change jobs, move when she chose, and have more "say" in her hours and vacation schedules. The military, on the other hand, took care of things like housing, health care, and job security—things that would be more difficult to guarantee on the "economy." The woman felt considerably better about her choice when she remembered that the *goal* was to live in Europe—and that any way that she chose to *reach* that goal would have certain tradeoffs.

We face many tradeoffs in life. When we don't examine the tradeoffs, we can get very frustrated. One man, for example, was shopping for a stereo system, and was shocked to find that prices were higher than he expected. He had a list of desired "features" in mind, and each of those features added to the overall cost. His *desire* was to find a system that had everything he *wanted* at a price he was willing to *pay*—but that system existed only in his imagination. He was faced with tradeoffs: He could choose to *give up* one or two features in exchange for a price that he could live with, or *pay more* in exchange for the system that had everything he wanted. Until he selected *one* of the available options, he was *stuck* with the one remaining option: An apartment without music.

We usually can't have it all. Women face the tradeoff between career and family life, and discover that television's favorite "supermom" is a myth. Men face the same tradeoff, with the additional social burden of being *expected* to devote long hours to the job at the expense of family. When we compare tradeoffs, it helps to focus upon our ultimate *goal*. The Army nurse's goal was to live in Europe. The stereo-seeker's goal was to have music in his apartment. The important question is not so much *how* we get there as *whether* we get there.

**5) There may be no perfect solution.** As the discussion of tradeoffs indicates, there may sometimes be several "good" choices but no "best" choice. Sometimes the options are more difficult: There may not be even a "really good" choice.

We often look for choices that will make *everyone* happy and give *everyone* what they want. We may want the choice that will solve *all* our problems *forever*. We may think that every choice must meet *all* the criteria that we set for it.

The truth is that very often, there *is* no "everyone wins" option. Most choices involve compromises, whether those are tradeoffs between the advantages and disadvantages to *you*, or between the needs and interests of more than one person. A compromise means that each party involved in a choice has to decide what advantages are the *most* important, and what he is willing to *give up*.

Once we realize that there is often no "perfect" solution, we become free to seek the best solution, or the least terrible solution. Sometimes even that is difficult. One woman faced the decision of telling a hospital whether or not to take "extreme measures" when her elderly mother was admitted for an emergency. She was, in effect, being asked to choose whether the doctors were to prolong her mother's suffering—or let her die. Neither of those is what one would call a "good" choice.

Nor was it easy to determine the "best" choice from the perspective of the mother, who was unable to communicate her wishes. The daughter's *desire* was for her mother to get better and be able to make her *own* choices—but this wasn't an option! (Fortunately, neither the daughter nor the hospital ever had to act on the final decision.)

Our choices often have an impact on others that may be considered negative, at least at first. When "Mommy" decides to go back to work, everyone in the family is affected. There is no "perfect" choice that will make *everyone* happy or give *everyone* what they want. The children may have to change their habits, and do some of the chores that Mom formerly handled. The husband may have to settle for a house that isn't as perfectly spotless as it once was, or for less elaborate meals, or he may be asked to help out in the home. Mom may have to choose between the value of a job and the approval of her family. Or, she may have to choose between the benefits of a salary and the cost of child-care. There may be no "perfect" decision—and the options may change over time. Once we realize that there often is no "best" decision, no decision that will be 100% perfect, we are free to do the best we can with the options that are available to us.

**6) The results of our decisions may not be immediately obvious.** Approval-hungry Adult Children often have a strong desire for immediate feedback or "gratification" from their choices. We want to know *as soon as possible* whether our choice is "right" and how it will "turn out." We want to see results, we want to have something to *show* for our work—something that we can show ourselves and something that we can show others to "prove" that we are doing something "worthwhile."

Thus we are often at risk of postponing long-term choices in favor of short-term demands. We may respond to the "squeaky wheel," the person who wants something from us *today*, and suppose that we will make the choice with longer-term benefits *tomorrow*. We think that we will embark on the "big" project once we have finished all the "little" projects. We'll go after our dreams tomorrow, when we fulfill all our commitments today.

Tomorrow never comes, because the "little things" never get done. No matter how many we do, there are always more. We can fill our lives with the pursuit of menial tasks—no matter how often we wash the dishes, for example, they always get dirty again. No matter how many demands we meet today, someone will always want something else from us tomorrow. Eventually "tomorrow" becomes "someday," and "someday" becomes "I guess it's too late for that now." If our heart's desire is to write that novel, it is only going to happen when we decide, not tomorrow but *today*, that the keyboard is more important than the dishes.

Immediate feedback is addictive. It is hard to exchange the gratification of a quick response for something that may not produce any visible fruits for months or even years. Recovery, for example, is a long-term decision: We won't see the results in a few weeks, or even in a few months. In the meantime, we face a thousand "choices" that are competing for the time that we are investing in our future.

We often postpone career or educational decisions for the same reason. It can be difficult to exchange the security of today's paycheck, in a job that we know we can do even if we hate it, for the uncertainties and delays of retraining for something new. Many people have declared, "I'd love to change jobs and do something meaningful, but it takes two years to retrain, and then I'd have to start at a lower salary, and who'd hire an older person anyway?" As one advice columnist once pointed out, you are *still* going to be two years older at the end of the retraining period; the question is, what will you *have* at the end of that two years? If you choose the long-term choice, the retraining, you will have a new skill and you'll be two years closer to your goal. Otherwise, you're just two years farther away from your dreams.

We may be afraid to make long-term decisions because we aren't certain that we really *want* a particular goal. We may think that the idea of retraining is *nice*, but what if we discover that we don't really like the career we've retrained *for*? We worry about *wasting* an investment of time and money on something that we aren't 100% sure of.

The reality, however, is that we can never be 100% certain of *anything*. What we have is questions—and our choices provide us with opportunities to *answer* those questions. As my husband once told me when I faced a job that I wasn't sure I could handle, "If you don't *try*, you'll always *wonder*." What changes our lives is *trying*—whether we *succeed* or not. If we do not *try*, nothing *changes*.

**7) Rules are not choices.** When we live our lives in response to the rules and requirements of others, we are not making choices. We are simply *conforming* to the choices that others have made *for* us. Often, those choices have nothing to do with *us*; they have to do with the beliefs and assumptions and desires of others.

We often believe that if we don't "obey the rules," we will stray into "sin." We believe that the rules are there "for our good." We may have learned that if we want to be members of a particular group, we must conform to the standards and expectations of that group. We believe that we *must* obey without ever asking *why*.

To learn how to make choices, we need to learn how to break the rules. Does that sound terribly wrong? It isn't. Most of the time, the rules that we have learned to conform to are not God's rules and have little to do with God's rules. They are the rules, beliefs, traditions, and demands of *man*.

We are often "bound" by the rules we grew up with. We make the choices our parents would have *wanted* us to make, even if our parents are no longer around to tell us what to do. We often feel as though a parent is looking over our shoulder—even if the parent is long dead. One woman was unable to dispose of her mother's belongings for nearly three years after her mother's death, because one of her mother's inviolable family rules was "never touch my things." The daughter found it terrifying to even consider breaking that rule; despite the fact that her mother was dead and she had technically *inherited* those things, she still considered them the property of her mother, not her own.

Many churches and denominations have developed their own lists of rules for what constitutes "good behavior" and "holiness." These often include dress codes, proscriptions against eating certain foods or drinking alcohol, rules against certain types of music or against dancing, rules about how people can socialize and what they can say, and rules about the "right way" to worship God. Some churches believe, for example, that we *must* speak in tongues if we want to talk to God, while others maintain that we *mustn't*.

Paul writes, "Since you died with Christ to the basic principles of this world, why, as though you still belonged to it, do you submit to its rules: 'Do not handle! Do not taste! Do not touch!'? These are all destined to perish with use, because they are based on human commands and teachings. Such regulations indeed have an appearance of wisdom, with their self-imposed worship, their false humility and their harsh treatment of the body, but they lack any value in restraining sensual indulgence." (Col. 2:20-23)

Why, indeed! Because we have been *taught* to, that's why. We have learned that we may be rejected, condemned, or punished for breaking, not the rules of God, but the traditions of *man*. Jesus, on the other hand, declares: " ' "They worship me in vain; their teachings are but rules taught by men." You have let go of the commands of God and are holding on to the traditions of men.' And He said to them: 'You have a fine way of setting aside the commands of God in order to observe your own traditions!' " (Mark 7:7-9)

God is not deeply interested in what you wear. If there were a "right" way to dress, we would all be wearing the sort of clothes people use to illustrate Biblical characters. He is not interested in how you style your hair, whether you wear jewelry or makeup, or whether you wear suits, skirts, or blue jeans to church. He is not going to send you to hell for listening to something other than "Christian" music (and "Christian labels" are not a guarantee of quality). He is not interested in the expression on your face but the condition of your heart. "God does not judge by external appearance—those men added nothing to my message." (Gal. 2:6)

When we begin to question, and finally to break, the rules and traditions of men, we can begin to learn what God is all about. We can begin to base our choices on *love* rather than on demands and requirements. We can choose without the restrictions of false boundaries and human threats. We will make mistakes—but we will learn to choose ever more wisely when we choose out of God's freedom rather than in man's bondage.

**8) What do you want?** Once we realize that our choices don't have to be guided by rules and traditions, or by assumptions about what "good Christians" do, or by the demands of others, we can begin to ask ourselves a question we may never have dared to ask before: "What do I want?"

It is not a sinful question. It is not "forbidden" by God. It is not necessarily going to lead us astray. It is the process of finding out the truth; how we *act* upon that truth is still a decision that remains to be made. Our desires are factors that we need to consider before making *any* decision.

We often suppose that *any* desire is a "fleshly" desire, because we have been taught to believe that we have no right to want *anything*. One of the things we need to learn, then, is how to distinguish fleshly desires from valid desires. For example, when I want tacos and burritos, I *know* this is a desire of the flesh—and my flesh usually suffers for it. I still make this choice, but with a full awareness of the consequences. God doesn't have to "punish" me for following the flesh; that particular sin punishes itself! However, when I face the decision to thaw, say, chicken or fish, the question "What do I *want* for dinner?" is a valid one. There is no "right choice;" there is no divine law that says that I "should" have chicken on Thursdays and fish on Mondays. If I don't know what I *want*, I am likely to be vaguely disappointed by what I get—but it will be my own fault.

What do you *want* to do? What are your desires, your dreams, your passions? Do you want to go back to school, study for a new career, embark on a new way of life? The first step toward identifying whether or not you *can* make a particular choice is to identify whether you *want* to make that choice.

We often think that we need direct, explicit permission from God to do *anything*. It is helpful to have a feeling of certainty in your spirit that the direction you are choosing is "right"—but if we spend our lives waiting for a burning bush to materialize in front of us, we are going to spend our lives simply *waiting*.

We may want God, or someone else, to *tell* us what we are allowed to "want" because we don't want to have to make these decisions for ourselves. Part of responsible decision-making, however, is to become aware of our desires and feelings, and then to choose responsible *actions*. God, as a functional parent, is well aware that a child will never "mature" as a decision-maker if all his decisions are mapped out ahead of time: "You may want this, but you mustn't want that." We often want God to tell us if a course of action is "right" for us—in other words, we want Him to reveal the *future*. But God very rarely reveals the future outcomes of our present choices; if He did, we would all be prophets. God will help us learn how to choose wisely based upon the information that we have available to us *today*; only by acting on *this* information will we ever discover what lies ahead of us *tomorrow*.

**9) God offers a multitude of options.** The question, "What do you want?" is an important question to ask when one begins to ask how one can best serve God. We often suppose that when we get saved, we are expected to "turn in" all our old dreams, interests, and desires, and "pick up" a whole *new* set. We may believe that we are supposed to "give up" our worldly careers and enter some form of ministry. We may think that we will be expected to learn an entirely new set of skills before we can "please God," and that our old ones are to be stored away in some forgotten attic.

The truth is that *God knew who you were before you got saved.* He did not wait until the moment of salvation to *begin* working in your life; He has been working in you since the day you were born. "All the days ordained for me were written in your book before one of them came to be." (Psa. 139:16) He knows what skills and talents you have, what dreams motivate you, what passions are likely to stir you in ministry. Your previous skills were not just picked up "by accident" before you could learn your "real purpose" in God's universe. They may well be an important *part* of that purpose.

Part of the problem is that we often believe that there are only a few selected ways to "serve" God. Service is not limited to such obviously "Christian" fields as ministry, teaching, missionary work, evangelism, witnessing, leading Bible studies, or volunteering in the nursery. In reality, we may serve God in an infinite number of ways. We may serve Him in the office, where we act as a living witness to His truth even if we *don't* roam the halls with a Bible in one hand and the other outstretched to collar potential converts. We may serve Him in the home, as an example to our children and loved ones. We may serve Him as a volunteer in a nonChristian organization, where our love of God's children leads us. We may serve Him as a teacher, as a writer, as an artist—in other words, with the dreams and talents that He gave us long before we ever knew Him. Having a dream doesn't mean that we aren't putting God first; instead, we can discover ways to put that dream to work in His service.

Paul tells us, "Just as each of us has one body with many members, and these members do not all have the same function, so in Christ we who are many form one body, and each member belongs to all the others. We have different gifts, according to the grace given us. If a man's gift is prophesying, let him use it in proportion to his faith. If it is serving, let him serve; if it is teaching, let him teach; if it is encouraging, let him encourage; if it is contributing to the needs of others, let him give generously; if it is leadership, let him govern diligently; if it is showing mercy, let him do it cheerfully." (Rom. 12:4-8)

The gift of "encouragement" is no less important than the gift of "prophesy." Each gift that is given us is one that we can practice "in proportion to our faith." Do you prefer to bake cakes than to work in the nursery? Do you prefer to sing than to teach? Would you rather paint posters than lead Bible studies? Would you rather coordinate schedules than witness on street corners? Instead of becoming concerned that we don't seem to "want" what we "should" want, we can make much wiser and more joyful choices for God when we seek to discover how to use the dreams and talents that we have and enjoy. "Then I realized that it is good and proper for a man to eat and drink, and to find satisfaction in his toilsome labor under the sun during the few days of life God has given him—for this is his lot. Moreover, when God gives any man wealth and possessions, and enables him to enjoy them, to accept his lot and be happy in his work—this is a gift of God. He seldom reflects on the days of his life, because God keeps him occupied with gladness of heart." (Ecc. 5:18-20)

**10) Choose to choose.** Making *no* choices is also a choice. When we delay or avoid making choices, we are making the choice to *give up* our rights and responsibilities. When we don't make a choice, a choice *will* be made for us, somehow. It may be made by the circumstances, or by others. It may *not* be what we would have preferred, and we may wish that the outcome could be different, and we may want to *blame* the circumstances or the people who chose *for* us. But the truth is that when we do *not* choose, we have only ourselves to blame for the consequences.

We need to get into the habit of choosing. Sometimes we won't have enough information to make the best decision. Sometimes we will be faced with conflicting decisions, or a host of options that look equally good—or bad. Sometimes we will fervently wish that someone would take a difficult decision out of our hands. But choosing is *our* responsibility. It was given to us by God, and we will learn and grow and become strong as we begin to practice our *option* to choose *among* options.

Sometimes our decisions will backfire. Sometimes the results will be disastrous. This can be discouraging—but we must not let that stop us from choosing again, and again. "Decision-making" is like any other skill: It must be *practiced* before we can become *good* at it. If we back off at the first sign of trouble, we won't learn how to choose more wisely the next time. The more decisions we make, the easier the process becomes, and the more we become willing to stand behind and defend our decisions.

Our recovery will begin to progress at a much more rapid rate when we become actively involved in our own choices. In the beginning, we often feel buffeted and swept along by forces beyond our control. As we learn how to make choices and decisions, however, we begin to discover that we *do* control many of those forces; it is simply a matter of getting the reins back into our own hands again.

As we build a better understanding of the impact of such factors as self-talk and self-image and emotions on our *choices*, then we will be better able to make *choices* about those areas of our lives. Choice-making is an interactive process: It is affected by other areas of our lives, and it has an *effect* upon those areas. Each step in each area contributes to faster and easier steps in every other area. The choice is yours!

## Setting Goals

When we begin making choices, it helps to have some goals in mind. Goals are like "destinations" on a map: We are *here* and we want to get *there*. *Choices* are the decisions we make along the way: Do we take this road or that? Each road has "tradeoffs"—This one is faster, that one is more scenic, the other is safer—but each will eventually get us to our destination.

We cannot reach a destination if we can't make choices about how to get there—and implement those choices. When I was a child, we used to plan elaborate summer trips, pinning maps to the walls and marking our routes with colored markers. But those maps didn't *get* us anywhere; we only reached our destination after we piled into the car and started to *drive*.

The choices, however, don't make much sense if we don't *have* a final destination in mind. At first, in the newfound freedom of recovery, we may enjoy the ability to simply "cruise" and enjoy the ride. But eventually—once we have cast aside our old "destinations" that were born of our belief in demands and constraints—we begin to ask ourselves where we *want* to go in life.

Besides knowing how to make choices, we need to know how to set goals. We are beginning to realize that we are no longer required to meet the goals of our parents, our spouses, or our church. But we may also fear the responsibility of setting our *own* goals. We may be terrified of setting a goal that isn't "God's goal for us." We may have failed at past goals, and doubt our ability to succeed at future ones. Our goal may be to simply survive and keep our head above water. But as we learn to look forward in hope to new and brighter destinations, our lives become filled with a healing sense of purpose, and we rediscover our *reasons* for living.

Goals have four components: They must be inspiring, well-defined, possible, and measurable. If any of these components are missing, we will only end up frustrated by goals that we can't reach, or goals that don't mean anything to us when we *do* reach them. To learn how to set goals, we need to learn what each of these components means.

• **Inspiring.** First and foremost, a goal must have some value to *us*. It won't help us to seek after other people's dreams, other people's demands. I have heard some ministers declare that we should *all* make a particular form of ministry our "highest priority." Another person's priority may not be *your* passion, however, and it may not be the priority that God has set for *you*. As we search for goals, we are searching for something that *we* can pursue with passion and enthusiasm.

When we are inspired and fulfilled, we don't mind working hard, putting in long hours,and giving of ourselves. Our "return" is not in money, or in praise, but in the joy we receive from doing what has meaning to us. God knows this! He *designed* us that way. He designed us to be motivated by passion, by enthusiasm, by inspiration, by the joy of fulfillment.

When we find goals that we care about, we will be motivated to make choices that will bring us nearer to those goals. Along the way, we need to learn to put aside the goals that we really *don't* care about, or that we *once* cared about but don't care about any longer.

One way to discover what we *do* care about is to discover what we are willing to give up for a particular goal. If the answer is "not very much," that goal probably has very little meaning. I have met many people who like the *idea* of recovery, but have no intention of spending the time or enduring the pain that is *involved* in recovery. Similarly, I have met many people who, upon hearing what I do, declare that they would "just love to be a writer too." But few are motivated to give up anything *else*—such as television time—to actually sit down and *write*. If a goal doesn't motivate us to do something, it isn't really a goal. It's just a nice idea.

Inspirational, and inspired, goals can be short-term or long-term. Today's goal might be to exercise for 20 minutes—and that may be part of tomorrow's *long-term* goal of better health and fitness. Today's goal may be to attend a parenting class, so that we can achieve tomorrow's goal of changing some dysfunctional family patterns. Once we identify what is *important* to us, we are a step closer to our *destination*.

• **Well-Defined.** Vague goals are discouraging. They may *sound* good, but we often don't even know where to begin. Many Adult Children enter recovery with some very vague goals, like "I want to be a better person," or "I want to be nicer" or "I want people to like me." Better than what? Nicer than whom? Which people?

Goals need precise definition. If we want to change something, we need to figure out what, exactly, we want to change. "Oh, everything, I guess," is *not* a specific goal. Do you want to change how you react to difficult situations? Do you want to change your tendency to "give in" whenever someone asks something of you? Do you want to learn better relationship skills? Do you want to change your self-image? These are all *defined* goals—and once we *know* what we want, we can begin to *work* on it.

We need specific goals in every area of life. Instead of saying, "I want to save the environment," we might say, instead, "I want to find out what I can do in my community to encourage recycling." Instead of saying, "I want to achieve world peace," we might say, "I want to find out how I can *contribute* to world peace (or improve conditions in my own neighborhood)." Instead of saying, "I want to serve God," we might say, "I really want to work with youth." Instead of saying, "I want to win the world to Christ," we might say, "I want to witness to my friends and neighbors."

Setting specific goals means learning to walk a fine line between *real* constraints and *perceived* constraints. Often, we have grown up with a host of "I can'ts" and "I'll never be good enough to's" that convince us that *big* goals goals are impossible for us. At the same time, there *are* some genuine, real-world constraints that make some goals impossible. We can always *test* those constraints—but we will find more encouragement if we start with *smaller* goals, such as "attending a workshop," and working *up* to the larger goal of "writing the Great American Novel."

• **Possible.** The next question we have to ask is "Is this destination *possible*?" Many Adult Children enter recovery with some highly unrealistic goals. They want to become "100% perfect," or find out how to "be happy all the time," or how to turn themselves into "people that everyone will love."

Not even Jesus was loved by *everybody*. In fact, quite a few people *hated* Him—enough to kill Him. If Jesus couldn't achieve that goal of "being loved by everybody," neither can we. Indeed, we can often judge our success as people as much by those who *hate* us as by those who *love* us. I often ask people who think that it is important to be "loved by everybody" whether they would be pleased to learn that Hitler thought they were wonderful, fantastic people—"His kind of folks." Most of them say "no." A more attainable goal, then, is not to be loved by *everyone*—but to seek the respect of people that *you* respect.

A 100% happy, trouble-free life is not possible. The perfect, flawless mate is not possible. Perfect children who never misbehave and upset their parents are not possible. An absolutely perfect, hassle-free job is not possible. A perfect self is not possible.

On the other hand, happy and healthy children *are* possible. A loving relationship *is* possible. Good and rewarding jobs *are* available. Self-improvement *is* feasible. When we realize that nothing is 100% perfect, we become aware of what we *can* attain.

Sometimes the "possible" component of a goal has to do with the amount of time and effort involved. If you want to become a brain surgeon, that is certainly possible. If you want to become a brain surgeon *tomorrow*, and you are an auto mechanic today, that is *not* possible. If you want to become "the most famous brain surgeon in the world," that is also *possible*—though less likely. If you *do* become that famous, however, it will *not* be because you *wanted* to become famous, but because brain surgery meant so much to you that you devoted yourself to it to the utmost of your ability.

Sometimes a goal may be impossible not because of the way that it is stated, but because of what we *mean* by it. Adult Children often declare that they want to be "healthy." This seems possible—on the surface. But what do we *mean* by healthy? For many, it means "having no needs," "getting rid of all painful emotions," "never having any more troubles in life," or "being a person who pleases others." These definitions are actually the exact opposite of being genuinely "healthy." *Healthy* people have needs, experience painful emotions, learn how to deal with life's inevitable troubles, and often no longer care whether everyone else "approves" of them. The problem, however lies with our *definition* of our goal. We can't get there, because the destination doesn't *exist*.

• **Measurable.** How will we know when we have "reached" a goal? Most towns have "city limits" signs that tell us that we have reached our destination. Goals need a similar sort of sign.

We often set "unmeasurable" goals. We want to be happy, healthy, and loved. But we often measure those goals by our "failures": Every time we feel unhappy, unhealthy, or unloved, we assume that we have "failed" to reach our goal. And since no one is ever happy, healthy, or loved 100% of the time, we have no way of assessing that kind of goal.

"Measurable" means that the goal has results that we can *see*. Those results may be tangible or experiential, but whatever they are, they are something that we can recognize and say, "Ah-ha. I've made it." For example, a person who decides that he wants to become a "better parent" has a meaningful and realistic goal. However, he also needs to set some *measure* of "better parenting." He might decide that one problem is his inability to manage his anger in a healthy way. A measurable *goal* might be to find new ways to handle anger. He will be able to determine that he has *reached* that goal when, instead of yielding to his usual temptation to storm out of the room when he gets angry, he reacts in a calmer and more constructive manner.

Suppose your long-term goal is to be a "famous writer." Writing is your passion—you are inspired by that goal. You know that if you are willing to work long enough and hard enough, "fame" is not totally out of the question: It's possible. But you *also* know that you are unlikely to become a famous writer *tomorrow*. You need *measurable* goals that are possible *today*.

Your first "measurable," then, might be to get something written. If you have nothing on paper, nobody is going to buy it or praise it. The next measurable might be to improve your skills through exercises or a writing class. The next measurable might be to *submit* your work; I have known more than one talented writer whose "talent" is shut away in a box in the closet. The next measurable might be "acceptance." Then you could move on to more prestigious, higher-paying acceptances. Step by step, you come closer to your destination.

This "step by step" process is important. Sometimes the "final destination" seems impossibly remote. We don't know how, or when, we will ever get there, and we get discouraged. When we break the "journey" down into measurable *steps*, setting ourselves a series of "mini-goals," we can begin to measure our *progress*.

The final thing that we need to know about goals is that *they can be changed*. Like choices, they are not etched in stone. Often, we stumble across new and more meaningful goals in our pursuit of our original destination. If we focus blindly upon our *original* goals, we may miss valuable opportunities. If we chase after the one star that we have set our sights on, we may miss other stars that come within our grasp.

All we can do in life is *set out* for a destination. Whether we will get there is in the hands of God—for He has not given it to us to see the future. As we learn how to make wise choices along the way, we may find that our destination changes, and the wisest choice is to pursue a new goal. It is no "shame" to abandon a dream when God sends us a better one.

# - 10 -

# A Time for Recovery

*There is a time for everything, and a season for every activity under heaven: a time to be born and a time to die, a time to plant and a time to uproot, a time to kill and a time to heal, a time to tear down and a time to build, a time to weep and a time to laugh, a time to mourn and a time to dance, a time to scatter stones and a time to gather them, a time to embrace and a time to refrain, a time to search and a time to give up, a time to keep and a time to throw away, a time to tear and a time to mend, a time to be silent and a time to speak, a time to love and a time to hate, a time for war and a time for peace... He has made everything beautiful in its time. (Ecc. 3:1-8, 11)*

AS WE WALK the journey of recovery, we will find that it is a "time" for all of these things. We will plant new things, and uproot old things. We will tear things down and build things up. We will weep and laugh, mourn and dance. We will embrace—and refrain. We will search things out and give things up, choose what to keep and what to throw away, feel torn and then feel mended, hold our peace and speak our piece. We will love, and we will hate, and after fighting battles in our hearts and with others, we will find peace. Through it all, we will discover that God has made everything, including us, beautiful in its time.

"Recovery" begins with ***birth***—with the decision to enter a life that we know nothing about. We did not know what lay ahead of us when we were physically born; if we had, we might have chosen to remain in the womb indefinitely. Many of us didn't realize what we were getting into when we chose to become "born again." And no matter how many books we read about recovery, we will not really know what we are "getting into" until we *get into it*. It is an experience that we cannot understand until we participate in it; we cannot "understand" it from listening to or reading about the experiences of others. The experiences of others can guide and advise you on that journey, but the journey is your own.

That means that the journey is uniquely yours. There is no single "right way" to recover. Techniques that are helpful to you may not be helpful to another, and vice versa. Your experiences in childhood were different from anyone else's, and your recovery experiences will also be different. Don't let anyone tell you what you "should" feel on this journey, or how long the journey should take, or where you should be at any particular time. Recovery is not a competition, and we do not recovery any faster by comparing our progress to someone else's.

Birth has its pangs. No birth is easy or painless. When we feel pain at the thought of moving into a new way of life, or as we take the first steps on that journey, we must realize that there is *nothing wrong with us*. It *does* hurt. We are making a difficult decision, a decision that involves struggle, turmoil, and even opposition. We are severing ties with an old way of life and even with old relationships as if we were cutting the umbilical cord to the past. Sometimes it feels as though we are being *torn* out of our old way of life and *thrust*, kicking and screaming, into a new life that we aren't completely sure we *want* yet. Everything is new, alien, frightening. None of the old techniques and coping skills "work" anymore. We don't know what to expect, and we *won't* know what lies ahead until we begin to *move forward*.

We also discover, as we begin to walk *forward* in recovery, that there is no going back. That can be alarming. We find ourselves "stuck" with a decision that we don't know enough about to be sure it was what we wanted. Now that we know what health *is*, or at least have a taste of it, we *know the difference*. We can never return to the old life in blissful ignorance. We can go back to old behaviors, but now we *know* what we are doing, and we will have to live with that. The pain of going *back* is worse than the pain of going *on*.

No birth ushers us into a "perfect" life. We didn't enter a perfect world or a perfect life when we were born the first time. We may have *hoped* that our "second birth" would bring our lives the perfection that the first one "missed"—but it didn't happen. We did not get "born again" into a life that was trouble-free or painless. Most of us have discovered that being a Christian means a *new* set of challenges and obstacles, as well as joys and resources.

Many Adult Children enter recovery because they are seeking "perfection." When we are told that we can "get better" we often hope that means that we will "be better"—and that *life* will be better as well. We may hope that *this time* we will find the happiness, peace, and security that we have been seeking. We may hope that "recovery" will be the answer to our troubles.

It isn't. Recovery does not remove us from hardship and pain; it does not remove us from *life*. Instead, it equips us with a new and more effective toolkit to help us *cope* with hardship and pain. Recovery means that we learn how to accept God's resources and guidance, so that we can experience God's growth plan for our lives.

Birth to a *new* life means ***death*** to an *old* way of life. When we are "born again," we "die" to the old life that we lived without Christ. When we begin the journey of recovery, we find ourselves "dying" to the old life that we lived in dysfunction. We "die" to many old habits, behaviors, beliefs, and even relationships.

This "death" is neither easy nor fun. Don't let anyone tell you that you should "enjoy" it or be filled with peace and contentment from the very beginning. You won't be. You *are* moving on to something new and better—but you are also leaving something behind. That loss hurts. That life was a part of you; those beliefs and habits were a part of you. That identity that you are leaving behind *was* you—the only "you" that you ever knew. You may feel torn apart, lost, even betrayed. You may wish that you could "reclaim" what you have left behind, because you haven't traveled far enough to *claim* anything *new*.

We have a right to grieve this death—and we *will* grieve. We will feel all the feelings that are involved in grief: Anger, sorrow, pain, fear, and that feeling that there is nothing left for us in the future. If we did *not* grieve, we would not be able to "let go." Grief is the transition process, the step that enables us to *release* the old, dead way of life and *embrace* the new, living life that we will discover and become a part of. Grief finalizes our losses, gives us a way to express the pain, and allows us to move forward by letting go. In recovery, we may experience several stages of separation and mourning, and each one is important.

Recovery really begins when we choose to ***plant*** some new and healthier ideas into our hearts and minds. You chose to read this book to bring some *new* ideas into your mind; as you read it, you may have identified some *old* ideas that needed to be uprooted and discarded. As we plant truth in our hearts, we ***uproot*** lies, so that the old and entrenched lies won't choke out the tender new crop of "truth" that is beginning to sprout within us.

Some of the lies that we believe have deep roots. They are not easy to pull out, because they go back to our childhood, back to a time when we had no *choice* but to believe what we were told. That planting and uprooting process often brings us feelings of shame, as we discover the lies that we have been operating on as "truths" for so long. We may feel "stupid" for believing these things; we may feel as though it is "our fault" for not having "discovered" them before. This, too, is simply another lie that needs to be uprooted and disposed of. We were not responsible for the planting of those misperceptions; it was *not our fault*. We were no more "stupid" for believing what we were taught as "absolute truth" than our ancestors were for believing that the world was round.

God does not measure us by what we "should have known yesterday." He takes account of the choices that we make *after* we discover the truth. If you discover a "lie" planted in your heart today, it makes no difference to God that you didn't discover it "earlier." *Now* that you have seen it, you can make a choice about it. God looks forward, not backward; He does not judge a field by the weeds it once contained, but by the harvest He knows it will one day produce.

We won't "uproot" everything "unhealthy" overnight. We may become frustrated with ourselves for not "producing results" as quickly as we think we "should"—or as quickly as others want us to. Only God knows how long the "season of recovery" will be for each of us, however. It may take us many seasons to "clear out" the various fields of our lives and "resow" them with a healthy and fruitful crop. Nor will we be ready to "believe," instantly, every truth that we have just planted. During recovery, we take this time to be caring gardeners, tenderly watering our crop, and tending *ourselves* as though we were a new garden. It may take many seasons for our "truth crops" to mature and be ready to harvest—but God is not impatient.

Recovery is also a time for ***"killing."*** It is the time when we "kill" our parents.

No, it is not a time to go home and shoot Mom and Dad—even though some of us may feel enough rage and pain to wish that we could do just that. The "parents" that we must kill are the "parents" who live inside our heads.

They are the "voices" that control us, that keep us bound to the rules and beliefs of the past, that refuse to give us "permission" to live our own lives in our own way—or, more importantly, in God's way. They are the voices that say things like, "How many times do I have to tell you? Now get it right!" or "I'm really disappointed in you; I thought you could do better in life," or "You're such a tramp; I've been ashamed of you since the day you were born," or "When are you going to stop being such a weakling and start acting like a real man?"

These voices *sound* just like Mom and Dad, or whoever gave us those messages in childhood. They control us just as effectively as our parents ever did. We listen to them, dread them, live in fear of them, allow ourselves to be shamed by them, and obey them. We wish that they would one day "approve" of us or "be proud" of us—but they never will, because they are our own memory of our parents' lack of approval, pride, and love. They fill us with guilt and shame, perpetuate our sense of unworthiness, and rob us of the ability to make our own choices.

Our perception of our parents often contributes to this bondage. We may "obey" the voices because we thought of our parents as "saints," and feel as though any sort of "disobedience" to their wishes would be a form of "sacrilege." Some of us are reluctant to do something as simple as bake a cake from a mix, because we know that "Mom would be horrified." Or, we remember our parents as merciless tyrants, swift to punish the slightest mistake, and we still live in terror of *making* that mistake. Even when our parents aren't physically present to enforce their will, our memories enforce it for them.

We may not want to *confront* those "inner parents" because we don't want to destroy our perceptions of them. If we thought of them as "saints," we may not want to destroy that illusion by recognizing the reality of our parents' behavior. If we thought of them as "demons," we may not want to give up the blame that we hold against them for "ruining our lives."No matter what we think of our parents, however, we no longer belong to them. We belong to a new, heavenly parent. We belong to God—the ultimate "functional parent."

Too often, when our inner voices come into conflict with the voice of God, God's voice loses. Or, we may interpret those voices *as* the voice of God: We "expect" Him to say something like "Get your act together if you want to win any favor from *me*." We may seek "permission" or "approval" from God *in the same way* that we sought it from our parents—and we wonder why we do not get it, because He won't *respond* to us in a dysfunctional manner.

It is time to "kill" those false parents, to rid our minds of them as we would rid our homes of destructive pests. We must let them go, bury them, mourn them, and move on. That thought is often terrifying, because even though we *hate* the voices, we may not know how to *live* without their "guidance." As long as they "whispered" to us, we always knew what to *do*—and more importantly, what *not* to do. When we "kill" our inner parents, we give up that false sense of security. We become responsible: We have to begin making our *own* choices, find our *own* ways to approve our work, and give *ourselves* "permission" to move forward in our lives.

We may believe that we are "dishonoring" our parents when we stop "listening" to them, and we feel guilty over that. Once we "do the deed," however, we can confess that we are no longer "Adult Children of Dysfunctional Families," but Adult Children of God, and answerable only to God.

Once those inner voices that filled us with shame and fear are silenced, we can begin to ***heal*** from the effects of those voices. Our wounds were opened and reopened with constant internal "reminders" of our worthlessness, our guilt, our imperfection. Now that the voices are no longer able to fill us with criticism, demands, accusations, and humiliation, we are no longer as vulnerable to the endless *hurt* they inflicted upon us. When we close the door to hurt, we open the door to healing, and our wounds are free to close.

Treating a deep wound, draining ancient infections, and closing that wound so it can heal, all involve pain. We have to *look* at our hurts before we can heal them. We can't "bandage" ourselves in the dark. Often, we were never "allowed" to experience the pain of our wounds *when they happened*—so we experience that pain *when we treat them*.

That pain can be scary, and we may wish we could avoid it. It can delay us in our efforts to recover, because we don't *want* to experience it. Many of us ask if there isn't an "easier" way, a way to heal *without* remembering (or reexperiencing) the hurt. Many of us wonder why God can't simply show us whatever we need to know, without "forcing" us to accept the pain that accompanies the process. One woman pointed out, "I hurt if I don't work on it, and I hurt if I do, so why bother?"

That pain, however, is like the sharp agony of setting a bone or lancing an infection, or the bitter sting of iodine. For a moment, it may seem *worse* than the pain of the original injury. But as we know from treating physical wounds, it is necessary. It provides cleansing, puts things back where they belong, and enables genuine healing to proceed. We may think we can "tolerate" the dull, underlying ache of a wound that has never healed—but that pain will *never go away*. The sharper pain that accompanies healing not only goes away quickly, it also removes the pain of the past.

Part of that pain comes from ***tearing down*** the walls that we have built to protect ourselves. Many of us have lived like snails, carrying our personal "strongholds" around with us wherever we went. Within those shells, nothing could touch us; we could withdraw whenever we felt threatened or vulnerable. At the same time, those shells were tight, constricting, painful in themselves. In recovery, we choose between the pain of *living* within impenetrable walls, and the pain of *leaving* those walls.

When we tear down those walls, we feel vulnerable and exposed. We hurt from fear itself, from the uncertainty of the life we are facing and from doubt about our own abilities to face it. We are like butterflies emerging from a cocoon, not sure yet what to do with our new freedom, our new resources, our new "wings." Everything is unfamiliar, and we are a bit weak and trembly, uncertain about what, exactly, we have "become." We are familiar with "crawling," not with "flying." We're not even sure, at times, that we *want* to fly. But, like a butterfly, we don't have the option of crawling back into that torn-up cocoon and reversing the metamorphosis.

So we choose to ***build*** something new, something better, something healthier. This time, we have different choices—we have our *own* choices. We are no longer stuck with the "blueprints," building materials, or even the construction tools that we "inherited" from our families. We can design our *own* lives, according to the plan that God has for us. We can select new materials, strong materials that we can place upon the firm foundation of God's Word. We can discover new tools, and we can take the steps necessary to learn how to *use* those tools. "For we are God's fellow workers; you are God's field, God's building. By the grace God has given me, I laid a foundation as an expert builder, and someone else is building on it. But each one should be careful how he builds. For no one can lay any foundation other than the one already laid, which is Jesus Christ. If any man builds on this foundation using gold, silver, costly stones, wood, hay or straw, his work will be shown for what it is, because the Day will bring it to light." (1 Cor. 3:9-13)

As we tear down and build up, tear down and build up, we will find ourselves ***weeping***, not just once but many times. As we walk the journey of recovery and discover how we were wounded, how often, and by whom, we feel the hurt not only of the injuries themselves, but of the betrayal of trust and the loss of illusions. We weep as we become aware of how deeply we have hated ourselves, as some of the hateful and self-destructive thoughts we have held come to the surface. We weep as we become aware of our true feelings about our abusers (past and present). We weep for what was, what wasn't, and what won't be. Most of all, we weep because, perhaps for the first time, we discovered that we have the *right* to weep, and most of us have a lot of overdue tears bottled up inside.

We also weep from joy and relief. As God touches our hearts and sets us from from old beliefs, from that old sense of worthlessness and unlovedness, the tears spill forth. We weep as we feel our burdens lifted and our chains removed. We weep as we look ahead, and see a future that is brighter and more glorious than we ever imagined. We weep when we realize that we are no longer doomed to failure, "stuck" with a hopeless and worthless self. We weep the way a prisoner may weep when he is suddenly, unexpectedly, brought forth from a dark cell that he believed he was sentenced to remain in until he died—and released into the bright light of a new day that he never thought he would see.

We also ***laugh***. As we move from bondage into freedom, we suddenly discover the *right* to laugh. We don't have to worry about what others think. For the first time, we realize that we have the right to *enjoy* life. Life isn't as "serious" and "bleak" as we once believed. It not only contains joy, it contains joy for *us*.

We discover that we have the right to be *ourselves*, and to explore who we really are and what we really want. We realize that we can act without fear of condemnation or punishment. We can act like children without having to listen to accusations of "childishness." We can explore our own tastes and interests without having to accept accusations of "foolishness" or "silliness." We can splash in puddles again, or kick piles of leaves, or walk along a fence, or catch snowflakes on our tongues. We can sing off-key, climb a tree, color in coloring books, build castles out of Legos® (my personal favorite laughter medicine).

We discover that "laughter" isn't something that we have to "wait for" until we finish the "serious business" of recovery. We discover, instead, that laughter is a very important *part* of recovery—that, in fact, we can't *truly* recover without it. As long as we believe that we don't have the "right" to laugh, a big part of us hasn't healed. But once we give ourselves permission to laugh, the laughter itself *brings* healing. "A cheerful heart is good medicine, but a crushed spirit dries up the bones." (Prov. 17:22) We may even discover that God has a sense of humor too!

***Mourning*** is a very real part of recovery. We have lost many things: Our self-image, our sense of being valuable to anyone, our belief that we could be loved, our innocence, our sexuality, our security, our trust, and perhaps most of all, our childhood. Part of recovery is *discovering* these losses, and grieving them, even though they occurred long ago.

Recovery creates its own losses as well. Even though many of the things that we lose *through* recovery are things that we wanted to get rid of for years, that process involves pain and mourning.

Perhaps the greatest loss we experience in recovery is the loss of *self*. Even though we may have hated ourselves, we were the "only self we had." At some point in recovery, we will wake up one morning to discover that the person we have "lived with" for all these years is suddenly, irretrievably *gone*—and we *don't know who we are*. We *used* to know what we thought, what we felt, what we wanted, and what was important to us. But suddenly we don't anymore. We don't know how to plan our lives because we don't know the person who will be *living* that life. We feel as though, in a way, we have "died." We sometimes wish that we could get our identity back, because even a "negative" identity feels better than *no* identity.

We are like some sort of crustacean that has just wriggled out of its old shell, and suddenly feels formless and vulnerable without that exoskeleton to give it "identity." The old shell may be lying there, visible, even within reach—but we don't fit back "inside" anymore, even though we may try. We don't know what to do with ourselves. We may find that our entire lives belong to the "old" identity—our career interests, our hobbies, our friends. When the old "self" no longer fits, the old *life* no longer fits either. We don't care about the work that we may have chosen to "prove ourselves worthwhile;" we don't want to associate with our old "drinking buddies;" and we don't need the hobbies that we may have taken on to insulate us from the need to "get a life." When *we* change, we may find that we have lost not only self but the entire "world" that this self was a part of.

This process may happen not just once, but several times, as we shed different *parts* of our old selves and old lives. Each time it happens, we mourn. But each time it happens, even as we are mourning, our "new self" begins to emerge, to surround us, and to lead us in new directions, almost before we are aware that it is happening. Just as we "woke up" to discover that the "old self" was gone, we are likely to "wake up" again to discover that we have begun to fit into that new self without even knowing it. All at once, we look around and realize, "This is who I *am*. This is *great*! Who'd have thought it!"

This is usually when we start to ***dance***. Recovery is not a "school" or "prison." It is not a process that we must pursue with serious diligence, to the exclusion of all forms of "frivolity" or "entertainment." Part of recovery includes rediscovering our ability to participate in joy, and to find joy in what we participate in. We need to learn how to have fun again—real fun, not what others *told* us to "enjoy."

We may start "dancing" in a literal sense. Adult Children are often tense and stiff; their body movements reflect the repressed emotions and buried fears that run their lives. We never knew how to express ourselves openly, physically; we were often afraid to. Many of us walk "hunched over," shoulders tensed against the world. We often keep our arms locked tightly to our bodies, or crossed over our chests when we have to face another person. We don't know what to do with our hands, and we want to hide our feet. Many of us felt "ugly"—too fat or too thin. We try to minimize our presence in the world, to blend into the background. Those of us who experienced physical or sexual abuse may have learned to *hate* our bodies; some have actually lost "feeling" in parts of their bodies.

As we recover, we learn how to start "living" in our own bodies once again. We no longer feel like strangers in our own flesh. We stop "hating" our flesh and begin to accept it (warts and all). Our stride tends to lengthen and take on more "swing." We walk taller, less fearfully. Our arms begin to swing a little more loosely, and we no longer use them as "shields" against the world. The stiffness leaves our muscles, and we begin to feel more physically relaxed and comfortable than we have in years. We are no longer so intimidated by people touching us or "invading our space." We can accept a pat on the back, a handshake, a hug. And we can dance: If our bodies want to "move to the music," whatever kind of music we prefer, we can let them. We don't have to feel embarrassed or stupid because we want to "move." Recovery restores not only our hearts and minds, but our bodies as well.

Through recovery, we ***"scatter"*** the old building blocks of our lives. We tear our old "homes" apart, idea by idea, belief by belief, assumption by assumption. We put those old, unhealthy perceptions as far away from us as we can. We dismantle our thought frameworks of "if only's" and "I can'ts" and "I mustn'ts." We strip our "strongholds" to the very foundation, and then we take a bulldozer to the foundation.

Then we ***gather*** new stones, new ideas and understandings and perceptions that will support our new lives. We surround ourselves with healthy ideas, healthy practices, and (as much as possible), healthy people. We begin to "build" with the building materials that God provides.

Many of us begin the process of recovery as "loners," thinking that we are supposed to "do it all ourselves." We are ashamed to go to others and ask for help, or admit that we have problems. We have been taught to believe that "strong people handle their own problems." We fear that others won't want to associate with us if they find out what is wrong.

Eventually, however, we find that we *need* people who will ***"embrace"*** us, without passing judgment on us or condemning us. We need people to support us and hold us by the hand, not to rescue us, but simply to tell us that they are there, that they care. We need people who will help us understand that *we aren't the only ones who feel this way*. We need to be with people who can help us realize that we aren't alone. We need support and love. Part of recovery is accepting that we *do* have these needs, and we have a right to seek out ways to get them met. If we can't find people who are willing to be supportive and nonjudgmental in our family, church, or circle of friends, we have a right to keep searching until we *do* find them.

At the same time, we may find that recovery is a time to ***"refrain"*** from establishing new, intimate relationships. We may discover that we don't know who we are, let alone who we are becoming—and that we no longer know what we *want* from a relationship. In the past, we may have sought people who could rescue us, or who would tell us what to do, or who would "imitate" the behaviors of our parents. Now, however, we are no longer attracted to (nor do we attract) the same kind of people that we once associated with. We no longer seek out needy people who made us feel "worthwhile" because we could "rescue" them; we no longer seek abusers who feed our sense of "victimhood." We no longer seek rescuers who will do the work of recovery *for* us, and we are no longer satisfied with people who do not have the slightest interest in what is going on in our lives. We find that we need to discover who we are before we can find out "who we want."

We may also find ourselves "refraining" from old relationships. We may no longer want to participate in the nonproductive (or even destructive) activities that we once shared with our friends—and we may find that our friends aren't interested in sharing our *new* life. We may find that our parents aren't willing to "let go" of their hold upon us, and do everything they can to reassert and reinforce their control. We may find that our own families aren't willing to support or encourage our growth and change. We may have to put some distance between ourselves and people who want to control us, manipulate us, intimidate us, or turn us into the person *they* want as opposed to the person *God* wants. We begin to discover what makes a healthy relationship and what doesn't—and we are no longer interested in retaining unhealthy ties.

Recovery is a time to ***search***. We search the past for answers, for truth, for understanding. We search our hearts for the feelings and beliefs that have been a part of us for so long. We search *ourselves* to discover who we really are, to find our resources as well as our weaknesses, our good qualities as well as our imperfections. We search the future for hope, opportunity, and growth. We search the Word of God for answers, and His heart for love and guidance.

As we search, we select the things that we are willing to ***throw away.*** Rarely are we able to identify, let alone get rid of, everything "unhealthy" all at once. But we begin the process. Little by little, we clean our closets and attics of outdated ideas, old baggage, long-cherished "sacred cows," and other mementos of the past that we no longer want around. We throw out old hurts, old accusations, old "blames." We find that we don't need our "good luck charms" and our defenses. Even when we choose to hold onto an unhealthy behavior for a little while, because we aren't quite ready to give it up and face the world without it, we know that eventually it will "go." This is not wrong; it is normal. God permits us to change at the rate at which we are *able* to change, not at the rate at which other people tell us we *should* change.

We also choose what to ***keep***. We begin to discover what is *good* about ourselves, what we have that is worth holding onto. We find out what is good about our relationships with others, and hold onto that. We keep the promises of God close to our hearts, knowing that they will be honored. We choose the dreams that still have meaning to us, and let the others go. We keep love, hope, and faith. We keep ourselves—even though we may have *wanted* to "get rid of ourselves" when we first entered recovery. We keep our joy—and our right to feel sorrow.

We often feel ***torn apart*** as we make these choices. We are caught between the old and the new, and we may feel as though we are ripping away a part of us as we "throw away" certain things. We hate to discard something familiar, something that feels "right," even when we know that it is destroying us—and we may fear to accept something new and unfamiliar in its place. We don't know where to turn or what to do at times. We feel torn between the commands and demands of the past, and the hope of the future. We may be torn between the demands of important people in our lives, and our desire to become a whole person in our *own* right. We are torn between "selves," between the old person that is dying and the new person that is being born. We may wonder how all these torn pieces are ever going to fit together into a new, whole pattern.

Yet we also ***mend***, however slowly. The things that we planted begin to bear fruit. The ideas that we chose to believe slowly become a reality. The truth of God's promises begins to manifest. Our hopes become real, our dreams become reality, our plans become established. We find ourselves *becoming* "new" people, sometimes with no firm idea of how we got there. Things begin to come together, and fit into place. Relationships begin to mend as new and healthy patterns replace old, dysfunctional ones. Our perception of self begins to mend, and our relationship with God begins to heal.

We begin to ***speak***. In the past, we may have kept silent when we feared that others would not like what we had to say. We may have spoken only when we were sure that we wouldn't make anyone "angry." As we progress in recovery, this pattern begins to reverse itself. Instead of keeping silent when we disagree, we speak up, and make ourselves heard when we think that something is wrong. We speak to change things, to make things right, to correct injustices and misperceptions. We speak up for ourselves instead of enduring abuse and pain in silence. We begin to speak on behalf of others. We talk about what we believe, no longer worried about whether others agree. We express our desires and needs instead of trying to pretend that we don't have them. We no longer agree with things that we know are wrong; instead we try to *change* those things if we can.

We may also become more ***"silent"*** on other issues. We may become less critical—of ourselves, and of others. We learn to apply the same healthy patterns of thinking to those around us that we have begun to apply to ourselves. We no longer "judge" by black-and-white or all-or-nothing thinking. We no longer expect others to meet *our* standards of perfection. We are less hasty to accuse, less hasty to defend ourselves when *we* are accused, and less quick to return one insult for another. We choose our words carefully, making sure that they are words of love, even when they may be strong words that others won't want to hear. We make sure that our words are free of malice, bitterness, or impatience. We are slower to condemn and quicker to forgive. We find new and healthy ways to express our feelings. We learn timing, balance, and a consideration for others that does not *preclude* our right to speak what is in our hearts. We no longer fear the words of our own mouths, or expect to be condemned by them.

Recovery is the time to discover what genuine ***love*** really is. It is the time to accept and experience the love of God, and to apply that love throughout our lives. It is the time to realized that we *are* loved, that we *can* love, and that we can love *ourselves*. Love is a vital factor in *every aspect* of recovery.

Yet oddly enough, it is a time to discover what we ***hate***. We *do* hate; every Adult Child becomes aware of buried hatreds, and usually feels intensely guilty for those hatreds. When we stop *pretending* to "love" what we actually hate, however, we can begin to resolve those hatreds. We can't change hate by pretending it isn't there. We can only change it by accepting it, confronting it, and applying the "resolution" skills we have learned. Accepting our hate, so that we can *do* something about it, empowers us to *love*.

Recovery is a ***war***. We sometimes feel as though we are fighting ourselves every step of the way—fighting our emotions, our self-talk, our perceptions, our fears, our assumptions. Our mind tells us to give up, to quit, that we are wasting our time, that we can't possibly succeed, that we will never get better, that we are selfish. We struggle against these messages on a daily, even hourly, basis.

We may also find ourselves at war with forces outside ourselves. Our worst opposition may come from our own families. Our parents may resent our recovery and regard it as an "accusation" or a "criticism" of their parenting. Spouses who want to control us (or to be "rescued" by us) may oppose recovery because they fear that they will lose that control or that support for their own unhealthy behaviors. Our children may oppose our recovery for the same reason. Our fellow Christians may tell us that recovery is bad, or sinful, or selfish, or that we are going about it the wrong way. We may become very discouraged when everyone around us tells us that what we are doing is *wrong*, or that it is hurting *them*.

Adversity, however, is not necessarily a sign that we are doing something wrong. It is a sign that we are "disturbing" the world around us. If that world is based upon false perceptions and unhealthy behaviors, it will resist change—and it will express that resistance through unhealthy and unloving ways. We have an adversary who will do everything in his power to keep us trapped in an unhealthy, dishonest world—his world—and keep us separated from the love and healing of God. Our adversary doesn't *want* us to experience the "abundant life" that Jesus promises (John 10:10). Instead, he wants us to experience that pain and shame and guilt and condemnation that Jesus died to release us from. Recovery is war with the devil—but we have God's promise of victory.

We also have God's promise of ***peace***. Through recovery, we will learn how to live at peace with ourselves for perhaps the first time. We will find peace from the swarm of bitter and condemning thoughts that have persecuted us for so long. We will find peace from condemnation, from anxiety, from fear. We will find peace from the "do more and try harder" mentality that has driven us throughout our lives. We will find the peace that replaces perfectionism. We will find the peace that replaces pain—and that gives us the strength to *bear* the pain that *will* come into our lives. We will find peace in our relationships. We will find peace in our relationship with God. We will find peace in the life that He has given us so abundantly, the life that He has made beautiful. We will find peace in the fulfillment of the promise of love. That peace may not come right away, but it comes "in its season."

# Appendix I: Resolutions for Recovery

---

### *Resolution I: Love and Self-Image*

- *I will be patient with myself, no longer expecting myself to change "immediately," but allowing growth to occur in God's timing.*
- *I will be kind myself, and no longer mistreat myself or abuse myself because I believe that I "deserve" unkindness.*
- *I will not envy others because I think that they are "better" than I am or have more advantages, or are more loved by God.*
- *I will not boast that I have no difficulties or negative feelings, or that my life is perfect and problem-free.*
- *I will not be too proud to look for help, to seek answers to my difficulties, to express my pain, and to seek healing and growth.*
- *I will not be rude to myself, call myself names, put myself down, or respond to my needs and feelings with sarcasm and criticism.*
- *I will seek my* ***best*** *interest instead of my selfish, frightened interest. I will do what is* ***healthy*** *for myself and others.*
- *I will not be angry with myself for not being "good enough" or doing "well enough." Instead, I will change those perceptions.*
- *I will keep no record of my wrongs, my flaws, my failures, and my imperfections. I will forgive myself.*
- *I will not turn to evil, self-abusive behaviors to punish myself for my failures or to numb my feelings.*
- *I will be honest with myself about who I am, and I will work to discover the* ***truth*** *about who and what I am.*
- *I will protect myself from harm, both from myself—through personal neglect or active abuse—and from others.*
- *I will trust God, I will learn to trust my own choices, and I will learn to trust others* ***wisely****.*
- *I will hold firm to the hope that growth, change, and recovery are possible through God.*
- *I will not give up on myself. I will stick with my recovery choices and follow through, even when they don't give the immediate "improvement" that I often seek.*

• *I will not consider myself a failure. I can* ***fail****—and still move forward to* ***success****.*

### *Resolution II: Love and Self-Talk*

• *I will talk to myself patiently, instead of continually pressuring myself to hurry up and get things done "already."*
• *I will speak to myself kindly, with consideration and respect rather than abusive language.*
• *I will not speak enviously or jealously of others, but thank God for the gifts and love that He has given me.*
• *I will not boast of thoughts or feelings or "conditions" that I do not have or that are not true.*
• *I will not be too proud to admit when I have made a mistake, done something wrong, or hurt someone.*
• *I will not speak to myself rudely, with put-downs, names, labels, condemnation, criticism, or sarcasm.*
• *I will not speak selfishly, attempting to defend my actions or win the love and approval of others. I will do my best to speak in ways that will benefit others, and that will be of benefit to me.*
• *I will not speak angrily to myself, scold myself, kick myself over every mistake, or chew myself out for every imperfection.*
• *I will not remind myself of my wrongs and mistakes, but forgive myself for them.*
• *I will not use "evil talk" against myself, including obscenity or profanity.*
• *I will speak the truth to myself at all times. I will be honest with myself about my feelings, my thoughts, and my personality.*
• *I will not speak to myself in a way that is harmful or destructive, nor will I tell myself that I deserve harm from others.*
• *I will remind myself that I* ***can*** *trust God even when I don't* ***feel*** *trusting.*
• *I will not tell myself that I am hopeless or that I have no hope for recovery. Instead, I will remind myself of my hope.*
• *I will not try to tell myself to quit or give up on myself, but will encourage myself to persevere.*
• *I will not call myself a failure or call only my failures to my attention. I will remind myself of my successes.*

## *Resolution III: Love and Emotions*

- *I will be patient with my feelings, and not get upset because they don't "change" or "get better" as quickly as I would prefer.*
- *I will be kind to myself in spite of my feelings, and not punish myself for having the "wrong" feelings.*
- *I will not envy others for being so "strong" that they don't appear to "have" feelings; I will be thankful for the gift of emotions.*
- *I will not boast that I don't have any bad feelings, that I feel no pain or anger or resentment. I will admit the negative (and positive) feelings that I have.*
- *I will not be too proud to express my feelings. I will not be too proud to cry, to admit that I am hurt, or to express my anger.*
- *I will not express my feelings to myself or to others in a rude way. I will not lash out at myself or others with rude language.*
- *I will not use my feelings as a selfish way to control others, to get my own way, or to make other people feel sorry for me. I will not let my feelings turn me into a "victim" or a "martyr."*
- *I will not condemn myself for having negative feelings. I will not blame myself or others for my feelings.*
- *I will not let my feelings lead me into evil actions of any kind, including actions that would be destructive to others or to myself.*
- *I will delight in my ability to feel, and learn how to recognize and accept my feelings for what they are. I will not deny my feelings to myself or to others.*
- *I will protect myself and others from the consequences of my painful feelings.*
- *I will trust the accuracy of my feelings, instead of supposing that there is something "wrong" with me for having them. I will let my feelings show me areas of my life that need resolution or healing.*
- *I will persevere in my efforts to understand and resolve my feelings, even when those feelings hurt.*
- *I will not fail to feel. I will not "stuff" my feelings, deny them, ignore them, or try to feel what I think I am "supposed" to feel.*

## *Resolution IV: Love and Forgiveness*

- *I will be patient in my efforts to forgive. I will realize that forgiveness doesn't always happen overnight or all at once. I will be patient in my efforts to forgive* ***myself*** *as well.*

- *I will act in kindness toward those that I need to forgive.*
- *I will forgive those that I feel envy toward, for "having" what I feel I do not have.*
- *I will not boast that I have "resolved" all my problems and pain, and that there is therefore "no need" to forgive.*
- *I will not be too proud to forgive.*
- *I will not forgive rudely, confrontively, or offensively.*
- *I will not forgive just because I want, selfishly, to be forgiven. I will forgive out of the sincere desire to do God's will and release others from my resentment and anger.*
- *I will not be quick to anger at others. I will try to remember the need for forgiveness* ***before*** *I yield to anger.*
- *I will forgive the "record of wrongs" I hold against each person who has hurt me in my life. I will also forgive my* ***own*** *record of wrongs, and never bring it up against myself again.*
- *I will forgive those who have done evil to me, not denying that it* ***was*** *evil, but allowing God to deal with it and heal it.*
- *When I forgive, it will be true forgiveness, and I will not claim to have forgiven something that I haven't.*
- *I will protect myself from the consequences of my own anger by forgiving myself for my "failures" and "flaws," instead of seeking to condemn and punish myself.*
- *I will trust in God's promise that He has forgiven me and no longer holds my sins against me.*
- *I will hope in the redemption God has promised me, and keep the hope that all my* ***future*** *sins will also be forgiven.*
- *I will persevere in my efforts to forgive, even when forgiveness does not come easily.*
- *I will not fail to forgive, but diligently seek out those hurts and bitternesses that I need to release—including the bitterness I hold against myself.*

### *Resolution V: Love and Relationships*

- *I will be patient with others, and not expect them to change or become what I* ***want*** *them to be on "my schedule."*
- *I will be kind to others, treating everyone around me with respect consideration, gentleness, and mercy.*
- *I will not envy others for having things that I wish I had. I will*

*not be jealous, or dislike others* ***because*** *of my jealousy.*

- *I will not be too proud to apologize or confess a mistake.*
- *I will not be rude to others, but will choose my words with care so that I do not speak with sarcasm, put-downs, or names.*
- *I will seek what is best for the* ***relationship****, not simply what I can* ***get*** *from that relationship.*
- *I will not be quick to get angry at others; I will not* ***assume*** *that others are deliberately trying to hurt me when I feel hurt.*
- *I will not keep a record of other people's wrongs, or remind them of things they have done wrong in the past, or constantly bring up their mistakes and failures.*
- *I will not bring any form of evil into my relationships.*
- *I will honor the truth in my relationships, speaking the truth in love and keeping silent when the truth cannot be spoken gently or kindly. I will not lie about my thoughts and feelings, and I will allow others to speak their thoughts as well.*
- *I will always protect those that I am in relationship with, and never do anything that would purposely harm them, and I will stand by them when they need help.*
- *I will trust others, knowing that even the most caring and conscientious person makes mistakes and may let me down. I will not trust foolishly, however, or fail to protect myself from people that I know to be abusive.*
- *I will hope for the growth and well-being of others, and hope for improvements in my relationships.*
- *I will persevere in my efforts to practice good relationship skills even when those efforts don't seem to be making progress or when they are not appreciated or rewarded.*
- *I will never fail to do my best in a relationship, regardless of whether others do the same.*

### *Resolution VI: Love and Choices*

- *I will be patient as I learn to make wise choices, knowing that this skill does not come instantly.*
- *I will choose to be kind to myself, and not make choices that are harmful for me. I will choose to take proper care of myself.*
- *I will not make choices out of envy or jealousy or because I wish I had what others have.*

- *I will not boast about the choices that I have made, right or wrong.*
- *I will not be too proud to make the right choices, even when those choices mean that I must reveal problems, weaknesses, or imperfections. I will not be too proud to change my mind.*
- *I will not be rude to myself when I make the wrong choices; I will not call myself "stupid" or other names, or curse myself or use filthy language.*
- *I will not make selfish choices, but seek the choices that are in the best interest of everyone involved, if that is possible.*
- *I will not get angry with myself every time I make the wrong choice, but accept that bad decisions are inevitable and move forward.*
- *I will not keep a record of my bad decisions, but forgive each one and move on to make* ***better*** *decisions.*
- *I will not choose evil under any circumstances.*
- *I will choose honesty over deception, openness over secrecy, truth over masks and illusions. I will choose to be truthful about myself and accept the truth about others.*
- *I will choose to protect myself from harm, abuse, and self-destructive behaviors—including the self-destructive behaviors of overwork and improper self-care.*
- *I will choose to trust God, and choose to trust my own decisions and judgment rather than relying upon others to choose for me.*
- *I will choose to hope even when I can see no reason for hope.*
- *I will choose to stand by my decisions, instead of abandoning them at the first indication that something may not be working out the way I want it to.*
- *I will choose to try, even when I fail—because it is better to* ***try and fail*** *than to* ***fail to try****.*